I0825181

# EYES *from* PENUMBRA

# EYES *from* PENUMBRA

## How Doing Hard Awakened My Soul, Freed My Mind, and Opened My Heart

**ADAM LACERDA**

Foreword by Stephen K. Bannon

War Room books may be purchased in bulk at special discounts for sales promotion, corporate gifts, fund-raising, or educational purposes. Special editions can also be created to specifications. For details, contact the Special Sales Department, Skyhorse Publishing, 307 5th Avenue, 4th Floor, New York, NY 10016 or info@skyhorsepublishing.com.



Visit our website at www.skyhorsepublishing.com.

Please follow our publisher Tony Lyons on Instagram @tonylyonsisuncertain.

10 9 8 7 6 5 4 3 2 1

Library of Congress Control Number: 2025941011

Cover design by David Ter-Avanesyan

Print ISBN: 978-1-64821-179-9
Ebook ISBN: 978-1-64821-180-5

Printed in the United States of America

To Paul C. DeMeo

For showing me every day of his life what it means to be a good man.

## Author's Note:

This is a work of nonfiction based on the author's memories and experiences. To protect the privacy of individuals, some names, identifying characteristics, and locations have been changed. Certain events have been recounted as the author remembers them; while every effort has been made to portray them accurately, some details may reflect the subjective nature of memory.

# Contents

# EYES *from* PENUMBRA

# Foreword

## by Stephen K. Bannon

The author of this book—with a compelling title—is a gentleman I met while I was serving a sentence in a federal prison in Danbury, Connecticut. I was convicted for refusing to cooperate with what I—and my lawyers—believed was an illegal Congressional subpoena compelling me to testify before Congress on the January 6, 2021, events in Washington, DC, concerning the 2020 election, despite me holding executive privilege. This was also despite the fact that the president of the United States' right to assert executive privilege had been well established. It is a right that US presidents have had for a very long time. Nonetheless, I was sentenced to four months.

At Danbury federal prison, it was my privilege to meet Mr. Lacerda, one of the smartest individuals I have ever encountered, and there I learned about the case that sent him to prison . . . *not* for four months. On June 25, 2015, he was sentenced to federal prison for twenty-seven years.

Adam Lacerda is a complex man, and, like each of us, not without human flaws. Adam founded a company called Vacation Ownership Group. As has become more evident over the years, vacation timeshares is a field fraught with deceit, exploitation by big banks and credit companies, and consumer dissatisfaction. Adam's company was helping these dissatisfied timeshare clients exit their timeshares.

He was sued in 2010 for allegedly stealing trade secrets. Believe what you will. The fact is that Adam Lacerda challenged some big corporate players and is now sitting in a federal prison, serving a twenty-seven-year sentence.

*Eyes from Penumbra* is Adam's reckoning with himself and the world. He has been motivated by his lengthy incarceration to learn and grow as a human being, and his insights into diverse topics are well worth engaging with.

In his candid and thoughtful memoir, Adam proves that prison can be a crucible for self-discovery, that tragedy can reveal our best selves, and that knowing yourself is the true foundation of freedom.

Everyone has a unique gift—but most never uncover it. Adam Lacerda has, and what a gift it is for us to learn from him.

# Prologue

*Bang Bang Bang!*

The loud slams on my door jolted me awake, followed by the click of a lock—a sound more effective in waking you than any alarm clock, despite being completely foreign to your senses. No matter how often you hear it, the sound can never be naturalized.

"Lacerda, court time!" a correctional officer, CO, screamed from the other side.

Waking at 5 a.m., following a sleepless night on a one-inch slab amidst a cacophony of screams that seep into your bones, echoing through the night while you stand on guard, vigilant against the attempts of the mice to make it from the floor to your bunk, is an indescribable type of disorientation. Even my brother, a United States Marine who slept in a desert foxhole during wartime, woke with more clarity than I did here.

Moving cautiously to avoid making noise, I put all my shower things on my plastic chair, picked it up while stuffing my feet into shower shoes, and stepped out of my cell, heading toward the open showers—a dismal sight. On my walk there, I wondered if, at some point, I would forget what it was like to shower without something protecting my feet.

Pulling back the curtain, I was met with a metal wall coated with a thick layer of soap scum hanging on like a snake's discarded skin, along with the stench of hundreds of men who had showered before. It was a harsh reminder of how much I missed the smell of fresh brewing coffee in the morning. The first few times you experience the shower, it is revolting, but like anything else, with time, you adapt in your head, taking care not to touch the walls or drop anything on the floor. The known stereotype surrounding dropping the soap in prison usually implies that an unwanted sexual advance will follow, but in this instance, it meant that you may contract something that you can never get rid of if you pick up the soap intending to continue using it. It is so unbelievably disgusting.

After a quick, cold rinse, I returned to my cell and did my best to prepare. Attempting to comb your hair and wash your face in a scratched, cloudy mirror with poor lighting is a frustrating reminder that everything is set to work against you. Inmates are provided with a green jumper as their prison uniform, and overnight placement under the mattress is the only way to press and iron clothes in an attempt to look presentable. I slipped the blasted jumper on and headed down the steps to make my way to the unit door, waiting for the officer to shackle me and painfully lock my hands between a black box—an invention by a former inmate that makes handcuffs more secure by restricting hand movement—before leading me to the transport bus, where further chaining would be required.

By this point, I had already been locked up in that hell hole for two years, having my soul tortured daily, waiting for sentencing day. The two years spent in limbo gave me clarity about the world I was now a part of, and I knew this day was going to be horrific. My judge was a tyrant from the very beginning. I'm unsure if he was different at the start of his career; perhaps he was, but the man he had become earned him the nickname "Hanging Hillman." It is no secret that many have attempted to hang themselves after going in front of him in his courtroom. My family, my lawyers, and I have been terrified of the man since our first encounter.

As the transport bus headed to the courthouse, my thoughts drifted back to the trial. Countless times, Hillman intimidated my lawyers and threatened them with being thrown in jail. You would think that was the worst that he did to them, but it wasn't. My lead counsel was removed with just three months to go before trial began, leaving me wildly unprepared, with a new lawyer who knew nothing and a denial of more time for him to prepare adequately.

I learned that hope can be an incredibly dangerous emotion. Undoubtedly, it has the power to keep a man alive and pushing forward, but when it seems lost, it can break you entirely. I had seen enough in the process to extinguish all reason for hope—yet still, a faint flicker quietly smoldered within me.

The back-and-forth that ensued between lawyers arguing about legal issues during the proceedings is a blur now, and perhaps that is because it never actually mattered. In the moment, my mind, working alongside my heart, created an artificial meaning to it all. You might call it ignorance. Everything happening in front of me was all for the show, as nothing would change the outcome, which was decided long before the day in question. The judge knew what he was going to do.

Being paraded in front of your family in shackles and a prison uniform is ignominious. The shame and embarrassment are overwhelming, and I imagine it feeling similar to that of your mother walking in on you masturbating as a child, or your friends suddenly pulling your pants down quickly in front of a girl you admire.

The only thing worse was having to see the pain that was etched in their faces while sitting in the well of the courtroom, seeing me dressed and shackled for the first time.

I kept looking up at the judge. He sat there staring at his computer screen, seemingly uninterested. Now and again, when I found the strength, I'd glance back at my mother, trying to appear calm, as if everything was going to be okay. I knew she was a nervous wreck about her upcoming statement to the court.

My heart broke for her. She looked fragile, the weight of the love for me aged her by decades at that moment. Up to this point, the judge had appeared to show no interest in anything outside of the stenographer's notes on the screen in front of him, but suddenly, a warmth came over him that none of us had seen before in all our previous interactions. He was thoughtful and compassionate when he spoke and seemed almost caring while addressing my sobbing mother.

"It's okay, dear, take your time," he said.

My mother wept through her plea to the court, constantly trying to catch her breath and steady herself. It was torture to be a witness to it, as a son's instinct is to protect his mother. I sat and watched a woman of strength who had cared for and loved me, every breath of my life, breaking right in front of me while at the same time, my father, the rock of our family, was at home, in hospice, dying.

"Your honor, I am losing my husband," she cried. "Please, don't take my son from me too."

It was impossible for tears not to fall down my face, too. The pain in the courtroom was infectious and palpable.

When the judge started to speak following my mother's statement, the change in his demeanor was still present and noticeable but also strange and unlike anything we had experienced at any time before. It was jarring and a stark departure from his former self. For the first time in this process, he addressed the prosecution in a challenging manner, and optimism flickered in the eyes of my family. He started to question the guideline range proposed by the government, twenty-seven to thirty-three years.

"Twenty-seven to thirty-three years seems excessive for someone like him," he said. "That's a sentence I reserve for level-six offenders who have spent their whole lives committing violent crimes; what do you mean by this?" he said, addressing the federal prosecutor.

While the prosecution responded, my lawyer leaned in and whispered in my ear, "Don't take the bait."

"What are you talking about?" I asked.

"He's allowing the government to clean up the record to hurt your appeal chances later," he explained. "He is also baiting you to admit guilt in your statement."

I hadn't seen this before, but it made sense once he said it to me, and I could see my circumstance more clearly. The judge was laying the groundwork to protect his decision from future challenges while also hoping his new demeanor would get me to slip up when it came time for me to address the court and say something that could be used against me later. This is why my lawyer had previously rewritten my speech three times, ensuring I had expressed remorse without admitting guilt.

My family was oblivious to my conversation with my lawyer. They sat there, holding hands, believing that things were finally turning around in this case, but I couldn't afford to get caught up in the illusion with them. When it was my turn to speak, I followed my lawyer's advice—respectful and remorseful, but careful not to cross the line.

The moment I finished, I could see the change on the judge's face, like storm clouds rolling in. The warmth disappeared, replaced by cold fury. I hadn't taken the bait, and he was furious about it.

The charade was over.

"Rise for sentencing," he ordered. His black eyes had taken on an evil sheen.

With vitriol in his voice, he attacked everything positive that had been said about me by character witnesses, by my mother, in the letters submitted to the judge on my behalf, from those who had worked for me or done business with me. It was all meaningless to him. It was as if it never existed.

After he finished publicly lamenting my existence, he decided to strike me with a final blow before telling me my fate.

"A man with your intelligence could have done anything with his life," he said. "But you chose this instead. Even when the FBI intervened early in this case, you somehow convinced everyone around you to stay the course and ultimately grew in size rather than stop what you were doing. Your influence over people and how you choose to use that influence makes you a clear danger, and I hope you take the time to look in the mirror at some point. Fortunately, you will have plenty of time to do that."

He sentenced me to 324 months and three years of supervised release. I guess twenty-seven years wasn't strong enough for him.

I could hear the noise of shock from the well of the courtroom as I collapsed into my chair, the world now spinning around me. It didn't feel real. How did it come to this? I have always been a good person: A good son, a good father, a good brother, a good friend, a good boss, and a good husband. I was my mother and father's son. I had been a law-abiding citizen my entire life and believed in our justice system. I had never abused drugs or alcohol. I paid my taxes and donated to those in need in my community, but now, now I was going to disappear and be forgotten by the world, still not understanding why.

I couldn't look at anyone nor see two feet in front of me. When the marshals stood behind me, they had to help me to stand, and they escorted me back to the holding cell to await transfer back to hell.

I was told later that my distraught and frozen family were unable to talk to my lawyer until later that night on the phone, and when they did, my mother said, "If I hadn't been there to see these proceedings firsthand from day one, I wouldn't have believed what happened. No American would believe that this is the US justice system. That trial was an absolute train wreck, and I had to watch my son crash and burn in slow motion, and not only not survive, today I had to identify the body."

I felt a profound sense of loss on the transport back, seeing the world through the windows, knowing it would be a very long time before I would be a part of it again. My mind was cloudy, and my heart was riddled with anxiety. I was clueless about how to move forward and make it to tomorrow. I started to daydream to avoid having a breakdown, and my mind began to revert to my childhood, specifically to one summer on the Cape, the time in my life when I had actually committed a crime.

Growing up on Cape Cod was a grand adventure for my brother and me. As kids, we often took our surroundings for granted, having known nothing else, but looking back now, I realize how blessed we were to call that place home. Summers were a blur of sandy beaches and blissful sun days, while our winters meant sledding on golf courses or skating on frozen cranberry bogs. In between, we embarked on a string of escapades straight out of a storybook.

My neighborhood was a child's paradise. New Boston Road, a quaint, winding lane, was the only way in and out of our secluded enclave. Nestled in its farthest corner was a blueberry patch that we would often pluck from, and everywhere else, there existed a treasure trove of wonder. In the center of the neighborhood was a naturally occurring makeshift baseball diamond, trails winding through the woods, marshlands, and towering trees begging to be climbed. The aftermath of Hurricane Bob added to the magic, which left behind a playground of fallen trees perfect for endless exploration and adventure.

I grew up in Dennis, Massachusetts, which is steeped in history. No matter where you went exploring, you would always stumble across a piece of it. We would explore for hours. It was an endless world in the woods, and randomly, we would come across small cemeteries. Tombstones dated centuries ago dotted the landscape throughout, and paths in the woods directly behind my childhood home would lead us to six different beaches, depending on where we decided to go. We lived outdoors, playing day or night until someone called us in, if they did at all. I grew up in the era before smart devices and social media, so the only thing that would keep us indoors would be watching an episode of *Saved by the Bell* or *90210*, and even then, my mother quickly reminded us that there was a world waiting outside.

"I'm not telling you that you should be outside right now, but if I were, it would sound exactly like this," she would say.

Three houses down from us was the Franklin family's summer home. Their kids, Philip, Laura, and Mark were close in age to us; Laura and I were the same age and she was who I was closest to, even though most of the time we were doing "boy" things and she had no interest. The start of every summer brought with it the excitement of their return. The friendships we forged were the kind that only childhood summers could create, making us feel like we were a tight-knit tribe.

That particular summer, the one just before Laura and I would be entering seventh grade, skateboarding was the "in" trend, thanks to Tony Hawk. One early afternoon, all the boys, including David, our year-round friend from farther down the road, were all in the Franklins' driveway, pretending we knew what we were doing.

"Kickflip!" someone would yell while their board flew in no discernible direction.

"Olly," another would yell as their board barely made it off the ground.

We sucked at skateboarding, but since it was something we all shared in our circle, we were perfect. We were kings of the driveway—future X Game Champions.

Now, like with any group of young boys who come together, at some point, mischief is impending, and we were no exception. Just down at the end of the round, as it headed around the block, was a new dirt road carved out by tractors to get to a new house built off the beaten path out in the woods. We knew it well because it had become the backdrop for some of our nightly games of manhunt. There were a lot of cool places to hide, but no one had lived there yet, adding to the intrigue.

Minutes before we were called in for dinner, Alan, Mark, and David hatched a plan: We should "borrow" some wood from the construction site to build our very own ramp to skate on.

"After dinner, when it gets dark, we'll go there and get what we need. It will be easy, and no one will know," David said to my brother, who was in complete agreement.

"Shit, I'm in," said Mark.

Being the youngest, I hesitated, but my protests were drowned out by their excitement, and my resistance was smashed with peer pressure and name-calling.

"Damn, bro, why is your brother such a girl? Maybe you should head in and dress up with Laura," Mark said to my brother. Ad hominem attacks were his specialty.

"What can I say, I got all the good stuff when I was born, and he got the shit left over," Alan replied.

"Shut up," I responded. "I got all the good stuff, and you got the crap."

"Way to steal my line, stupid," he replied.

For some reason, at this age, I was never very good at the back-and-forth insults; regardless, he always came out on top. The most famous picture on the wall of our house is me, at around age two, holding a glowworm doll, clearly crying my eyes out, and my brother standing next to me with his arms flailing out, offering a "what? I didn't do anything" expression. I don't remember taking the picture, but it always made perfect sense when I looked at it. Don't get me wrong, I love my brother and think the world of him, but as a kid, he was the type to climb up in my highchair with me and sit on my head while I was eating.

I voiced opposition again, but they were demanding, and I agreed to be their lookout, which felt like a win at the time. All I had to do was keep watch, which, for some reason, I thought would absolve me from any wrongdoing. Ignorance is bliss.

I stood halfway between the construction site and the road, anxious like a man with a bloody nose in shark-infested water.

"Guys . . . GUYS!!! I think I hear a car coming down the road," I said loudly, still attempting to make my voice sound like a whisper.

"Yeah, there is a road directly in front of you, and the world is full of cars, moron. If you hear a clown laughing or a lion growling, that would be something worth reporting," Alan said. He sure did have a way about him.

We successfully transported all the wood we needed back to the Franklins' driveway and called it a night. The next morning, my brother and I raided my dad's workshop for tools and went straight to the Franklins. We spent the rest of the morning together until just past lunch, building our ramp. It wasn't perfect, but it worked. For the next forty-five minutes, we were kings of our makeshift skatepark until reality came crashing down upon us.

The first warning sign was my dad's truck. Its distinct diesel engine rumbled in the distance long before we saw it. He waved to us as he drove by, a look of confusion crossing his face as he noticed our creation. It wasn't until he returned a few minutes later from what looked to be the job site down the road that we started to feel as though we may have a problem.

He parked at the fence on the road and hopped out of his truck, heading toward us.

"Hey boys, nice ramp you got there," he said, his voice tinged with suspicion. We all grinned and shot nervous looks at one another, aware of the brewing storm. "Where'd you get the wood?" he asked.

Silence fell. My father, the shop foreman for Shepley Wood Products for over thirty years, had immediately recognized the stampings on the side of the plywood and knew that we had taken it from the construction site. We were busted.

"It looks like you boys did a lot of work putting this thing together. I hope you saved some energy because now you are going to take it all apart." He didn't raise his voice at any of us, not once, but his evident disappointment in us was enough punishment for me. I wasn't present for my brother's reprimand, but it ended with him being punished for a month, and he had to pay back what was damaged to the job site.

When he finally turned his attention to me, he said, "Go get your skateboard and bring it to me now." I obeyed, handing over my prized possession under protest. He looked at me and said, "I hope you gave this thing a kiss goodbye because your skateboarding days are over," he said firmly. "This belongs to me now, and no, I will not buy you another one; no, you cannot buy another one for yourself, and yes, this conversation is final and without room for debate." Damn, he knew me well, but he left an opening. I debated internally whether I should pluck on that string and decided that you can't achieve anything if you don't at least ask. I swallowed hard. "When can I have that one back then?"

He responded almost before the question came out of my mouth, as if he knew it was coming. "I'll give it back to you when you graduate high school. Maybe you can ride it to college. But let me be clear: if I catch you on one of these things before that time comes, you will wish you were never born. Understand?"

"Yes, sir." Well, shit. That killed that.

That day marked the end of a skateboarding era. Over the years, I found new hobbies and eventually forgot all about skateboarding. It lost its appeal and was only brought up at some later time in a conversation with a friend when discussing the past.

When the actual graduation day came many years later, I had forgotten all about the incident and returned home, still in my cap and gown, to see my father standing in the middle of the backyard, waiting for me with a big smile. He wasn't a man of affection, but on this day, he walked right up to me, wrapped his arms around me, and gave me a massive hug—a Dad hug. "I'm proud of you, son," he said.

Then, with a rare grin, he told me he had a gift waiting for me and to stay where I was. He disappeared in the shed and then reappeared a minute later, holding something in both hands that looked oddly familiar, although I couldn't quite make out what it was. As he approached me, I recognized the scratched-up pattern on the bottom of the board, and it hit me like a ton of bricks.

"Holy shit, that's my old skateboard. Wow, I forgot all about it." I was shocked.

"I didn't. I told you I would return it to you when you graduated high school, and today you did. A man's word is everything, son," he said, handing it back to me.

I didn't fully recognize it then, but that skateboard was one of the greatest gifts my father could have given me, not because of what it was but because of what it symbolized. It was a testament to the values he had instilled in me my whole life: integrity, responsibility, and the weight of one's word—these lessons I later used to survive.

He also slipped me a wad of cash.

"Here, don't tell your mother. Have some fun with your friends and remember our deal. If you are ever in a situation where you are about to drive after drinking or are about to get in a car with someone who has, stop and pick up the phone. I do not care what time of night it is, and I will come and get you, no questions asked."

"I know; thanks, Dad."

"Seriously though, don't tell your mother."

"Of course not." I smiled.

I often wondered why he always did this. Anytime my father would slip money into my pocket, he would always follow up with "don't tell your mother." Even when I was in college.

"Here is some beer money, don't tell your mother."

I found it funny because my mother didn't care. If anything, she would want him to give me more. I guess this was just another way for him to set something to the side as ours or to make an interaction between us special. And looking back on it all now, he accomplished what he wanted to achieve. I did always feel special.

* * *

The transport bus pulled back into the detention center, and reality returned. I was just sentenced to more time in jail than I had lived on the earth, and today was going to be the start of an arduous journey that I was in no way prepared for.

Life as I had known it was now in my review, and only the harsh terrain of the unknown remained ahead. The moment I stepped off the transport bus and entered the elevator, shackled and bound, I knew I existed on the fringe of society. It was going to be many years from this moment before anyone could recognize me as a valuable member. I was removed, a convict out of sight and out of mind to the rest of the world.

As the elevator doors opened and I was forced into the R&D section of the detention center, I could feel in my heart and soul that I was entering the Penumbra.

# *Chapter One*
# Entering Oz

Becoming part of the prison system felt like being Dorothy caught in the violent twister in *The Wizard of Oz*. I was ripped from the only life I knew and hurled into a strange, artificial world where nothing made sense. However, this distorted version of Oz was not colorful or magical; it was grey, bleak, and dangerous. The characters weren't made of straw or tin; they were hardened men, broken souls, and authority figures wielding unchecked power. The rules were unspoken and irrational, yet strict and unbreakable. This world was controlled chaos, and staying alive became my mandate.

Survival instinct kicked in full throttle, and my brain became a scanning machine, constantly running threat assessments to develop self-protection plans. Initially, I was like an untrained soldier on a battlefield, engaged but unsure exactly what I was looking for. However, understanding this illogical world was not optional; it was required to stay alive, and thus, it became a top priority.

This is what I have come to know:

At the top of the pyramid, far above inmates and internal politics, are the ones who carry the keys: the corrections officers.

About 5 percent are genuinely competent individuals who want to make a difference. Inmates can point these officers out. They stand out for their honesty, desire to help, and belief in redemption. They are exceptional human beings, compassionate, educated, and sincerely invested in rehabilitation. They treat inmates like people. Yet, despite their character, they hold the least amount of sway over institutional policies. This slim percentage is usually stuck in lower-level positions and lacks the authority to be effective. Five out of a hundred. Think about how tragically small this number is.

Another 5 percent of the staff are decent folks with bigger dreams. For them, the job is a steppingstone, not a career, and while they are not trying to help per se, they are polite, professional, and just trying to get to the next chapter in their lives.

The rest? The 90 percent? They form cliques like high school kids. They talk behind each other's backs, feud like mean girls, and openly trash one another in earshot of inmates. Many are having affairs on the clock, disappearing off-camera. Others nap through their shift or binge-surf the internet. Despite being entrusted with monitoring the inmates, there is no accountability, and anything they say goes. If you did a random audit of the typical corrections officers of any compound, you would likely find that, on average, thirty hours of a forty-hour work week is spent online surfing the net, paid for by the American taxpayer. The only thing they all seem to be able to come together on is their mutual disdain for the incarcerated population.

Half of them are lazy, incompetent, lack qualifications, and are there for a paycheck and nothing more. You wouldn't hire these individuals to do yard maintenance, nor would they do the job because they would see it as too labor-intensive. This is why, despite repeated requests year in and year out, I have been allowed only *one* dental cleaning in twelve years. Getting help from staff is nearly impossible. Almost every employee actively obfuscates their duties and has mastered the art of passing the buck. You'll often hear: "Send a cop-out." (A cop-out is a written request, which is usually ignored.)

If you ask an officer, they will send you to your counselor. The counselor will send you to your case manager. The case manager will pass you off to your unit manager, who will forward you to an associate warden. They will take your name down and do absolutely nothing. When you return later to check on it, you are told to file an administrative remedy against a specific department. You will never do this, as it will open yourself up to retaliation from those within that department.

The other half is a mix of staff with military backgrounds, others with vendettas, and pure criminals. The veterans have figured out that they can receive a double pension from the government. They're generally solid, disciplined, fair, and focused. They won't mess with you if they see you are doing the right thing, but if they catch you doing the wrong thing, they'll bring the hammer down. As expected, they're often militant and can be harsh in their ways.

Those that arrive with a vendetta have an axe to grind. Bullied in their youth or slighted by society, they now enjoy punishing others. These are the power-drunk guards, both men and women, who thrive on controlling, humiliating, and emasculating. I once had an altercation so over the top, I had to ask, "What happened, man? Why are you so hostile?" All my property ended up being taken and tossed around the unit. Unfortunately, these folks often rise quickly through the ranks, hating the inmate population more with each year that passes, eventually becoming the very people you're forced to deal with when all other avenues of help have been exhausted.

The criminals masquerading as federal officers abuse their positions of authority and badges daily. They smuggle in contraband, steal funds, abuse inmates, and weaponize their positions for personal gain. They shift blame expertly, often pinning misdeeds on the very people they are tasked with supervising because they know that no one outside of this world would believe the word of an inmate. How is it that drugs, cell phones, and other contraband are so prevalent in an institution? Inmates are known for being incredibly resourceful and coming up with ingenious ways to introduce contraband into the institution, but when the facility performs a mass shakedown (nightmarish contraband search that involves messing with everyone's personal property in the name of finding illegal items) and finds forty-plus phones with chargers in a week, is the public supposed to believe that the inmates are making their way down to a local Walmart and buying them? The fact is, for many officers, successful shakedowns are good for business. If they find illegal items in inmate property, they are rewarded career-wise and now have an inmate who needs to purchase more.

Many of the officers in some of the institutions are active gang members, which means that the ones enforcing the rules in these places belong to the very groups the rules were meant to dismantle. It's no wonder that the Bureau of Prisons pays out hundreds of millions annually in civil and criminal liability. Hundreds of staff are indicted yearly on criminal charges, and even that's barely scratching the surface. It's like removing one flea from an infested dog's back.

I will never forget one officer in particular, Officer Martinez. This man fit into several categories mentioned above: unqualified, vengeful, thirsty for power, lacking intelligence, and engaged in criminal activity. He thrived on conflict. If you rubbed him the wrong way, he would find a reason to write you up what we call a "shot." A shot is a disciplinary infraction in prison, similar to receiving a ticket, albeit with more dire consequences. These disciplinary reports vary in severity, from minor infractions to actions that can send you straight into solitary confinement. The range of infractions goes from a 100 series to a 400 series shot.

Here are a few examples:

- 100 series: Murder
- 105 series: Rioting at the prison
- 113 series: Possession of an illicit substance.
- 201 series: Fighting
- 219 series: Stealing
- 312 series: Insolence to staff
- 324 series: Gambling
- 409 series: Unauthorized touching. (An example would be if you kiss your son or daughter on the head while having a visit with them. Most officers would not commonly write this up, but a CO like Officer Martinez would.)

Getting a shot often leads to time in solitary confinement (the SHU), loss of visitation privileges for six months, loss of calls privileges for six months, loss of access to the commissary for six months, and/or a transfer to a higher security institution if they so choose.

I and many others witnessed Officer Martinez, on countless occasions, plant contraband, drugs, and phones in an inmate's property while he was shaking them down, pulling them right from his pocket to justify the write-up. He either found the items earlier in a common area within the unit and was targeting an inmate based on suspicion or dislike, or he brought it inside the institution himself. Either way, it didn't matter. The paperwork would say that the contraband was found in the inmate's living area in their property, and that was that.

Being in prison is hard enough, and this guy desired to do all he could to make life harder. He'd strip you of your contact with family, bury you in solitary, and add months or years by removing good time earned for anything that ticked him off. Perversely, the more he did this, the more praise and promotions he received. There is no way to fight back for us inmates—you can't beat the guys with the keys. Filing a grievance guarantees retaliation; however bad it was before, rest assured, retaliation would be even worse.

Officer Martinez was finally caught in his misdeeds and was convicted of raping a female inmate at the adjoining women's camp. He is now doing time in prison himself. He is not an outlier. FCI Dublin has shut down this year because a widespread rape ring was exposed, involving the warden and other top administrative staff. Over 116 million dollars was paid out in damages to the victims. Officers pled guilty to assaulting inmates on a large scale. But for all these officers caught, too many are not.

Knowing who is who among the staff is essential, as is understanding the social order among inmates.

Prisons in the federal system are divided by race and regional affiliation, with inmates organizing into "cars." There are Black, White, and Hispanic cars, each with internal factions tied to gangs or hometowns. Each car has a "shot caller," the unofficial leader who governs decisions and enforces the rules within their car. Simply put, they make the call for what occurs within their factions. This can include coordinating an assault on another inmate or group. The higher the security of an institution, the more severe the prison politics.

Status is mainly determined by the behavior exhibited within your case. Those who kept silent took a plea or went to trial without cooperating against friends or business partners are given respect. They're considered to be solid and stand-up men. "Rats" are people who snitched on their loved ones, sometimes including their mothers, to get a lighter sentence. There is a reason why Sammy "The Bull" only received a five-year sentence for murdering fifteen people in cold blood.

In a high-security prison, Rats are often assaulted and checked into protective custody for their safety. They are not safe for long in the general population. At lower security facilities, they are still shunned but allowed to exist in the general population. Ironically, they are some of the most dangerous inmates at those levels. Not because they are violent but because they are deceptive, manipulative, and always scheming. Nothing about the criminal justice system changes a Rat's behavior because they are taught that they will benefit if they tell the government everything they want to hear. They most commonly move contraband and report on anyone they know to gain favor with the investigative unit within a prison (SIS). They provide so much information that what they say carries weight even when they lie, which allows them to take advantage of the situation further. To sit their sentence with minimal hassle, they play both sides. They drop notes and provide anonymous tips to get people locked up in the SHU under investigation all the time.

The sex offenders (SO) are another group of inmates, referred to on the inside as "chomos," which is short for child molesters. There are two kinds of SOs, "clickers"(child porn) and "touchers" (hands-on abuse). Even among themselves, they are divided by disgust, but none garner any respect from the rest of the inmate population. Many of their crimes are so vile, so grotesque, I can't speak of them on these pages. Ironically, I don't believe any of them got sentenced to more time than I did. Higher security prisons make them a protected class and designate specific locations for them because otherwise, they will only last minutes in the general population. In low-security prisons, they exist quietly, knowing they are one misstep away from violence.

Inmates are not allowed to move from one area to the next unless it is a scheduled "move." When a move is called, you have five minutes to shift location. The doors within the prison are temporarily opened and inmates can move from their units to the library, the gym, the education center or vice versa. The moves are never on time, which causes stress and chaos as you can be stuck waiting around for the move to take place or you can be completely caught off guard and need to make a run for it. As they open all doors at once, anywhere between four hundred to eight hundred people are crowding together to get in or out of a few small doorways at the same time. This is also where a lot of illegal activity takes place, whether it be drug dealing or any other sort of "prison transactions" as people are running in and out of the units in order to try and make it back within the five minutes.

* * *

Prison politics dictate everything. You live with your car and race, watch TV with them, eat with them, and walk the yard with them, and if you cross those lines, there are consequences. Every shot caller tries to keep order and discipline within their car, showing strength when they think it is needed. They use their political clout to secure the desired jobs for their own, such as kitchen, maintenance, commissary, and laundry, because all those perks translate into power and income.

The economy on the inside is one massive illegal market of earning, buying, and selling stamps. Specifically, compound stamps that have long expired for real postage but are eternally valuable on the inside. You could always buy a flat book of stamps from a commissary for the standard rate, but it loses value the second you walk out. Twenty stamps are considered a "book" worth ten dollars (each stamp is worth fifty cents). Five books? Fifty bucks. Do you want a laundry contract (have someone do your laundry for you), to get a haircut, or have something repaired? You pay in stamps. Want more than prison fare (a hockey puck they claim is a burger every Wednesday, chicken every Thursday, or a fish patty every Friday)? You can buy stolen food from the kitchen with stamps and create your meals yourself.

The institution is physically falling apart, and nothing ever gets fixed. With millions in their budget and an army of slave labor, you would find it hard to believe that the conditions would make the third world look like a resort, but it's true. Toilets leaking or running for months on end. Sinks that do not drain or work. Mold, sometimes black mold, everywhere. Power outages, 110 degrees in the unit in the summers, ice machines that don't produce ice, steam leaks everywhere in the winter, ceilings falling, roofs leaking, and it takes six months to replace a TV that has burned out because "We don't have any money for a TV." Truth is, fifty of them randomly "go missing" and "no one knows how." Theft is rampant.

The idea of rehabilitation? It's mostly a facade. Programs exist on paper to justify the budgets they have been given, but they aren't adequate for a lesson in a middle school classroom. With each passing day, the clarity deepened: I had destroyed my life long before I learned what it truly meant to live it.

# *Chapter Two*
# A Lit Fuse

Why will a man on his sailboat, lost at sea, praying for the wind to come and save him, instinctively tug at the loose frays on his sail? When standing on a cliff looking down at the ruins of a city that used to be your life, it's impossible not to contemplate how you arrived at such a moment. Where did I fail along the way? What is the meaning of this life, if there is one at all?

There will always be more questions than answers in life. Still, one thing that has become abundantly clear is that mankind is repetitively destructive.

When going down this road of exploration, initially I was not finding the answers I needed, which meant I was susceptible to repeating the same mistakes. I had already lost everything, but being incarcerated meant that those mistakes could now be fatal, and I could feel my survival instincts on high alert, working overtime, keeping me focused. Still, I wondered how much weight these instincts held over my decisions when I was unaware of their presence.

Everything I cared about was destroyed: My family, good name, business, and, worst of all, I was taken from my daughters. More than anything else, I wanted to be a good father and couldn't wait to pass along the wisdom and lessons my father taught me. The fact that I couldn't brought me more pain than anything else I have yet to experience, including the loss of my father. Everything was destroyed without a single bad intention in my heart. Why? How?

My journey of self-destruction and reflection on it are potent examples of the destructive tendencies that exist within all of us. I am sharing this with you so you can understand the importance of recognizing and acknowledging these tendencies to prevent further harm in your own life.

How and why are difficult questions to pose, and when I finally could, I found it equally difficult to be true to myself when answering because feelings of shame consumed me. These questions create an endless barrage of memories, highlighting the destruction of things you cared about deeply. How many opportunities in your life have you squandered? How many relationships have you destroyed? Friendships? Did you even take the time to see where you were at fault?

It's logical to assume the importance of understanding where we come from to better predict where we are going, but looking at universal repetitive and self-destructive patterns, I question whether society is capable of learning from the past; the weight of history's lessons should be a constant reminder for us, but they don't seem to be.

Man's propensity for self-destruction is embedded deeply. Throughout history, humanity has demonstrated this quality as an emerging paradoxical force. The duality of creation and destruction permeates every era of our history, which is both awe-inspiring and troubling. Males exist to elevate our species to greater heights through leadership and strength. Yet, they are also more easily manipulated to follow others. (A man is also nothing without a woman, and I will elaborate further on this in a later chapter.) Looking at nature and its natural order, men are designed to lead and take charge, shown throughout the animal kingdom. But when you look closely at humanity, the male species' righteous path will almost always lead to a path of destruction. Indeed, wisdom greater than our own wanted mankind to take a righteous and virtuous path, but how many times did mankind alter that path and turn it toward destruction? Did a blueprint that showed us how to maintain civil societies exist? Or are we ill-fated to endless chaos and disharmony?

There have always been those who spend their entire lives studying history. They seek knowledge and try to learn from previous mistakes to avoid repeating them in the future. But the same cycle has repeated for thousands of years, with the newest generation looking back and wondering how our ancestors could have been so foolish.

No one can successfully argue against man's destructive nature. Will we ever break this pattern? Will my children's children be looking back at us wondering the same? Are we doing now to our children what we did to the women in Salem, Massachusetts, in the 1600s? The people believed at that time that they were killing witches. Today, that seems crazy, but is it any different than surgically operating on a child to change their sex, or is the argument at present nothing more than a modern-day witch trial? History will judge us. Still, at every juncture, we can choose to supercharge our self-awareness and understand our patterns as the driving force behind self-improvement. I was drawn to look at these times for answers, knowing that the lack of understanding is the culprit for our propensity toward destruction.

History has provided endless examples of remarkable achievements and reveals our dark impulses that transform those achievements into regret. Every society, at one point or another, rose from remarkable advancement only to fall and destroy itself. Besides the comforts of our technological advancements, what makes us different from Mesopotamia, ancient Egypt, or the Roman Empire?

How far back does this destructive pattern go? When we look at our most primitive origins and prehistoric battles for survival, we can see the development of rudimentary tools. Created to help us cut wood and hunt for food, these tools quickly became weapons against those who sought the same. Naturally, as society evolved, so did our weapons and conflicts.

The earliest recorded example of this behavior is the story of Mesopotamia, 3000 BCE. At this time, the Sumerians were among the first to develop a complex society on Earth. They accomplished this through constant warfare to acquire more fertile lands and water from the Tigris and Euphrates rivers. To grow, they needed to destroy everything around them, which led to crops being ruined, infrastructure destroyed, and thousands of people dead. Again, they only exist now in the pages of history.

Nearly three thousand years later, the Roman Empire had many historians who studied the mistakes of Mesopotamia and used what they learned as a guide forward, hoping to reign supreme for thousands of years. Like those who came before them, their roads, aqueducts, and legal systems were revolutionary, setting the foundation for future civilizations. Still, their rise to greatness was yet another of the paradoxical nature of humanity's advancement, all of which came on the backs of violence, conquest, and subjugation. To grow their civilization, they had to destroy countless others. In the famous battle of Carthage, a rival of Rome was utterly razed to the ground, their people slaughtered and enslaved, even going as far as to salt their lands so nothing could ever grow there again. Is anything more destructive? This is why, if you want to vacation today in the Roman Empire, you can stand outside the ruins of a once magnificent coliseum.

Searching through the past started to feel futile. How would I find answers for the present and future in a past where it was clear that a state of antebellum never existed, and looking at the state of the world in the present shows no indication of moving away from this insanity?

Einstein once defined insanity as doing the same thing repeatedly while expecting a different result. As sharp as he was, this definition is flawed at its core. When we look at human history, we see a pattern of repeating the same mistakes across generations. Does that make us insane?

If you take a ball and toss it up and down repeatedly only a few inches into the air, even though it is a trivial task, I expect something different will occur, and I will drop it at some point. It may take a day or two to do so, but eventually, I will tire, my motor functions will shut down, lactic acid will fill my arm, and I will drop it. Given Einstein's definition, thinking like this would have made me insane, which is why we cannot classify our species as such, although we have not obtained enough insight to see ahead to our purpose. If humanity were without purpose, we wouldn't be able to reflect and rise. Our repeated mistakes don't signify a lack of reason or insight; they highlight our growth potential. Where we need to improve is the foresight to recognize in what ways our growth can breed destruction and then account for it moving forward.

Take Benjamin Holt, for example, a man who, in 1904, revolutionized agriculture by inventing a continuous track for tractors. This innovation allowed humanity to feed a growing population and utilize farmland in terrain previously considered too rugged to reach. His invention was a true leap forward, meant to benefit mankind. Yet, almost immediately, the British Military co-opted his design, which led to the invention of tanks in warfare—a perfect instrument of death.

This pattern emerges repeatedly everywhere you look. Nuclear energy, developed initially with the hope of providing clean, endless power, became the atomic bomb. The internet, designed for sharing knowledge and fostering communication, has become a battlefield of cyberwarfare, disinformation, and hate. Chemical research for medical advancement became nerve agents and mustard gas; weather satellites became spy apparatuses. Biotech for medical treatment became COVID-19.

The realization that not only have we not escaped our propensity for destruction but that the more advanced we become, the more accelerated that destruction seems to be is incredibly scary. The world has never been more dangerous than today, yet we have the advantage of being able to learn from our past and can radically change course.

In ancient Egypt, the Pharaoh could not understand why Moses wanted to leave to be a religious nomad in the desert. Egypt, the epitome of advancement, believed itself to be invincible, and the Pharaoh thought Moses was insane. At that time in history, Egypt led the world in technological advancement, agriculture, science, education, architecture, and medicine, and the fact that Moses wanted to take his people and leave for the desert wasn't something the Pharaoh could fathom. It would be like working on a mega yacht and telling the captain you would like to leave on the lifeboat with your co-workers to float out into the unknown ocean. This is how the Pharaoh saw Moses's request, and he denied it. You know the story of the plagues and what followed until, ultimately, Moses and his people were freed.

If I asked you, "Where is ancient Egypt today?" what would you say? It exists only in a museum. It exists now in our history books. A lot can be said about this, but it is much easier to point out the obvious. Ancient Egypt neither had nor followed any blueprint, and that is because God did not provide one to them. They ended up destroying themselves. But what about those who did? What about the Children of Israel?

The Torah, the Bible, the blueprint given on the journey into the desert, is still followed today by Jewish people worldwide. Comparing these two nations, one with and one without concrete directives, leads to an unmistakable contrast in the outcomes of both people.

Fast-forward to today, when remnants of ancient Egypt can be viewed from behind glass, but the Jewish people have endured millennia and currently stand at the forefront of all human advancement. These are vastly different fates and a testament to the power of adhering diligently to a higher purpose via a purposeful guide.

Purpose. Meaning. Direction. A guide to life. Are these the factors that work? Or that would help me? How was I going to choose a new direction, and did I know enough about myself to choose the right direction? How would I know?

## *Chapter Three*

# Know Thyself: Nosce Te Ipsum

This maxim, inscribed at the Temple of Apollo, a revered site in ancient Greece known for its association with prophecy and wisdom, is one of several aphorisms said to have been delivered by Apollo. It has transcended cultures and epochs, shaping philosophical discourse, personal introspection, and ethical conduct throughout history. It continually evolved throughout every generation, providing insight into its enduring relevance.

Socrates, one of the greatest philosophers in history, believed that self-knowledge created the foundation for virtue and ethical behavior, and choosing not to take on this difficult journey would leave a person without an understanding of their place in the world and the inability to make moral decisions or live a virtuous life. And this philosophy was what the founding fathers had in mind when crafting the Constitution.

Epictetus and Seneca, Stoic philosophers, believed that this path was the means to achieve tranquility and self-mastery, thus attaining *eudaimonia* or the "highest human good," a state of flourishing and fulfillment. Influenced by them, Cicero, a Roman philosopher, believed that understanding oneself was crucial to being an effective leader, as seen in much of his writing on ethics and personal duty.

During the period of late antiquity, Christian theologians such as Augustine of Hippo incorporated these previous teachings and saw the journey inward as a path toward God. Augustine concluded that to grow spiritually and achieve divine understanding, one must self-reflect and confess one's sins.

The Renaissance brought with it a revival of classical thinking, emphasizing individualism and our potential within. Humanists like Erasmus and Michel de Montaigne revisited their understanding of "know thyself" through the lens of personal growth and intellectual development. For Montaigne, self-knowledge was about recognizing the fragile parts of us and working on better understanding the complexities of individual identity.

Every interpretation of this ancient maxim throughout history has merit and is worthy of study and analysis. It has traversed a long and varied history and has become the cornerstone of philosophical, religious, and psychological thought. However, as humanity continues to evolve and the world is forever changing, the call to understand oneself has never seemed more important than now and is paramount if a harmonious world is desired.

There is no way to look at the history of this maxim and solutions previously put forth and apply it to the technologically advanced world of today, a world dominated by social media, instant communication, and constant external influence. This is why only a handful of people can achieve this internal transformation, leaving the rest to live a life where true meaning and purpose elude them. Suppressed by a lifelong struggle with external influences, the most beautiful parts of our soul remain tethered and hidden, revealing themselves only through small, fleeting actions—often so subtle they go unnoticed.

At some point or another, everyone fails at being whoever they believe they are supposed to be, an expectation passed from generation to generation, imposing itself on the blank canvas of our lives. Emphasis on what's essential for an individual is grossly and deliberately lacking when it needs to be the highest priority in life. Understanding who you truly are is the winning recipe. Only self-comparison matters, despite being led otherwise, and until we recognize this, we remain on a futile path. No one will ever be able to shine when standing on someone else's sun.

The greatest qualities humanity has to offer, the best versions of ourselves, are inside of everyone, and the key to unlocking that part of yourself is a most challenging journey, often taking decades of life experience and self-reflection, and many tools available to assist us in this process are grossly outdated. If any of the philosophers previously mentioned were alive today, they would not understand the world we are living in. It would seem like an alien planet. A man like Socrates could never consider the effects of TikTok, social media, or any of the modern-day external influences when attempting to bring us down the path to enlightenment, thus making the previous guides he created obsolete. None of the philosophers were able to take a long and visceral look at life in a digital era before bringing forth solutions.

Many people live their lives without realizing their full potential, failing to offer the world what they could. However, it's never too late to embark on the journey of self-discovery. By recognizing the importance of understanding oneself, we can avoid the regret of unfulfilled potential and strive to make the most of our lives.

Factions in both government and the private sector intentionally create roadblocks to this journey of self-realization. The most powerful in society obtain more power with a weaker population. That way, when the wolves descend, everyone will look for a shepherd to guide them. They want to be your shepherd.

When the world is telling you who you are and where you are supposed to be, how can you know any different? The ruling class have erected a wall you cannot climb, with armed guards at the ready. As previously stated, Montaigne believed we needed to be self-aware of the complexities of individual identity to find the most authentic version of ourselves, but how is that possible today when those who seek power continually create complexity and discourse surrounding individual or independent thought? This is why there is a deliberate action to place everyone into a category or group, hoping to enslave them to their assignment as a measure of control.

Questions were clawing their way to the surface and I realized that to become truly self-aware I needed to identify within myself the things in life I was certain about, that which I knew to be true deep within my heart and soul, and in attempting to do so a memory from my past came to mind.

## *Chapter Four*

# Inside of Us All

When my girls were toddlers, my mother continually pestered me until I brought them for a visit. "Bring me my grandkids" she would text quite often. My parents adored playing the role of grandparents. It became the joy of their lives, and my father had never been softer or warmer than when his granddaughters were in their home playing with dolls on his lap. It was surreal for me to watch.

On this one occasion, it had been a while since I had brought them for a visit, and I arrived at my childhood home, tired and hungry. I deposited the girls with their awaiting grandparents and went straight to the fridge. Inside, there was not a single thing that I enjoyed. It was stacked from top to bottom with everything the girls liked. I had officially been replaced. Despite my hunger, I was happy; I loved watching my parents spoil my girls.

But I was hungry.

"Hey, Mom, I'm heading to the DPM."

"Why? Did you not just see the fridge? It's stocked to the brim."

"Thank you, but string cheese, squeezy yogurts, and juice boxes will not cut it. Do you need anything?" I asked.

She didn't respond. She was in full Grandma mode.

The Dennis Public Market was only two minutes away from my parents' house, at the end of the only road into my neighborhood. Pulling into the parking lot was nostalgic for me, and it brought me back to the thousand times I had done it before, whether as a child on a bike or in my car while in high school.

I got out of the car and headed toward the entrance, noticing an elderly woman almost frozen directly in front of my path to the entrance. The only movement I saw from her was a slight swaying back and forth, and I was instantly concerned, wondering if she was having a health-related issue. I increased my walking speed until I was standing directly behind her. She was still unaware of my presence. I was about to place my hand on her shoulder and ask her if she was okay when I heard her speaking. I was quickly able to identify that she was praying. I was going to continue past her, but desperation in her voice somehow anchored me next to her, listening.

It felt intrusive, but I remained close, sensing that I was meant to be there for some reason. After another minute of swaying and praying, she tilted her head slightly and raised her hands halfway in the air, crying out, "Why? Why, God, why did you bring me such tragedy?" The bellicosity in her tone was clear, her pain real, and I felt an emotional wetness begin behind my eyes.

The social norm would have been to continue walking on, leaving her to her prayer. Still, whatever her tragedy was, I had inadvertently absorbed some and felt compelled to involve myself. That's the thing about tragedy in life. Buried within is a short-term solution that can erase all the programmed behaviors within. The catalyst can ignite the spark of the most significant part of us, even if only for a moment.

I took a step closer to her, and she could see me. Our eyes met for the first time, and I took her hand as softly as I could.

"The power of tragedy and tragedy alone is that it evokes humanity's best and inspires change."

I watched as the pain lifted from her face, leaving her eyes like storm clouds fading from the sky. She didn't smile but patted my hand softly, saying only, "Thank you." Her gratitude was a testament to the power of human connection in the face of tragedy.

This is one of the things that I know in my core to be true. Tragedy was not brought into the world as a means of destruction. Instead, it brings with it a transformative power: an awakening that strips us of the cloak of outside influences we all wear and unleashes that which we have suppressed and kept dormant—the best version of who we are, our truest self. Tragedies serve as a reminder of our shared humanity, for in the face of this form of adversity, we set aside our perceived differences and come together to support one another. Most people believe that tragic events in life exist to teach us how to survive in the world, but I do not agree. These difficult moments exist to motivate some of us to want to change the world.

Sadly, there is no shortage of evidence in our history of this magical awakening. Whether we are talking about the horror of September 11, 2001, or the catastrophic damage caused by Hurricane Katrina in 2004, the days following were extraordinary. All backgrounds united. First responders and regular citizens, including firefighters, police officers, medical personnel, and our everyday neighbors, risked their lives to save others. We stood as a people, united in these times to donate blood, help with search and rescue, and provide support for victims' families. Churches and communities opened their doors. Governments, NGOs, and small businesses contributed billions of dollars to help rebuild and provide food and shelter. The sense of unity and resilience was unmistakable as everyone came together.

But when time passes, as it tends to, the awakening of shared tragedy begins to fade away like the sun on the horizon, and people revert to the person they believe they are supposed to be. The salvation of your internal imprisonment morphs from a calling into a whisper. The freedom tragedy grants you disappears like the fog being burned off by the sun, and we are all right back where we started—where we are told to be. That doesn't change what just occurred. In those moments, the truest version of us is revealed as proof of its very existence. We just have to be self-aware enough to recognize it.

## *Chapter Five*

# Follow the Compass

It's possible for the best version of us to emerge without the catalyst of tragedy, but having spent over a decade on this journey, I will tell you that it is difficult, painful, and rooted in self-discovery. I hope to save some of you from the long-term pain I experienced by offering a modernized roadmap to the gold at the end of the rainbow.

The most accessible place to begin is through an identifying question.

Suppose you could go back once and change anything from your past. What would you change? Be raw and honest. The answer is not for anyone but yourself.

Please put this book down for a few minutes and think about the answer; it is vital to your internalization of this process.

If you have jumped to reading instead of doing this quick exercise, know that you are avoiding the answer, which is step one to never getting there. For the rest of you, welcome back.

If you said yes and flashes of bad choices from your past invaded your mind, you are still the person you believe you are supposed to be. You have not yet freed yourself.

For those who said no, you did so because you are connected to your authentic self and know that you would not have been able to become this person if not for every experience that came before.

Many readers may feel stuck and believe they are fated to repeatedly make the same mistakes in life. You are not, but understanding the why will help you change course. You feel as you do because you are still on a path in life that others intended for you to be on. You are not traveling the road you are fated to follow even though it is always directly in front of you.

Life sent me down a long, painful road, a journey I wish on no one. It was a deadly obstacle course devoid of light, leaving me scared of falling to the edge of nothingness with each step.

Darkness is often described as the absence of light from a person's life, literally and/or emotionally, but I suspect those who define it in these terms haven't experienced it from the inside. If they had, they would know it is far more complex.

True darkness is a belief, a conviction, that never again will light return to your life.

Whenever we are thrust into an experience saturated with an unnatural darkness, something primal begins to stir within, trying to help us claw our way out of the darkness. Instinct propels the mind forward, beginning to analyze every day before the darkness falls so we can frame it in a way we can hold it. We hope that by framing our view in as optimal light as possible we will minimize the guilt we may feel from our actions or choices and help relinquish our responsibility. It is easier to be the victim. If I am, I don't have to change. I can also blame others and exercise anger. However, all options are futile and will not stop the cycle you wish to break.

The process is excruciating, but like anything in life, reshapes you into your future self. When tragedy ran into me like a raging bull, I met darkness full on and because of it, I am who I am today.

Despite my personal experience, which I will be underscoring, the essence of my writing emphasizes that growth, perspective, introspection, and self-discovery can all be achieved without having to experience tragedy in one's own life.

Ideally, you shift and live the life meant for you before a raging bull forces the shift. And that is what I want to encourage you to do today. Regardless of where you find yourself, embrace change, for it is the key to unlocking your true potential and living the life you were meant to live.

For me, it became about recognizing the gifts provided to me within my own experience and utilizing them to help myself and now others become who we truly are. Life is a barrel of lessons; the sooner we learn them, the less expensive they are.

When you encounter a barrier in life that seems too high to climb, you must build a pair of wings and fly above it. After an initial period of despair, I remembered what I believed and began searching for a pair of wings, knowing they had to be hidden somewhere within the dark.

Armed with the foundational beliefs that had been instilled in me long ago I went searching deep within to find them.

No matter how you view yourself currently, understand that it's impossible to truly know yourself without honest self-reflection. Identifying who you are and why you do what you do is challenging. I don't recommend doing this without guidance.

Because if I asked you to reflect on something you deeply regret in your past, how can you be sure you aren't circumventing feelings of guilt about your behavior at the moment? Would you recognize if you were? Perhaps you are in a space where you are trying to practice "self-love" and healing and thus being kinder to yourself rather than helpful, or you are naturally inclined to look for fault elsewhere as a defensive reflex. The point is, if you can't see yourself, there is no possible way you will be able to reflect on past events either.

The problem with attempting to self-reflect without proper perspective is that it will run you in a circle, leading you back to being the person you believe you are supposed to be. It's a vicious circle, the path laid before us by external expectation. When the Marine Corps changes a civilian into a warrior, they take them down a meticulous course, breaking them down and rebuilding them into a fighting machine. The lessons embedded within my experience will help you break down your preconceived notions of who you believe you are supposed to be, and the "machine" you will become is an engine of change.

I had my first breakthrough at the beginning of this journey. It was the moment some light flashed into the darkness, and this flash came from my ability to correctly identify the unique talents I possess. These talents are undeniably present, whether you attribute them to a higher power or not.

Our parents often spot these gifts in us as children before we can be considered self-aware. Still, it isn't until we immerse ourselves in society that we may be able to identify our uniqueness further.

I knew that answers were not going to come easy and if I wanted to understand the man I was looking at in the mirror, I was going to have to start in the early days and reexamine my life from a critical lens.

## *Chapter Six*

# Talent Me Forward

As a child, my communication skills were noticeable to everyone around me besides myself. Inwardly, I knew I could identify feelings or thoughts even if one wanted to hide their emotions from the world. Facial movement and body language spoke to me more clearly than words, and it was as if I was destined to hear the radio clearly despite everyone else hearing static. The caveat was that I had to tune in, and the only time I did choose to tune in was when I needed or wanted something. However, once I tuned in, I could easily communicate with anyone, as I was hearing precisely what sometimes wasn't even being conveyed. At an early age, I could identify the incredible influence I wielded. My mother thought I had the gift of gab cloaked in charisma, but my ability to transfer my emotions from one person to another proved far more significant as I matured.

From a young age, I always appreciated having money in my pocket. I remember collecting all the fives and singles that would come to me inside holiday and birthday cards and putting them into a tight roll. My mother took anything of more value for the bank and I may have kept only thirty to forty dollars, but rolled in half, it felt to me like a million. My imagination would run wild, and it was glorious.

The summer of '94 was the first time I met with a venture capitalist looking for an investment in a new venture. I was ten, and the venture capitalist was my father. I wanted to find a way to earn my own money and came up with the idea that I could cut grass around the neighborhood. I practiced what I would say for hours before he got home. When he did, I didn't give him time to take off his work boots.

"Dad, I need to talk to you, it's very important."

He shot me a look that seemed more like an acknowledgment that he recognized the look on my face. He knew I was about to ask him for something.

"Important, you say? So important that I can't take my boots off first?" he asked.

"You should be happy I wasn't blocking the driveway," I said.

He laughed. "Okay, hit me with it."

I gave him my pitch and told him I needed him to buy me a mower, and I would pay him back with the proceeds I earned. I had practiced for hours and realized within seconds that I didn't need to. I could see pride on his face, and he loved my initiative.

"I'll tell you what, I don't want any of the money you earn from your clients. That is yours. I want you to also cut our lawn, and every time you do, I will apply a ten-dollar credit to what you owe me until you no longer owe me anything. That is my only offer. Do we have a deal?" he asked.

Ten dollars? I was going to charge twice that amount in the neighborhood. I considered protesting the amount, citing some child labor laws I knew nothing about. I knew my efforts were worth more, but I also knew my father, and the fastest way to get him to change his mind would be by saying anything other than:

"Yes, thank you, we have a deal," I said with artificial excitement.

"It's a good thing I didn't take these boots off. Put your shoes on, and let's pick out your mower."

While we were picking out the mower in the store, my eyes went to the weed whackers. We already had one at home, but it wasn't mine. I was about to pitch him on buying me one of those when an idea came to mind. Yes, we made a deal, but there was nothing in our terms that said I couldn't renegotiate at a later point.

The following week, I gave our lawn its first manicure. I worked hard on it, and it was hot. It was worth more than ten dollars. When my father came home that evening, he was pleased.

"Looks like that mower works well. The yard looks good," he said.

He gave me an opening. "Yes, the yard looks good, but it is sort of like making a cake without icing," I replied.

"I don't understand," my father responded.

"Well, we made a deal that I would cut the grass, but when I finished, I noticed it also needs to be weed whacked. Now, I am not going to ask for one because you already purchased the mower, so instead, I am wondering if I could borrow yours, and I will charge a discounted price. Five bucks, making the total weekly credit fifteen dollars. Is that okay?"

He didn't blink. A deal was struck, and I decided to follow through with the rest of my plan. The following week, I upped the ante again.

"We have a problem," I said as if the world was about to end.

"We do, huh? What problem is that?" he said, his voice riddled with skepticism.

"Well, you bought me a lawn mower that doesn't have a bag, and as you can see, all of the dead grass is starting to build up on the lawn, and Mom is getting mad at us for tracking it in the house." Little did anyone know, I intentionally tracked some in earlier in the day to set the stage. (Sorry, Mom, if you're reading this. I can hear her now. "You little shit.")

I continued, "We didn't buy a mower with a bag on it. If we had, I would have simply walked it out into the woods and dumped it. But as it stands, if you want this stuff cleared, I am going to need to borrow your tarp, rake up everything onto it, and drag it out to the woods."

"You can borrow my tarp, no problem," he replied quickly.

"Slight problem. That is almost as much work as mowing is, and that wasn't the deal we made. I am willing to do everything, but I think I should be able to earn another ten-dollar credit, which means I will earn a twenty-five-dollar credit each week." I remained silent while he thought about what I was saying.

This was when my father began to look at me differently, realizing he would have to think hard before making a deal with me. In hindsight, it would have been much better for me to wait to show him this side of me until my teens rather than showing my cards early. It would have allowed me to get away with a little more for a little longer.

When winter came, I converted my mowing services into shoveling driveways and walkways for my existing clients. They were happy to keep me in business, which gave me the confidence to approach my dad with the same offer.

The next day, he came home from work with a plow on his truck. I remember thinking that it better not break because the cost of my services would now be double.

My knack for entrepreneurship wasn't born out of a desire for cash. My family inspired it. Before starting my venture, I worked for my grandfather on the weekends. He was a lifelong businessman in the car and restaurant industries, which helped fuel my ambition. My favorite place he owned was the Dunes restaurant on Route 28, where I washed dishes for him for twenty dollars a weekend. It was highway robbery, so you can imagine where my idea to protest under child labor laws when my father offered me ten dollars came from. I was trained to think this way due to my grandfather being cheap. But I loved the work, and soon enough, I was helping to prep, cook, and bus tables and was even allowed to serve breakfast when the crowd was light.

By '96, I was always working and doing something, and my family took notice of my work ethic. My grandmother and grandfather had divorced long before I was born, and I was much closer to my grandmother. Little did I know that competition started brewing when she discovered what my grandfather paid me. She ran and operated the Tony Kent Ice Arena on the Cape and my brother and I grew up playing hockey. It didn't take long for her to offer me a job working for her. A real job. She paid me minimum wage, and I would earn an actual paycheck with taxes taken out and everything. I felt so important. Later, Gramps.

At first, I started out in the snack bar because I already knew every inch of it from my time at the rink, and within no time, I was wearing many hats. Being a good skater, I was a skate guard for public skating and "teen rock night." I would clean, work in the pro shop sharpening skates, and change out the glass for different events. By fourteen, I was taught how to drive the

Zamboni. Yes, driving one is awesome, albeit I only was allowed to do so a couple of times with adult supervision.

I was saving money, but I wanted a car the day I would get my license, a few short years away, so all my free time went to work. I added whatever I could, including picking up a small early morning weekend gig at the Donut Shack a hundred feet from the Dennis Public Market. I was pushing coffee and crappy donuts for tips, but the locals on the Cape were always hard-working and generous, and customer service became something I was able to fine-tune. A few days before I got my license, I became the proud owner of a 1991 Oldsmobile Cutlass Supreme. It wasn't lovely, but it was mine. I paid 100 percent of it on my own, and the feeling was powerful.

With a car, I wasn't limited to jobs within biking distance. One afternoon, I hopped in my car and began to comb the town for after-school employment. I dreamed of upgrading the vehicle to suit the dates I planned to take beautiful girls out on.

I spent hours looking but wasn't finding anything that was suitable. I pulled into the drive-thru of a Dunkin Donuts to get a coffee from my friend Danielle. While waiting for her to bring me my coffee, extra cream, extra sugar, I noticed a Now Hiring sign in the Radio Shack across the street next to the bowling alley. I had never been inside a Radio Shack and decided now was as good a time as any. I wasn't dressed in a business manner, so I would have to turn up the charm to compensate.

When I went in, the store manager, Hassan, greeted me. He was dressed nicely, and I took notice of the precision with which he tied his Windsor knot. I instantly regretted not looking more presentable, but there was no turning back now.

After chatting with him a bit and learning about the job and pay, it seemed like the opportunity I was looking for. The hours would work perfectly for an after-school gig. There was only one problem.

"Listen, you seem like a great kid and perfect for this type of work. Tandy Corporation has a minimum hiring age of eighteen, so I am sorry, but I can't give you a job," he said.

I didn't expect to hear a "no," and I must tell you that I was not a fan of it at all. I decided to redefine what it meant. He just needed to know more.

"I am sure they have that policy for a good reason, but if you get to 'know' me a little more, you will quickly learn that I am a reason people would change their policy. Look, you're the manager of this store here, and I am going to guess that the more volume this place does, the more money you make and the better you look, right?" I was arrogant in my teenage years, flaunting my talent like a child wielding a gun.

He smiled, and I continued.

"Plus, if I turn out to be as good as I am telling you I am, then you are going to look like a good leader with good instincts, and if not, all you would have to do is fire me. So, let's go ahead and make a call to whoever the big boss is and get me some sort of waiver. I promise you will be happy you did," I said, awaiting my "yes," placing my hand out to be shaken. "Deal?"

"I like you, kid. I can't promise you anything, but I will see what I can do, okay?" he said, shaking my hand.

Not okay. I wanted to start tomorrow after school.

"Let's be honest for a second," I continued. "You have to be good at sales to become a store manager like this, right?" I asked.

"Yes," he said.

"You don't have to be modest. Clearly, you're a beast, and if you want this to happen, then you can make it happen. I am going to buy some shirts and ties and will be back tomorrow ready to blow the roof off this place. You'll see; you won't regret this."

I started the next day and a discussion about his conversation with whomever never took place.

## *Chapter Seven*
# Doors Open

Learning the products, electronic parts, and pay structure was a journey of its own. The prospect of earning more with each sale was a motivating factor. To sell, I had to understand. And I did.

Before long it became as natural as breathing. Someone who was coming for a replacement battery for their cordless phone would end up leaving the store with a brand-new home phone system, possibly with a new cell phone, plan, a new TV with warranty, and a new subscription to Direct TV as well. And they left happy. See, if I fell in love with the product and features, it was easy for me to get anyone to feel as I did about it. This was the gift God gave me. I was able to connect with the products I was selling on a personal level, which made it easy for me to connect with potential clients as well. I was upselling, but with purpose.

Tandy tracked the efficiency of their salespeople by a measure of ATP (Average Ticket Price). When I worked there, the average ticket price for a sales representative in Massachusetts was around fourteen dollars per receipt. That meant that the average customer would spend $14.00 when they shopped. Hassan and I were located off the beaten path and were not considered a high-volume store like one in a mall would be. Roughly forty people would come in on my shift. Still, at the end of my first year, my ATP was above ninety dollars; at sixteen years old, I had the highest overall average in the state. Hassan's bosses took notice and were paying close attention.

"See, I told you I would make you look good," I told Hassan.

My father was proud of me for keeping my word. I started there to earn enough money to cover my bills, which I was doing, plus anything I wanted.

After two successful years at Tandy, I was offered an exciting opportunity by Radio Shack. They wanted to provide me with a position managing my store with room for advancement, offering a career path as an alternative to college. However, as the first person in my bloodline to go to college, I did not feel comfortable bringing this choice to my mother. She was already so proud of me, making me proud of myself. I respectfully turned it down, valuing the pride and support of my family over a potentially lucrative career path.

In 2002, I began my first year at UMass Dartmouth. The first two years of college were magical. I can't think of a time when I had more fun, but as my sophomore year ended, I started wanting to get more serious with my life. "Fun" seemingly lost its luster, and without consulting my parents, I began to look for a transfer option. Ironically, the law didn't speak to me, which was why I had initially signed up for UMass Dartmouth.

I have never had a solid relationship with my biological father, Al. My stepdad, to whom this book is dedicated, married my mom when I was three, but because Al was part of the faculty at Boston University for over thirty years, I would not be charged tuition due to their policy for families of faculty. Thus, I decided on a transfer to BU and accepted the free tuition. Upon doing so, I felt terrible. It was the first time in my life that I took the "easier" road. It did not sit well. Going to BU for free because my biological father worked there felt wrong, and I was incredibly angry that I made this choice.

Toward the end of 2004, my brother finished his final deployment to Iraq and was honorably discharged from his service as a United States Marine. He was dating a girl from Myrtle Beach at the time and decided to move in with her, but whenever I spoke with him on the phone, I knew something was off. He kept talking about me coming down and spending time with him, but it didn't feel like that was what he was asking me to do. It felt more like he needed his brother but was reluctant to admit something he was trained to perceive as weakness.

I looked for colleges close to him, and when I found one that worked I immediately submitted another transfer down south before BU had responded. There weren't as many options as there were in New England, so I decided to be creative. By transferring credits from UMass to both Horry-Georgetown Technical College and FMU (Francis Marion), I was able to earn credit toward an associate's degree and a bachelor's degree at the same time for no additional cost. Because of the transferred credits I only had two classes at HGTC before obtaining that degree.

The girl I was then dating, who became the mom of our two beautiful daughters, followed me to South Carolina.

With school and relationships then sorted, I needed work.

I called my old bosses at Tandy, who previously had offered me an opportunity to stay, and explained my situation, hoping they knew of something in that neck of the woods. Not only did they hire me back on that call, but they also offered me a regional trainer position, which had me covering four stores close to where I was living, helping elevate their salespeople's numbers while also training on new products. The required hours were the same as when I worked part-time after school, but the earning potential was slightly better than before so long as I made some sales, too. Work was sorted.

However, the very reason I moved down to South Carolina was not. I was losing Alan, my honest, funny, and honorable brother. Two years went by, and he worsened with time. The aftermath of war was seriously affecting him, and despite my life taking shape in South Carolina, his was not. I convinced him to return to Cape Cod, which seemed the better option for him at the time.

At that point, I had finished school, become a dad to a miniature clone of myself, and bought my first home, so while my brother returned home, I stayed in Myrtle Beach.

In the early months of '06, I headed to the North Myrtle Beach store just like any other day, ready to sell and train. Radio Shack was trying to modernize to compete with outfits like Best Buy, and added AT&T, known as Cingular Wireless at that time, to its list of products. I had to train the staff in how to sell it.

I stood at the front door entrance, where endless opportunities to make money would be walking by every second, and I modeled this for the staff. I noticed a man coming toward me wearing a black suit, a salmon dress shirt, a matching handkerchief in his breast pocket, and a Verizon Wireless bag in hand.

I moved as he began passing the storefront, with my staff watching.

"Excuse me, sir, are you okay?" I asked, with a tone of concern.

He looked puzzled. "Yes, I'm fine. Why?"

"Well, it looks like your bag is weighing you down. What do you have in there, bricks?"

"No, just a phone. Pretty light."

"Is it? If you knew what you had just gotten yourself into, you'd realize it's much heavier than it seems. Come inside, let me show you the mistake you just made, and you can thank me after."

Curiosity got the better of him. He forgot all about wherever he was heading, and I seized the opportunity.

I could tell right away he was in sales. A fisherman can always spot another fisherman from afar. He kept throwing objections at me in the middle of my pitch, not because he objected but because he wanted to see how I would handle them. I caught on quickly and decided to preempt what I knew was coming. The classic "I need to think about it" line.

I was going to have to gamble a little. I interrupted him, "What do you do for a living, sir, if you don't mind me asking?"

"Not at all; I am one of the owners at Burroughs and Chapin."

I recognized the name and knew sales were connected to their organization, but I wasn't a local and needed to learn more about the company. I went with what I knew best: sales.

"Great, I love working with a successful salesperson. Do you know why?"

"Why?" he asked.

"Because a successful salesperson will never get to the end of something and tell you they need to think about it. If we like it, we will use it, and if we can afford it, we buy it. Simple as that."

He smiled, and so did I. We both knew that now he wasn't going to be able to get to the end of this thing and spring that on me. If he did, he would essentially be calling himself unsuccessful, and I knew his ego would not allow for it. All that was left was to show him a better offer, and I did. He ditched Verizon and signed a contract with Cingular. Sorry, Verizon; nothing personal.

What I did then took it to the next level, changing his perception of our interaction from something impressive to something he desired. At the register, we had a promotional Mont Blanc pen for sale for $100.00. The proceeds were meant to go somewhere good, but I can't remember exactly where. As he was about to sign his contract, I pulled one of the pens out and asked, "Shouldn't you be using this?"

This time, an exhausted chuckle, "I don't need a hundred-dollar pen," and he proceeded to sign with the pen attached to the counter by a chain.

My staff was watching.

"Are you sure about that?" I asked. "I could be wrong with my assumption, but a man who dresses like you and is an owner of a company like yours, wouldn't that make you a man with a valuable signature? I mean, you are wearing a pretty nice Cartier watch, and that is probably because you value your time. That being the case, how could you not also value your signature? Am I mistaken?"

Now his laughter was out loud. "You little shit, not bad, not bad at all." At this moment, I finally understood when my mother would say this to me, but there was a difference in me from then to now and something my staff could see. I believed in what I was saying and the product I was moving; otherwise, I would not be pushing them on him. I had studied Cingular for months in preparation of their rollout and knew the coverage area and signal strength in Horry County. It far outweighed Verizon at that moment and time. I was also going to offer him a service plan that gave him much more for far less than would be the case with his new cell phone. As for the pen . . . I wanted to be that person. I wanted to become someone whose signature mattered, and that person was supposed to be someone like the man in front of me, except he didn't see it. I used passion, not pressure.

After he threw me a curveball, he handed me back his credit card, and I handed him the pen to sign the receipt for it.

"Come and work for me," he said, dead serious.

# *Chapter Eight*
# Head in the Lion's Mouth

I declined.

Fear had, uncharacteristically, set in. I was a new father with a new home. I had bills. This was no longer only about me. I had a family to support. He tried to sway me. He spoke of my wasted talent, room for potential, and unlimited possibilities. Finally, he handed me his card and thanked me for the fun experience.

He did return, but on that day, I was training in another shop, and I did not follow up. I left the exchange in my past and forged ahead.

Months passed. One day, I received a call from a woman named Laney Herrington. Her voice was loud and forceful, yet polite. I learned that she got my name and number the night before.

Top executives from the hospitality industry, essentially the good ole boys' club, had one of their annual dinners where they glad-handed each other on being masters of the universe. The man from Burroughs and Chapin had been in attendance. As Laney tells it, her boss, the Vice President of Sale and Marketing for the largest hospitality corporation in the world, sat and listened to Burroughs and Chapin go on and on about a young man that he met and who had a talent he had never seen before. Drinks flowed, and he became more animated throughout the night, lamenting how he couldn't convince me to come and work for him. Laney's boss acquired my first name and where I worked, and early the following day, he came straight into her office with those two pieces of information and told her to "find him and get him in here."

She spent all morning on the phone trying to track me down. I don't know why talking to her was different than talking to Burroughs and

Chapin. Maybe it was because I was relaxed at home, or the seed had already been planted months before, but she was persistent and kind. Eventually, I agreed to a meeting.

When I first stepped foot in the behemoth's corporate center offices, I was mesmerized by the luxury. It was like stepping into a five-star gold crown hotel, with its opulent decor and bustling atmosphere. Laney met me at the entrance and brought me right up the stairs to her office. The loud noise of business being conducted around me was infectious, and the smell of fresh popcorn filled the air. Once we sat, she pressed a button on her phone, ordered in coffee for us both, and began her recruitment process. Occasionally, a beautiful young female would alternate with others and come by, making their presence known, saying hi to Laney, and welcoming me as if I was already employed. It was a schmooze fest and about as subtle as a gun, but there was no denying they captured my attention.

Eventually, I had enough of the bells and whistles, and I said bluntly: "You haven't technically offered me anything yet, but I assume the job is mine if I want it?"

Laney smiled and nodded.

"Okay, show me what you are offering. Let me see your pay structure."

She laid out their commission-based pay sheet, and after a glance, I was almost in disbelief at how much money I had the potential to make. This was a different animal, after all.

"Ms. Herrington, I would greatly appreciate it if I could take a few moments to speak with some of your staff. I want to get a feel for this place before I give you an answer."

She hesitated for a moment. No one had ever asked her this before, but she agreed. I thought about my newborn at home and knew I had to do some due diligence first. I began walking around the 25,000-square-foot sales floor, talking to the employees who were not currently entertaining a client. I asked how they felt about working there and how much each made the month before. The answers varied: $4,500, $8000; one guy I came across with the same name as my brother told me he had made $19,000 the month prior. Every one of them seemed like a dullard to me. I had heard enough.

I returned to Laney's office. "You did your job well. I'm in and will give my current employer two weeks' notice."

Five weeks from that day in the summer of '06, I was ready to see my first client. Almost immediately after deciding to change my career, something inside me changed. I was nervous. I knew I had an incredible talent but lacked the experience to match it. Was I going to be able to rely on my talent alone? I couldn't take that risk. Every free moment that followed, I read books, mainly focusing on sales and behavioral science. I was determined to understand people and how they make decisions, believing that the better I understood them, the more my talents would be elevated. This dedication to self-improvement became a defining part of me.

It became an obsession, taking up more of my time than college courses ever could. The deeper I went, the more interested I became.

# Chapter Nine
# Why We Do

Physician and neuroscientist Paul MacLean's framework of the Triune Model divides the brain into three regions: the midbrain, the neocortex, and the reptilian. Each plays a pivotal role in our decision-making process. Understanding these regions provides insight into how we think, feel, behave, and, most importantly, decide.

To simplify:

Reptilian Brain: This part of the brain is responsible for skepticism and survival instinct. This is the voice you hear when a telemarketer calls, warning you not to trust them.

Neocortex: The logic center of our brain. When we use this part, we rely on logic and reason to make our decisions.

Midbrain: Our emotions reside in this brain region, driving our emotional decisions.

I needed more than this basic three-part explanation, so I delved deeper until I realized this:

Selfishness is seemingly unaccounted for in this model, and unless we are aware of it, we cannot overcome it.

Socrates believed that self-knowledge is the foundation of virtue and ethical behavior, and this is a piece of the puzzle that is needed to understand better who you truly are. It is our nature to make choices based on selfish reasoning. If this has you defensively examining "selfless" actions you have taken as a countermeasure, know that you moved into the reptilian portion of your brain.

You can examine the actual "why" behind the "selfless" actions that came to mind, or you can ask yourself if I am intentionally pointing out that we are selfish because I want you in your reptilian brain.

Spoiler alert: I am.

Some years before the COVID-19 pandemic, there were many bird flu outbreaks globally. During this time of craze and panic, there were only a handful of deaths around the world, which was horrible, yes, but in the scheme of deaths from infectious disease on a worrisome scale, nominal. For such a nonlethal event in our history, for whatever reason, there wasn't an airport anywhere lacking people wearing masks, which created more hysteria surrounding the bird flu; people were terrified, so even more people began to wear them.

Ironically, at that exact moment in time in our history, over one hundred million people in the world had died from AIDS, but still, no one wanted to wear a condom.

If you are mulling this in any capacity, you are using the neocortex of your brain.

Our natural inclination toward selfishness is constantly influencing the choices of our lives, and when you can accept that as an uncontestable fact, in that moment, you will gain total control over it and be able to factor that into your future decisions. This is an essential step in discovering your true self because this lack of understanding is weaponized against you in every facet of your life to guide your choices in a manner that someone else chooses. Whether it is your government, big tech, big pharma, the fashion or food industry—all are stoking the flames of your selfish desires. Are you now wondering, "How many choices have I made truly independent from outside influence?"

To show you how easy it is, as you are reading, you have just transitioned into your midbrain. Self-understanding will come when you recognize this in real time and can choose for yourself if that is where you want to be. We will delve more into this at a later point.

When I examined my selfishness, I discovered that my Achilles' heel was not money or financial gain but a better standard of life, recognition, and accolades.

My father killed my love for money itself.

When I was around seven years old, before my parents purchased the house we were renting, my father pulled out seven hundred-dollar bills and laid them neatly on the dishwashing machine for our rent payment. This was the most significant amount of money I had seen in one place, and it excited me. I was drawn to it.

I looked up at my father, eyes shining like he just laid out a treasure map.

"Whoa, I would do anything to have that much money," I said.

He looked at me awkwardly. "You would do anything, huh?" he asked.

Excitement shot through my veins. The year before, I had told him I wanted to sell lemonade for money, and he brought home all the wood, taught me how to build my lemonade stand, and gifted me my pitcher and cups. So, I was hoping he would give me some project or chore that would allow me to earn it.

"Okay," he continued. "Since you will do anything for money, as you told me, this is what I want you to do.

"Take this and put it on Hondo," he said, handing me our dog's leash. "Then I want you to load him in the truck so we can take him to the vet."

"Why are we going to take him to the vet?" I asked.

"Because you are going to tell the vet to put him to sleep and kill him. You did say you would do anything for money, so this is the price. Do this, and I will give you the money."

Shock and fear sizzled through me; I started crying.

My father stood looking at me in silence, letting me cry. I cried harder and harder, and he stood there still. After about a minute, he put his arm around my back and guided me to the kitchen table. He waited patiently until I calmed. I will never forget what he said to me.

"Never again do I want to hear you tell me you would do anything for money. Money doesn't mean anything, as you just learned. Money will come and go in life, but it's only money. Do you understand me?" he asked.

I did, and from then on, money was never a motivating factor. Accolades, however, filled that void and became my "kryptonite."

Determination was propelling me toward my goal—the top.

# *Chapter Ten*
# A Sweet Scent Turned Sour

The system that the largest hospitality corporation that I was just hired to work for used was a powerline based on their APG (average per guest) and being new meant I was at the bottom of it. Ranking dictated your ability to choose a client, and being at the bottom meant that opportunities to see clients of choice were nil. Any clients at all for newbies during slow months were rare. Cynthia Rice and Niles Bronst held the top two spots, with an APG of just over two thousand. Al held spot three with 1,950.

Time to sink or swim.

By the end of the first month, I had closed 68 percent of my opportunities, had an APG of over five thousand, was number one on the powerline, received my first check and monster bonus check, and was hooked.

Every morning at the start of the day, there was a morning meeting and, amidst blasting music, those who closed a client the day before were called up to be celebrated and given the chance to talk about their success. Everyone would clap and cheer while some funny song one of the managers picked played for you as you made your way to the front. It felt like an awards show, and I got one or two awards every morning, as I often doubled down when I could see more than one client in a day.

Attention was being paid, and higher-ups were calling my VP inquiring about his new employee. The numbers produced in my first month for a frontline salesperson were unprecedented for veteran staff, never mind a rookie. The top sales associate in the country usually operated at a 20 percent close rate and a two-thousand-dollar APG; I was doing more than triple that in my first month.

And that was my warm-up.

At the close of my first year, I was 2007's Rookie of the Year and received every award the company offers: President's Council, President's Club, the Big 10, Salesperson of the Year, etc. It was terrific, but it still came in as a distant second to the birth of my second daughter. Those two munchkins kept me focused even though their mother and I had ended our relationship shortly after my second daughter was born.

Sales reports are shared with every site globally; thus, everyone knew my name. When I attended award ceremonies at exotic destinations of the company's choosing, people I had never met from places I had never been were seeking me out, wanting to meet me and discover my secret. I didn't have a secret, though. I loved what I was selling and had been doing a lot of work to enhance my natural talents, making dealing with clients effortless.

By '08, as my name recognition grew, so did my responsibilities. Before long, I was giving podium presentations, training new hires, coordinating dinner parties and event weekends, and developing sales pitches to be implemented for the masses. My dinner party events carried an average APG of over twenty-two thousand, and in January 2008, I did the impossible; I had a 100 percent close rate for the month. Out of the twenty-three days that I worked that month and twenty-seven clients I saw, twenty-seven clients purchased.

Before the close of 2008, I was promoted and offered a leadership position in Atlantic City. After I accepted, they began construction on a brand-new three-million-dollar sales center which coincidentally was one that remained open and flourished when the market crash occurred, and other sites had to close. In 2009, the most prestigious honor someone in my position could be given came: I received the ARDA award nomination. It made logical sense. If I was already the top salesperson for the most significant hospitality corporation in the world, then by default, wouldn't that make me the top in the world? Yes, it would.

You may think I was the happiest person on earth at that moment. Awards were my thing, and they were now flowing. Everyone around me was constantly recognizing me. I had abundant money, owned two homes, and had two beautiful young girls.

But at this point, I was miserable.

As I refined my skill set and climbed the ranks, my bosses had me develop new pitches. To do so, the veil was lifted, and I no longer saw the product I loved and sold but the whole picture. The entire picture was a house of cards, smoke, and mirrors, sold as a dream but designed as a nightmare. That way, when the clients returned to us later, there would be a more significant opportunity to fix the problem by selling them more.

"We have a fiduciary responsibility to our stockholders to make money," I was often told. They were trying to pull me into their web to help create new methods of selling problems and, thus, solutions. The "solution" was always more money, investment, and dependency. It didn't just feel wrong; it made me feel sick.

I had done so well and spent so much time enhancing my skill set because I loved the product. If I loved something, I easily made others love it, too. That combination, plus my thirst for knowledge and understanding people and their decision-making process, made me incredibly competent and unbeatable, or as my judge called it, dangerous.

He was wrong, but he was batting for the other side and deliberately ignored my moral compass.

This moral compass did not allow me to continue selling products that I now knew were destroying lives. I realized I had been lied to, as had most of my colleagues, and it was only my talents and the lure of me creating more for the company that showed me what was afoot.

I quit.

# *Chapter Eleven*
# Awakening a Sleeping Giant

Quitting an extremely lucrative job when you are a dad of two with no other prospects is a daunting decision. It's a leap of faith, a step into the unknown. I finally understood what Nathaniel Hawthorne spoke of in his works about the struggle between conflicting identities and unsustainable consequences. But it's also a testament to the courage and determination to pursue truth.

Burroughs and Chapin were right; I was wasting my talent.

I had the idea to use my talent to help those who wanted out of the products I had sold them. It was more than just a good idea; it was a calling. I knew all the lies and some of the protocols I had designed myself—I could help them reverse out, should they choose. I set up shop, driven by a deep sense of purpose.

Past colleagues flocked to work with me. My product was not to sell but to unburden those unhappy with a product they bought. I was no longer working for the accolades; I was working for the people. It was a profound shift in my mindset, a transition from self-serving goals to a greater purpose. It felt empowering to be making a difference in people's lives.

Within a month of moving into an office, I received my first lawsuit from my previous employers. They were keenly aware of my talent and ambition and did not want it working against them. It was a frivolous complaint, and they lost, but within that first year, they had to shut down the sales center in my city. I was not their competition, yet with someone to help counter their "solutions" to problems they created, they were losing.

I did not realize the level of corruption in the industry I had entered. It was like awakening a sleeping giant. I was young and naive, and I believed in fairness. I was wrong. The giant was not interested in fairness; it was interested in maintaining its dominance.

Over the next three years, I simultaneously built a company and fought this corporation. The company's success grew from my home office to a massive 25,000-square-foot corporate office and sales center in New Jersey and other large offices in Cape Cod, Massachusetts; Nashville, Tennessee; Charleston, South Carolina; and Evansville, Indiana. We also employed workers in satellite offices in Colombia, India, and the Philippines. At one point, we had over five hundred employees.

Whenever I opened a new office, my previous employer filed two lawsuits—one in state court and one in federal court—the same suit they had already lost but didn't care about. It wasn't about winning; it was about exhausting me financially, which billion-dollar corporations tend to do. I was ready and prepared for it. I knew I was in the right, and I was prepared to fight my case. They lost every case against me. They had to close the sales center I helped build.

But despite being prepared for a fair fight, I wasn't prepared for ego and corruption within the Department of Justice. A company such as theirs is quite political and has provided hundreds of millions of dollars in political contributions over the years. Favors were called in.

When the attorney general's office came in, they did their investigation and once it was completed, I was cleared. Directly following came the Real Estate Commission. I was cleared as well. Then, the FTC, Labor Board, and the IRS followed with a forensic audit. It was stressful, yes, but as my dealings were honest, I was cleared of it all. The only minor issue in all these investigations was a window of time related to the transition of some staff from independent contractors into full-time employees, resulting in me paying a couple thousand dollars in taxes. It was justified, and I settled it immediately.

I was twenty-five years old when I started this business and was still learning.

"Finally, this is over, and we can get back to work," I thought, not realizing that this was just getting started.

They came for my family.

One night, around 8:30 p.m., I was sitting in my living room after a long and hard day, watching the news, when I heard an unexpected knock at the door. My five-year-old stepdaughter exited the kitchen and looked at the glass beside the front door.

"The pizza man is at the front door," she said excitedly.

"What? We didn't order pizza," I said, confused.

My alarm wasn't set, and my front door wasn't locked. In my neighborhood, it was never a thought. I saw a man holding a red pizza bag and assumed he was at the wrong house, but something felt off. Instinctually, I opened the door, but only enough to see out and let the man know he had the wrong address. My foot was planted behind the door and my ex-wife was pushing against it alongside me. The moment I did, he made a mistake and told me, "You didn't order a pizza." From the corner of my eye I saw a man in black coming from behind the bushes, gun in hand. The pizza man dropped the bag and slammed into the front door, his partner in crime right behind him.

My planted foot stopped the door dead in its tracks, and I stiff-armed it simultaneously. Out of sheer luck and divine intervention, my returned force was delivered split seconds before they went in for a second hard push, and it caught the man's hands in the door, crushing them; he screamed. When he removed his hand, the door shut, and I could turn the latch on the lock, yelling for the girls to lock the slider in the back simultaneously. It was 8:30 p.m. in a nice, well-lit neighborhood, and the men weren't about to stick around. They took off running full speed to a white car parked down the road. I was in disbelief.

Business had no place becoming personal. Business dealings had no place becoming violent.

I was dumbfounded, wondering if I had brought all of this on myself. If I concluded I did, would I have admitted it to myself?

# *Chapter Twelve*
# Where Was I Reaching?

Mastering brutal honesty in life is a challenging task. We often spend our lives telling half-truths to maintain a sense of whatever we are telling ourselves we are maintaining. Yet, what usually offends us most is when others lie to us. Embracing brutal honesty empowers us to take control of our life and steer it in the direction we truly desire.

I want you to practice avoiding your reptilian part of the brain and recognize that no one else is in your mind but you. No one knows what you're thinking or can hear you.

Understand that most people live their lives keeping honesty on the fringe, the Penumbra, believing that being fully honest is not good. A lifetime of external influence teaches us this and will help us justify this choice, but just because something is more challenging doesn't mean we are meant to avoid doing it. There are consequences to everything. The bill always comes.

I am reminded of a young woman who worked for me. She texted me after she was already late for work, telling me she wasn't feeling well and wouldn't make it on time and would arrive in an hour or so. Recognizing the behavior pattern of this young woman, I didn't believe she was sick, so I said: "Yeah, something tells me this has nothing to do with being sick, and you have 'clubinitis,' am I right?"

"Yes, sir, you're right, I am sorry. I am calling in still drunk from the night before, and I am going to be running late," she responded.

You may assume it would be better for her to lie to me, as you would to your boss if you were in that situation, but you would be wrong. I preferred the truth because the truth is what allowed me to trust the information and helped me to make the best choice possible. In this instance, I told her to take the day off. What could have happened if I did not get the correct information? I possibly could have put pressure on her to get to the office quickly, which would have put a woman who was still drunk on the road, putting her and others in danger. What if she made it, and I put her on the phone with clients? The fact is, she didn't want to get into trouble or lose her job, so she made a selfish decision for herself in her reptilian brain to not be truthful. Luckily my challenge made her shift to her neocortex and answer me using her logic on the second go around.

Thinking back on all the moments of my life leading up to my fall from grace reminded me of a *Where's Waldo* book. You may have a similar experience when you begin to self-examine. There is so much to look at on each page, but only a tiny part within each chapter will help clarify who you are. You are looking for Waldo; the rest of the landscape is a distraction.

I cycled back to a memory of me in my corporate office on the sales floor, giving a morning meeting to my staff before the day began. Successfully transferring your emotions to 150 people at one time early in the morning is no small task, and I was always looking for a hook that would get everyone engaged.

The goal of meetings such as this is inspiration. You want everyone to feel that it is in them to become the most successful person in the room by realizing that the only thing standing in their way from achieving this is a lack of perspective. It is in understanding that the difference between success and failure can be measured in millimeters. This realization adds hope and optimism, knowing that even small changes can lead to significant success.

To help them visualize what I was saying, I would hold up my thumb and index finger separated by a couple of millimeters so they could understand that the difference between success and failure was a nominal distance in any other circumstance. I wanted to make an impact and for what I said to them to stick.

On this particular day, I began, "Okay, everyone. I need you all to do me a favor and listen to my directions closely. Follow my directions exactly as I give them to you. I want all of you right now to raise your hands above your head as high as you can," I directed.

For those of you reading, do the same and then keep reading.

"Now . . . raise your hands a little bit higher."

You, the reader, as well.

I watched an entire sales floor of people raise their hands a bit higher in the air—a couple more inches. I smiled and asked a very straightforward question.

"The instructions were clear, so why didn't all of you just do that the first time?"

My point was made. This was the difference I had been speaking to everyone about—the difference between the ultra-successful and those who are not—these extra inches. Not getting those extra inches on round one is why they were not where they needed to be. That little bit is the difference.

"Because if you asked me to raise my hand," I continued, jumping on the table before me and reaching toward the ceiling with everything I had. "Well, you're lucky; there isn't a ladder around this place. Now get out there and get those extra inches," I concluded the meeting.

I knew I was lacking perspective in my life, and because of that, there had to be a reason why my mind was taking me back to the memory of this meeting. What relevance existed within this moment connected to the life choices that landed me in my position? I started to analyze the meeting itself and my true intentions of having it. I took myself through the decision-making process.

Where was the selfishness?

That's the thing about being truthful with yourself; at first, it can be difficult because you have spent a lifetime out of practice, but once you realize that the conversation with yourself is private and confidential, it becomes much easier to do. When I first began to analyze the purpose of the meeting and others like it, I could have argued with myself back and forth that I was doing it to benefit everyone. I started the conversation for the collective good, but in the end, you can't put lipstick on a donkey and call it a horse. I didn't run this meeting for the benefit of anyone other than myself.

## *Chapter Thirteen*
# Use Them Wisely

Through the natural course of maturing, my talents coalesced to forge a life of success. I made concerted efforts to use them for a better purpose than my previous employer did, but with age comes wisdom, and looking back, I see a young man in his early twenties trying to break through the glass ceiling, ignorant of how sharp the falling shards would be.

Ego and envy surrounded me at every turn, and I was the source watering the seed. As my success level rose, I could see it all around me, including those who worked for me. As a result, I began to contemplate our capacity for envy and its role in our lives. It didn't take me long to realize the importance of understanding envy and how, like selfishness, it was not included in the Triune Model when analyzing how we made decisions, yet without understanding it, we would never be able to understand ourselves and others fully. Selfishness influenced my choices and envy from those around me brought evil to my front door.

It's easy to look at other people, see what they have, see the talents they were blessed with, and be envious of it all. The emergence of social media has made it impossible to ignore, and the capacity to monetize ensures that you don't. Whether you like it or not, the propensity for envy resides in us all, and we are so terribly influenced in this digital era that children as young as six are already looking over the fence to see if the grass is greener on the other side. Fuel is being poured onto this fire at every corner of our lives, and the lack of perspective is making it more challenging to put out the flames.

Look to the modern-day movie star, for example. We can see their lives—what they want us to see—in high definition twenty-four hours a day, seven days a week. Many stars trade large, scripted segments of their lives for millions of dollars a year, and this illusion is made to look like real life. The stark contrast to actual reality creates difficulty in avoiding envy.

An actor's talent is the ability to convince you that they are someone they are not. In other words, they lie to you convincingly about who they are to entertain you. This is their talent. We need to be able to turn them on and off in our lives as we choose, but only if we are deliberate with our choices; most of us get taken in by their facade and confuse it with reality.

Did you know that there are more addicts, overdoses, suicides, and divorces in Hollywood than anywhere else? Hollywood is the shining example that misery does indeed love company.

Yet, they preach—about what skin product to use (when they have surgery), who to vote for (when they are clueless and disconnected), and how to date (when they are changing partners like underwear).

We'd be fools to listen, yet millions of people still envy their lives because of what is shown on the surface, in good lighting, and endeavor to mimic their choices, not knowing the reality of the consequences that follow.

With the light of proper perspective shining into your life, envy would dissipate, and inner peace would consume the space in which it resided.

Here's the thing about talent: It's equally dispersed to everyone in the world, only its form differs. I almost went down the Hollywood Road once in my life. I wanted to pursue a career in modeling. Who knew that you had to be good-looking to be a model? I should have tried comedy. Either way, my talent level is not lower; its form is different.

This is why not wholly understanding your talent and its value is problematic. Society assigns value to talent based on the times, but it is all an aberration invented to serve those seeking money and power. Think about this relative to the times. If you went back a few thousand years to watch an actor during that era, do you know what you would be watching? The answer: a court jester. A court jester ranked just above a prostitute in social status, and I am willing to bet that if the technology existed where their photo could be captured at one of their shows, no one would have that picture hanging on their bedroom wall.

How society assigns value to a person's talent means nothing and is, again, nothing more than an external influence trying to dictate your path. The only value in the talent we are given exists within who we are. When we understand that the value comes from within and is not something that society can define for us, we can identify its meaning and better understand why we were given it. When this occurs, no monetary value would exceed its worth.

The majority of people live the life they think they should be living, acting how they are told to act, so how could anyone expect a different result?

We could elect to do things differently.

Instead of using our gifts for the sole purpose of making money or being selfish with our talents, we can avoid "more money, more problems" by doing the opposite.

The easiest way to identify whether you are using your talents selfishly is if you can sense envy beginning to form around you. Once you can determine the capacity for it in yourself and others, you can weigh it and your inclination toward selfishness into all your decisions, bringing clarity to choice.

# *Chapter Fourteen*
# Identify the Why

President Donald Trump is a perfect example of a man who has taken many public actions under constant scrutiny. Whether or not seeing this name in print here makes you joyful or angry is irrelevant to the example. Ignore your midbrain and emotional reaction because that reaction you just had seeing his name has been programmed into you. It doesn't matter if you are conservative or liberal; those in power have found a way for the everyday person to hear this name and bypass their neocortex. I want you to be aware of it, put yourself into your neocortex, and follow my example.

By all accounts, Donald Trump has lived a life most people would envy. For starters, he is a billionaire. He has a supermodel wife, incredible children and grandchildren, and has built an empire. He is the president of the United States and sits among the very few who share this honor in history, yet no one out there currently envies him or his life. No one wakes up in the morning and wishes they were Donald Trump; there is only one honest reason why.

The path that Trump is currently on is not one of a man being selfish or using his talents to enrich himself. I am not saying he hasn't done it in his life back when everyone did envy him; I am talking about him as a President. I am not saying you must like him or even believe his actions are good for our people or our country. On this, the government is divided. I am telling you that for better or for worse, he is not doing it for himself, and the lack of envy is an incredibly accurate metric. Donald Trump believes he is doing this for the betterment of the world. We vote and have elections to put people in place that we believe will make the world better.

While I was on my quest to enhance my talents, I never stopped to think about why I was given them before those in a powerful position spotted them within me. I had no idea what I wanted out of life or what to do with my life and allowed myself to be wined and dined, so to speak, into a high-paying, high-pressure section of the sales industry, understanding what 95 percent of the rest of that industry did not. I understood that the definition of a sale is the successful transfer of emotion from one person to another. Now let me ask you: Were you able to absorb this paragraph, or do you still have some emotions brewing surrounding the name Donald Trump and the fact that he was used as an example? A more interesting question to ask yourself is whether the power class in this nation wants you to react.

Understanding your thought process and decision-making is crucial to comprehending the world around you. Whether you realize it or not, the functioning of the world is influenced by a select few who excel at influencing others. Nothing significant happens in the world without a "sale" taking place. Consider, for instance, a presidential campaign. It's a powerful reminder that you, as part of the public, play a significant role in shaping the world.

In my own life, those in control were beginning to surround me. My selfish use of my talents created envy everywhere, and even though I could sense it, I was still blind to its extent.

What came next started as a whisper, a subtle inquiry that I was not supposed to notice. But it quickly morphed into a full-blown witch hunt.

As my former employer's first civil suit ended, they were blindsided when the judge ruled in my favor. Their case had been built on lies, and the judge saw right through it. The aftermath forced their true colors to the surface. While the judge was delivering his closing, my former employer's general counsel was standing brazenly in the well of the courtroom, mocking the judge and spouting outrageous comments. I was sure the judge could hear them, though he did not react. But I deeply felt the sting of their arrogance and the complete disrespect they showed without fear. Instead of accepting their defeat gracefully and preparing to appeal, the lawyer representing them, in a last-ditch effort, stood and announced, "Your Honor, I think it is important for the court to know that these guys are under investigation by the FBI."

The words hit me like a sledgehammer. The FBI? Why? My lawyers were just as stunned, and you could see it all over their faces. They quickly stood from their chairs to inform the judge that no one knew of any such investigation and questioned, " If that's true, how would opposing counsel know about it?"

Crickets.

At that moment, the truth became clear: my former employer and their allies in the industry were behind it all. The FBI case that would soon follow was the civil case rebranded and made into a criminal one. After the FBI invaded my home and office to make their presence known, it took us far too long to learn that the sealed criminal complaint was from them and not from those who were doing business with me. They were mad they didn't win in court; they were angry they didn't exhaust me financially; they were mad they didn't scare me away, and at this point, I believe they were mad I was alive. They wanted to destroy me.

I once viewed the FBI as heroes, the men and women in white hats who fought for justice, but when I look back, I feel like perhaps I should have seen it coming. While they were tearing everything apart in my home and office, I had a flashback that came to me like a bolt of lightning striking water. I was sitting in my former CEO's office. There was a picture on his desk of him shaking hands with the current FBI director, and only in that moment did I feel the scope of leverage being used against me.

Truth no longer mattered; orders had been given, and they were out to annihilate me, my reputation, and my company, using every tool. They started online, with press attempting to make me seem guilty before I had a chance to defend myself. They launched smear campaigns, released press statements, and paid bloggers to flood the internet with harmful content, poisoning the narrative for anyone who searched for the company name.

I updated my knowledge of SEO, latent semantic text, anchor keywords, metadata, and more. After the family went to bed, I spent my night creating content and coding to counteract the results in Google and other search engines to sink their attack. As part of my update, I learned what types of actions or tricks in the SEO work Google would punish and lower the results of and started to do those very things to the content which was meant to hurt me.

Behind the scenes, however, the lead agents on the case started working hand-in-hand with my former employer, creating direct lines of communication between my clients and each other. They would use their collections department to contact my clients and begin an onslaught of lies and threats, doing everything they could to convince them that my clients were being scammed, and would then provide them with the number to the lead agent in charge on the case. This would be very scary and believable to the average person. The agents would then echo the same lies even though they didn't know the industry or understand the truth, thus sending them back to my former employer to help them recover their business and become witnesses.

Simply put, the trap was built and set.

It's common practice that in any large and successful business, you must let go of some employees, whether for poor performance, excessive work absences, or failing required drug testing. No one is angrier at a company than the terminated. Find them, and you can stoke flames in whatever case you want to build.

As Sheva, my best friend, says, "Beat the data, and it will confess."

The government tracked fired employees and cut in with prized offerings whenever possible.

Jim, an incredibly talented man, had to be fired after his addiction to opiates got out of hand. Sadly, he was not safe for clients anymore. His life continued south as his addiction progressed to heroin, with multiple overdoses, hospitalizations, and cellulitis; he was homeless and living in a tent in the woods until he was imprisoned for using faulty checks. In exchange for his testimony, Jim was freed.

His friend, Brett, another talent wasting away, seemed to have more hope. Instead of firing him, I paid $20,000 for his rehab with the hopes that he could save his life. After completing rehab, Brett returned to his old, productive self. But when he started using it again, I had to fire him. This was particularly hard for me, as I was cheerleading his recovery, but ultimately, the safety of my clients and employees came first. I did not hear from him again, but I did hear from his mom, who called me for help after he was arrested for forging prescriptions in NYC. He was freed in exchange for his testimony against me.

Watching Brett on the stand, testifying against me with utter lies, cut more profoundly than most of the ugly things I witnessed. Up to this point, I wouldn't have been able to believe he would lie, and here he was, lying against me and doing so with zest. The power of incentive. He wanted to be free and exchanged appreciation and honor for it. Sadly, he has since died of an overdose.

As I waited for trial over the next three years, the government tracked and incentivized whomever they could. But I, too, was preparing a solid defense against this house of cards.

Eight weeks before the trial, the judge disqualified my lawyer, who had been there from the beginning and prepped for the trial for nearly three years. The claim was a conflict of interest, and despite it being utter nonsense, the judge removed him, ordered no communication between him and my new counsel, and denied more time for my new lawyer, who was coming on the case with zero knowledge and only eight weeks to prepare.

These facts are objectively sickening from a human right, judicial, and procedural point of view. But on top of that, the money I had paid to my old lawyer was gone, and I had staggering bills for a lawyer who, self-admittedly, didn't know enough to defend me.

And that is how I entered the trial for my life.

## *Chapter Fifteen*
# Over Before It Started

The prosecution paraded coached witnesses to the stand, distorting the truth and dismantling my life's work. I couldn't help but feel the crushing weight of injustice. Apart from a single childhood lookout experience, I had never committed a crime. I believed in law and order and upheld it in my own life.

It would have been comical if it wasn't so terrifying.

Much of what was on offer was tripe, but I had an underprepared lawyer, and the judge blocked evidence proving my innocence while allowing the government anything they asked.

The judge was clearly in collusion with them. His bias was evident in his rulings and willingness to grant the prosecution's requests, even when unfounded or unjust.

After days of this, something crossed my lawyer's face, and he interrupted the proceedings. "Your honor," he said. "I think we have a problem here. I will ask you to excuse the jury to address it."

"All right," the judge responded, turning toward the jury. "Why don't you all take an early lunch?"

What clicked in my lawyer's mind was related to one of the counts they were holding against me: money laundering. Despite having an in-house accountant and being cleared by the IRS in a thorough audit, they still tacked on the outrageous claim. It sounds bad and dirty, and even if it's not true, it accomplishes a lot for them. Having the book thrown at you leaves your reputation in tatters (maybe he didn't do everything—but he must have done something!), and even if just one count sticks, they win.

During the testimony, my lawyer noticed that the money laundering charges didn't even apply to the mail and wire fraud claims they had stacked against me. What they had stacked on me was related to stocks. It was absurd—absurd that they had charged me with it, absurd that testimony was allowed to a jury for days about it, and absurd that it took my unprepared defense weeks into trial to notice it.

The judge began to examine the indictment in the case. "It appears you are right, Mr. Cedrone," he said.

The prosecution was able to see it, too. "Yes, your honor, we see it. We made a mistake. Please grant us the evening to see if there is any case law on this situation?" Granted.

There was no case law, and as a matter of law, all those charges had to be dismissed immediately, as the jury had already heard days of testimony on this made-up claim that didn't make sense. But this was not a room for justice, and instead of dismissing the trial or restarting it with a new jury, they just continued.

To top it off, embarrassed by this glaring mistake, the government punished me for it. Whenever there is a criminal trial, the government gives you a notice of forfeiture, letting you know what they will take from you if you lose your trial. When they served initial search warrants, the FBI took around half a million in cash and accounts, which I kept in reserve for tax obligation at the end of the year. The notice of forfeiture I was provided included the fake money laundering charges that were now dismissed, which meant I was never given a notice of forfeiture. Thus, they could not forfeit the money I set aside for tax obligations.

Instead, seemingly as punishment, the judge ordered a forfeiture against me for *five times* the alleged amount of the crime: an $11,900,000 forfeiture two years after being sentenced.

The government learned much about who I was during their investigation and trial. They had witnesses testify that they believed me to be brilliant, but they were mistaken because a genius wouldn't have ended up in this situation. They knew I had an incredibly successful career in sales, was well-spoken and influential. They also learned of the complexity of the process I had created, and that I was the only one who could articulate it in a way others could understand clearly, so they had an insurance policy ready. They collected on this policy on the first day of my defense.

Ten minutes before I took the stand in my defense, they filed a motion to detain me for the rest of the trial. From that point on, I was to be a prisoner, trapped in a system that already decided my fate. The psychological impact of that moment was devastating. The sudden loss of freedom, the uncertainty about the future, and the separation from my family and responsibilities left me in a state of shock and despair.

Just a second before the jury came out, my belt and ring were removed, and my wallet was sent to my family in the courtroom. I was now in federal custody and would not be returning home at the end of the day; I would be going to jail. My mind was spinning. Who was going to take care of the kids? My dog? What about the offices and my staff? I was in shock, barely able to think straight, riddled with anxiety as the jury was taking their seats. I couldn't even hear what was happening around me.

I can't imagine what the jury saw when they looked at me, having no idea what had transpired seconds before they came out. They were looking at a wreck of a man who, until this point, was described by the prosecution as a competent, charismatic salesperson who was now struggling to put himself together and having difficulty answering questions coherently. It was clear to them that something was wrong, but they weren't allowed to know what, so I am sure what they saw looked like guilt.

And from then on, I was continuously descending into the darkness that never let up.

I was lost now, knowing that they were never going to allow me to win.

# *Chapter Sixteen*
# When It Rains It Pours

I was thrown out of a living nightmare into actual hell. High-security prison in the federal system is a place where survival meant more than just staying alive; it meant staying human. Most fail at that. I knew nothing of the brutal politics that ruled this world. The men around me were hardened criminals, many of them killers, rapists, and gang members who had lost their humanity long before. The strong preyed on the weak, and unspeakable acts of brutality were a daily occurrence. I witnessed men being raped, others fighting, slashing, or stabbing one another, tossing boiling oil in each other's faces; the sounds of suffering echoed through any space devoid of a camera.

I was an outsider in this hell on earth, trying desperately to navigate a world designed to strip away my dignity. This is where I began to understand the true meaning of darkness.

A few months into my imprisonment at the detention center, while awaiting sentencing, my father was rushed to the hospital in what appeared to be the onset of a stroke. It was not. It was large B-cell lymphoma. Thanks to his service to this great country, he was exposed to Agent Orange in Vietnam. Within seven months of me losing my freedom, the strongest man I knew, my beloved dad, was gone. I wasn't allowed to say goodbye or pay my respects.

My brother, a marine, was also beginning to deteriorate. During his time in Iraq, he was injured but, like many Marines, he rubbed some dirt on it (metaphorically speaking) and continued to push forward in war and, later, in life. Alan never sought medical attention, even when symptoms became noticeable. Losing my father and me at almost the same time did not help him. My mother was trying to hold everyone together. The pressure became too much for her to bear. One night, she drove to the liquor store, bought a bottle of vodka, opened it, and took a swig right there in the parking lot. Over a decade of sobriety was erased in that moment.

And just when I thought I had felt the worst of it, an emotional blow came that nearly broke me: my first Christmas at this prison, I received Christmas letters, and among them, written in red and green crayon was this:

> Dear Santa,
> I have been a very very good girl this year. Better than any of the girls in my class and you would like to hear that I have been a good big sister. I promise I will continue to be. All I ask is that this year you do not send me any presents. I do not want them. All I want is my Daddy back.
> Thank you very much, Santa.

I cried so hard in that moment I was scared I was going to vomit up my stomach. But being nervous that someone would hear me and sniff weakness was something I couldn't risk. I knew I needed to do everything I could to keep the wolves from descending, so I somehow pulled myself together to survive.

Trying to emotionally balance all of this from behind prison walls was unbearable while also trying to prepare to be sentenced, unaware that a flaw in the Federal Bureau of Prison's security calculation system was about to send me—a first-time, nonviolent, white-collar offender who had never abused drugs or alcohol—into a high-security prison.

It is difficult to describe the actual state of my emotions following, and to survive I had to suppress the horror.

I did write this poem, though. It may give you a glimpse into how I felt then.

Depression
A heart that doesn't beat, candles without fire,
What once was known as the truth was delivered by a liar.

A mind that's scared to dream, a cup you cannot fill.
I'm an object designed for motion remaining frozen, remaining still.
Comedy without laughter, crying without tears,
looking at a calendar that has lost all of its years.
hearing without music, visualizing without sight,
Trapped inside the darkness like the sun being trapped by night.
The world no longer spinning, Stars remiss from shooting.
I'm forgetting the feel of comfort and what used to feel so soothing.
Touch that has no feeling, food without any taste,
Being stuck inside one's inner self while all potential goes to waste.
Time in the clock is frozen, a ticking without any time,
This is an area of no crossing, devoid of any line.
An end with no beginning, the finish without a start.
A trip that is meant from taking, but never will depart.
Strength enough to be weak, enough courage to be a coward.
All that tasted sweet, turned, and now is soured.
A thirst you cannot quench, pain with no relief.
Walking through your life with faith and then losing all belief.
View has lost its color; all is in black and white.
Everyone seems taller, but there is no way to measure height.
Longing for the pain to end questioning if I am enough to save?
Or am I a sail without the wind to guide, an ocean without its wave.

# *Chapter Seventeen*
# A Lifeline

At some point, many of us have heard the well-intentioned platitude, "Now you have nowhere to go but up." That was not true for me. I was floating in darkness, clueless to what was up or down. All sense of direction was lost in the abyss like a black hole sucking the life from me; the gravitational force of despondency kept me from escaping.

True darkness is a belief, a conviction that light will never return to your life again. For many, many months, I could no longer see the possibility that light would return.

The only awareness of myself that remained was a voice inside my head. It was difficult to hear in the early stages, but I imagine that, like with any lost sense, time develops other senses to compensate. I had lost my foresight and gained this voice. As time passed, I could make out more and more of what that voice was saying, and I began to wonder what was talking to me. What part of myself?

I knew that my sight, sense of touch, sound, smell, taste, and mobility had nothing to do with it, for even if I lost any of these senses, this same voice would still be there. That was when it hit me. The voice was my soul.

Whether it was survival instinct or divine intervention—perhaps both—is something I will never know, but one day, the voice was so powerful that I went to the mirror. I didn't realize how long it had been since I had looked at myself.

Only one question emerged.

"Who the fuck are you?"

With my senses still dormant, answering truthfully was easy.

"I don't know, but I do not like whoever I am looking at," I answered.

And then, for the first time in a very long time, the fog lifted, and I saw. I saw that I had the power to choose. And so, I did. I would do the time as I decided to instead of letting the time do me.

That is when I found my wings. I remembered something more that I knew in my heart to be true: In every obstacle is opportunity, and what I needed to do was surrender to God's plan so I could see the opportunities more clearly. I listened to my voice more, knowing that doing so would lead me to an elevated life of raw and honest truth, which would allow me to use my God-given talents for something greater. But to be successful I had to learn how to exert control over the fuel which propelled me forward.

## *Chapter Eighteen*

# First . . . to Fall

Competitiveness has always been at the heart of my drive; I've never been content coming in second place. I needed to be the best, and the most successful, for the recognition that followed was the fuel that propelled me forward.

I now know that my competitive drive, which had always been a source of my success, was also a catalyst for my hidden selfishness. Like most of us, I viewed selfishness as a negative trait, something I couldn't see within myself and wouldn't admit to, despite it being a shadow that lurked behind me, influencing my decisions and clouding my judgment when it mattered most.

When my world crashed, I had to confront some hard truths. Throughout life, I recall many examples when others described me as someone with an uncanny ability to read and influence others, even going as far, in some cases, as referring to me as a genius. These moments played in my head like vignettes. If true, how could I have allowed so many people into my life that were never worthy of my trust? Why did I marry a woman that was not trustworthy? Why did I build a team with members who lack integrity and loyalty? How did I take on a job with a corrupt organization? How did I not see these character traits when they were so obvious? Genius? Far from it.

As I pondered these inconsistencies, I realized that my competitive fire was also an accelerant of my selfishness, even though I subconsciously denied its existence. The shadow behind me was present but out of view, shaping decisions and clouding critical and essential judgments.

I was blinded by my ambition and trying to build a life I thought I should live. As a result, the top concern in my life was talent, identifying it in others and recruiting it to my cause to help me achieve the goals I laid out for myself, and how they could make me bigger, better, and more prosperous. I ignored everything else, even when its ugly nature was revealed. I couldn't see anything past my desire to win.

Every individual has a weakness, a trigger that can lead to disastrous decisions. My competitive nature and the desire for recognition guided my choices, leading me to undesirable consequences. Looking back, making decisions in such a state was akin to being intoxicated.

I have always had this weakness.

As a child, waking up to a snowy day on the Cape was as exciting as the holidays. On one such day, when I was around nine years old, my dad had something thrilling in mind when he called in sick to work.

"Get on your snow gear and meet me outside," he said with a grin.

I could hear his truck warming up and figured we would go sledding. However, when we stepped out the back door, I saw a rope and a snow tube tied to the back of the trailer hitch. We were going tubing around the neighborhood. My older brother went first, and I watched as he laughed and glided behind the truck, amusement written all over his face. After a good run, my dad decided to change it up. He was approaching the corner and noticed a nice snowbank piled up from the snowplows earlier. He hit the gas, sending my brother into it while making the turn, and Alan went tumbling. Alan stood up, still laughing, and I could hardly contain myself; I almost jumped out of the truck before it came to a complete stop—my turn.

The excitement was palpable, and I was determined not to fall off like my older brother. My competitive nature kicked in, and I didn't want to lose, unaware there was no competition. After the same run, we made it around the block and approached the turn that tossed my brother off. I tightened my grip, refusing to let go, and when we hit that bank, I was stubborn and immovable. I hit a patch of ice on the snowbank, which shot me forward more rapidly and sent me under the truck's back tire. It ran over my left side, and I was lucky it didn't kill me.

The hospital trip that followed was chaotic. My left side was bruised, swollen, and terrifying to look at. Fear covered my father's face like a mask.

It was obvious he was devastated and guilt-ridden, and I could see how much pain what had happened was causing him. He just hurt someone he loved more than anything in the world. He was trying to act silly to make me laugh while we waited, pretending to take a sip out of the urine jug, but I was not fooled.

After a long night, a barrage of testing, and having to down the most disgusting drink of my life, the doctor finally came in with news everyone needed to hear.

"Adam is pretty banged up, and we need to keep him overnight as a precaution, but it looks like he will be okay," he said. "What happened?"

As quickly as the relief came across everyone's faces, nervousness replaced it. Instinct took over. No one asked anything of me, but for some reason, I knew I had to speak. I jumped in with a story.

"My brother and I were wrestling on top of a snowbank, and I slipped and fell as my dad backed out. He didn't see me, and I went under the tire. It happened so fast," I said. That ended up being the story I told for years. I didn't fully understand why then, but I felt like I needed to protect him, which was protecting us all.

But looking back now, I see it all so clearly. The accident was a fluke. Any other kid would have let go when they hit that snowbank. But I couldn't. I wouldn't. My competitive drive wouldn't let me, and the choice it guided me to almost took my life.

Then and now.

## *Chapter Nineteen*
# Find the Weak Spot

The me that didn't let go of the rope that day was the same person who was running that office meeting, shifting people against one another like pieces on a chess board in an attempt to separate the weak from the strong. Once I could do that, I would put all my attention into the strongest of them to better serve my cause, effectively leaving the rest to sink or swim.

Reflecting on my past actions, I realized that my approach could have been different. Instead of pitting people against each other, I could have fostered a team spirit and focused on collective growth. My failure to do so led to the emergence of envy, an emotion that spread like a virus among those who felt left behind.

As I reflected, I faced how I used my talents, and despite my growth and accolades, I was no longer proud. I used my gifts for the same reason I hung on to that rope.

Life can be a series of endless mistakes with moments of scattered bliss. We have all heard that we learn from our mistakes, but that statement is only partially true. We *can* learn from our mistakes, but only if we are fully honest with ourselves, and that is something we cannot achieve until we know who we are. This journey of self-discovery, of understanding our motivations and emotions, is a powerful tool for personal growth and transformation.

I knew if I was going to survive prison, I had no choice but to do the same.

I pondered the works of Epictetus, a former slave whose teachings were recorded in the *Discourses* and *Enchiridion*. Epictetus emphasizes the dichotomy of control and discusses how our thoughts, judgments, desires, and actions are within our control, while external events, the actions of others, and outcomes are not. Focusing on what we can control and accepting what we cannot is a crucial practice for achieving inner growth. For anyone familiar with AA, "accept the things you cannot change" is a common expression, and now you know its origins.

We may not be able to choose the talents God bestows on us, but we can choose how to use them, which is where I started by focusing on what I could control while blocking out the rest.

To do the same, you, too, need to identify your talents and reflect on how you've used them to achieve objectives in the past while remaining honest with yourself about your motivations. The journey to self-discovery requires commitment and discipline, but the rewards of self-awareness and personal growth will justify the efforts.

It's crucial to understand and accept our capacity for envy and selfishness. These emotions often share space in our minds. Overcoming them is necessary to achieve a state of *apatheia*, a term from Stoic philosophy that refers to peace of mind. This state of mind allows us to make decisions based on reason rather than emotion.

It's easy to identify the area in our lives where our selfishness runs most rampant, and we can locate it by performing a simple, private exercise. No one has to know anything about it or the results, so when you begin to recognize your selfish areas, do not feel shame or fight it, because understanding and controlling the selfish part of yourself will become a far greater strength than weakness, empowering you to make better decisions.

We are all imperfect, which makes us beautiful. So free your mind, allowing anxiety and concern to dissipate. If you can lie down or get to a comfortable spot, I recommend that you do. When you start, ensure your eyes remain closed, like you are about to nap. Once you are calm and your mind clear, I want you to imagine that when you awaken the following day after a night's sleep, you will do so with an incredible ability. You are now able to see up to twelve hours into the future. You can see anything you want up to half a day ahead of you.

What would you look for? How would you use this extraordinary gift? Erase any preconceived notions of morality or that which is "appropriate." No one but you is in your mind, and this exercise is only for you. Let your mind take you on the journey it wants to go. Embrace your imperfections, for they are what make you unique and powerful.

Focus on where your mind goes. Would you look for Powerball numbers or the stock market results? Would you use your power for sexual gain? Would you be heroic? It doesn't matter where your mind goes. It only matters that you let it go there unburdened from control. Wherever it goes is the treasure map to your selfishness and where it leans the most, and it is this piece of information you need to assimilate so you can weigh it properly in your decisions.

As mentioned previously, the Triune Model is a potent tool for comprehending your mind and, consequently, yourself. It is the master key that can unlock your potential and put you in the driver's seat of your life.

Often considered the second founder of Stoicism, Chrysopsis believed that logic and ethics were inseparable, and that the universe operates according to a rational and purposeful order. Because of this, human beings must use logic and reason to guide their lives, helping them make moral decisions even in complex and ambiguous situations.

The section of the brain that controls logic is the neocortex. It resides in the outermost layer of your brain and is divided into four different lobes, which are identified as follows: frontal, parietal, temporal, and occipital. They are the powerhouse of rational thought and decision-making. Here, you can analyze complex information and consider long-term consequences. For example, this is the part of the brain that creates a list of pros and cons to help you decide whether to continue pursuing a relationship (side tip: if you are crafting this list, he or she is not the one).

The midbrain, or the mesencephalon, resides in your limbic system and is the custodian of emotions and memory. When emotions are high, the limbic system influences decision-making, often leading to a choice based solely on emotion and nothing else. Losing awareness of your emotional state and its influence on choice can be catastrophic, forcing you to ignore rationale. This area also controls arousal, which can influence decision-making. You may have heard the expression "thinking with the other head," which generally means deciding based on arousal rather than rational thought.

You need to open your eyes and be aware as this is the tool used by the powerful. Messages designed to bring forth an emotional reaction are done with the hope that you ignore logic and are swayed in their direction. Politicians live in this sphere. Abortion, racism, feminism, and trans-rights, to name a few, are all topics harped on to make you emotional with the hope that you make an emotional decision. Those in sales often use third-party stories to transition you into your emotional state before trying to close you, and you must remain aware and vigilant. Whenever you feel fueled with emotion, you must force yourself into the reptilian part of your brain before making any choice. When you begin to calm down, it will be easy to transition into the neocortex and think about things rationally.

The reptilian section of the brain is also known as the basal ganglia and is the most powerful and the most dangerous part of our brain, as it is where our fight-or-flight responses are encoded. The basal ganglia also control behavioral traits associated with dominance and territory, such as aggression and defense. It's where our survival instinct resides, and our skepticism is born. When the primary goal is survival, it is unsurprising that this part of our brain yields the power to override rational thought in a heightened-stress situation. This brain area will convince you to ignore the math and fold a winning hand when you should go all in. This area can be dangerous to us if we rely on it to help guide us in situations that are not life-threatening because it removes logic and rational thinking from the decision-making process.

Understanding and controlling your mind is crucial. Without this control, you'll always be influenced by external factors, and your true self will remain elusive. By learning how you process information and using that knowledge to make decisions, you can take control of your life and your self-discovery journey. Cultivating logical and rational thought gives you the most power and the ability to overcome less advantageous instincts. I had studied. I was practiced, and I felt ready to conquer the world ahead.

## *Chapter Twenty*

# He Who Is Lost Offers Insight

Time quickly started to blur as it moved past, but I will never forget the arrival of a younger white kid who came off the bus from Washington, DC. Those from DC have a heavy presence on the east coast of the federal system because every crime committed in DC is considered federal. Anyone that has done time in this system will confirm that the DC car is well known for extorting and raping inmates. I have no explanation as to why it is most prevalent among this group of men, but it is. Hence, they set their sights on this kid the moment he arrived. Clearly, he didn't have "clean" paperwork, meaning there was no chance anyone would step up to protect him.

In the beginning, other inmates watched him like wolves surrounding their prey. At first, they noticed his commissary spending power and leaned on him for months until he had no money left to spend. Once he was broken, there was only one thing left that they wanted. He was small and weak, and the fact that he was straight wasn't going to help. They came for him.

What I found to be baffling was that he didn't put up any fight. Any animal will attack when backed into a corner, but he did not. I didn't understand. Months passed like this until one day, I was walking past him on the track, and I took the opportunity to speak to him for a bit, hoping I could offer some support.

"Why are you letting this happen willingly? Why not fight back or at least check into the SHU so they can send you somewhere else?" I asked.

His answer was short and full of defeat: "This isn't something I am going to be able to hide from. I just want to survive and make it home."

"I want to survive"—powerful words saturated with meaning far beyond anything he could understand. His statement revealed an answer that previously eluded me: the reptilian part of our brain.

This primal part of our brain, where our survival instincts reside, is meant to save us in moments of life-threatening danger. It is also responsible for our many destructive choices while unaware of its influence. Every time man has made a dangerous choice throughout history, it was almost always under the guise of survival and for selfish reasons. This means that our propensity for destruction, under the facade of safety, lives within the reptilian part of our brain. Finally, I was finding answers to some of my lingering questions.

I had another lens now. Allowing survival or selfishness to hijack our choices and blur our clarity leaves us in a less-than-ideal state despite the desire stemming from survival mode and seemingly giving us no other choice.

This man looked at it through the lens that he "just had to survive." His reptilian brain told him this daily and allowed him to withstand repeated rape. His logical brain was shut down—he couldn't see the logic in checking in to the SHU and saving himself from this emotional and physical torture. To "just survive" was to allow whatever would be.

The very thing given to us in our creation meant to save our lives when danger is upon us is also the lit fuse of destruction if utilized for anything other than lifesaving.

My sight was clear, and my understanding of the world changed forever. Not understanding our minds and how they view the world can be catastrophic and lead to disaster. The world has become hypersensitive, whether you recognize it or not, making every feeling we feel more intense and urgent. Financial stress and falling on hard times can be emotionally difficult for a family. Stress, fear, and shame can consume you, and as a result, your survival instinct comes into play in life and can take control of your decisions moving forward.

I could also recognize this in the person in the bunk beside me. Given that he was living next to me, you already know where this trajectory would lead him, but I could now see clearly how his reptilian brain guided him there. His business had fallen on hard times, and he could not secure a loan to keep things going. He was on the verge of losing everything he had built and would no longer be able to make payroll. Desperation hydrated the seed of survival, and he contacted an old friend from his past who had lived a nefarious lifestyle. He purchased a couple of kilograms of cocaine, hoping to sell it and spin enough profit off it to turn things around and keep his business going. This is an example of the power the reptilian brain has over you and your decisions, and this is the consequence of not being aware of the power that section wields.

You must be mindful of it so you never let it control your choices.

My true self and purpose revealed themselves, as they will to you once you find your true self. Something remarkable happened when I finally crossed that threshold and could look in the mirror again.

In the earliest stages of this journey, whenever an opportunity presented itself for me to cry privately, even if for a moment, I did because of the grief and despair I felt within. I had gone through so much and knew it was natural to think as I did. Anyone who could go through what I had without emotion would have something seriously wrong with them, as many around me did, and over time, I learned to numb those emotions and put them away, so they did not consume me.

After my true self was revealed, a profound shift took place. Uncontrollable emotions would rise to the surface, and felt behind my eyes like a shaken soda about to have its cap removed. Still, they were not emotions derived from self-pity but something deeper and more meaningful. It was as though I had tapped into a previously unseen beauty around me, connecting me to the world in a way I had not felt before.

I saw everything clearly, and whether it was a heartwarming story, a random commercial, a moving scene in a movie, or even a tale of triumph on one of those singing show competitions, something would stir inside of me. Tears would well up, but I fought them back, so no one took notice. But I noticed. I felt different. I was different.

Where I was previously blind to life's subtle, beautiful nuances, I was no longer.

My old pains were no longer my driver; I am driven by a deeper appreciation for the beauty in life's minor, often overlooked corners. It was time for me to turn my gaze outward, to look at the world in front of me with fresh eyes and see if I could begin to understand it as I had come to understand myself, which seemed impossible the first day I arrived at this gladiator school.

When first being released into the general population of a high-security federal prison, it's jarring to discover how little you know or understand about the world you just entered. The memory of that day still haunts me: being yanked off the transport bus after a long and hard day, ushered into Receiving and Discharge (R&D), and waiting for hours in a holding cell, unsure of what was coming next. I was on edge, tired, hungry, nerves running high, trying to act calm while having no idea what to expect.

Eventually, my name was called, and the Special Investigation Services took me to be interviewed. Their job was to figure out whether it was safe to let me into the general population or if I was going to be the type of guy who'd get stabbed the minute I stepped foot onto the unit. If I had the wrong kind of case, if I were a rat or a sex offender, then that would mean I would likely end up in hospital, maybe worse, before that day came to an end. Unlike lower security institutions, the prison politics here were confirmed, with high stakes.

"Are you in any gangs?" SIS asked, flipping through my file like he had seen it all before.

"Do I look like I'm in a gang?" I shot back, too exhausted to filter my expression.

He paused, looked me over again like it was the first time, and then squinted back to my paperwork. "No, you don't. I am just going through the motions as it has been a long day, but I must ask why you are here. This is a white-collar case and a small one at that. Who the fuck decided it was a good idea to send you here? Did you piss off a politician or something?"

"I have no idea, sir," I replied, feeling worn down.

"Do you have any money left?" he asked, shifting gears without warning.

I went right to my reptilian brain and started thinking about why he was asking me this question, unsure of his motives. I remained silent.

He leaned in slightly. "Look, I'm only asking because if you do, you need to keep it to yourself in a place like this. Play broke. Don't spend a lot at the commissary right off; people will be watching."

"Understood," I said, feeling like I was being let in on some inside information I hadn't asked for.

"One more thing," he added. "Did you cooperate with the feds on this case? Testify against anyone?"

"No, I didn't."

"Alright then, that's all I got for you."

He handed me a new, red prison ID, took me out of the compound exit, and pointed me toward laundry. "Head over there, and they will give you some fresh gear and boots," he said, turning away. I felt like I was being pushed through a machine without knowing how it worked.

Word travels fast in prison, so fast that those from the Boston area already knew that I was arriving, and by the time I got to laundry, one of them who worked there was waiting for me. How they knew about me or that I went to trial was beyond me, but they knew, nonetheless. When I came to the window, a Boston guy came from the back, telling the kid with tattoos all over his face that he had this one while grabbing a newer bedroll from a rack different from the one I would have been handed.

"Here you go, brother. If something doesn't fit, bring it back later, and I'll get you. By the way, I'm Johnny," he said and put his hand out.

"Adam," I replied, shaking his hand.

I thanked him, took the pile of stuff, went through the metal detectors, and arrived in my unit. Walking in felt like I had entered a different universe. I came when everyone was busy doing something, so the unit was only half full. I was lost in the moment's silence because I didn't know where to go or what to do. I felt eyes on me and saw a small group of white guys in the corner playing cards, all looking in my direction, so I walked right up to them, attempting to appear confident.

"Hey, I'm Adam, and before you ask, no, I am not a rat or sex offender; yes, I have all my paperwork, and I went to trial and got twenty-seven years." I could see their faces ease a bit.

One of the guys who barely looked up from his cards said in a thick Russian accent, "That's nice, but we're not the ones you need to worry about. I think Sean is upstairs. Hold on, and I will check. He will want to meet you."

They brought Sean down the stairs from the top tier a few minutes later. He was built like a tank covered in tattoos, including a massive swastika on his leg. I swallowed hard. "What's up, kid? I'm Sean. Where you from?" he asked, sizing me up.

"Massachusetts," I replied, trying to stand my ground.

"Ah, so you're part of the Boston car then," he said casually.

I blinked. "What's a car?"

Sean laughed out loud. "Wow, you're green as grass, aren't you? Don't worry; you'll learn everything soon enough, but first, let's find your cell."

Sean marched over to the officer's station and had them switch my assignments so I would be in a "white" cell, compliments of the racial politics that rule over everything in prison. I didn't ask questions. I was too tired, too overwhelmed, just trying to keep my head above water. When we walked into my new cell, Sean turned to me.

"Hand me your bedroll," he demanded.

I shook my head. "Oh no, it's cool, bro. I can make my bed and everything. Thanks, though."

He shot me a look. "I'm not asking so I can help you make your bed, moron; give me the damn roll."

Confused, I handed it over. He laid it out on my two-inch mattress and started rummaging through it methodically. He was looking for something specific, which made no sense to me. After a few seconds, he pulled out a hidden shank. My stomach dropped. What the hell was that doing in there?

Sean held it up, inspecting it, and then looked at me. "This is a pretty good one. You're not a rat. Otherwise, this wouldn't be in there," he held it toward me, offering it up.

I forced a laugh, nerves creeping into my voice. "Yeah, like I told the other guys, I went to trial, but if it is all the same to you, I have no interest in adding more time to my sentence on my first day here, so would you mind taking that with you?"

Sean smirked, amused by my naivety. "Fucking newbies. Don't worry; I'll hold onto it. You just let me know when you need it."

Need it? Jesus. I spent the rest of the day getting settled, moving into my cell, and meeting everyone I would associate with on the unit. Every conversation was a test, a chance for them to figure out whether or not I was worth keeping around. By the end of the day, I was still in one piece, and I took that as a good sign.

On my first walk across the compound to the dining hall, I had to pass through multiple metal detectors again, and there were two guys behind me having a conversation I'll never forget. They had to have been in a GED class of some sort.

"Hey yo nigga, how many feet is in a mile, man?" one man asked the other.

"What?"

"Feets, how many feets is in a mile?"

Naturally, my mind spoke 5,280 feet, and I almost said as much to them but decided not to interrupt.

The other man paused, thinking hard about how he would answer. "A mile? Aw, come on nigga, you can't measure that. That shit's a trick question. Ain't no two people's feet are the same size; you can't measure that shit."

I was stunned.

"Ah fuck, you right. You got that. They are trying to trip us up with that shit."

I stared straight ahead in disbelief, thinking, *Where the fuck am I?*

I knew I had a lot to learn about this new life, and it wasn't going to be an easy lesson.

# *Chapter Twenty-One*
# Shots Fired

"You've got five minutes," my brother said, pumping his BB gun, glaring down at me in bed with mock authority, checking the non-existent watch on his wrist.

"Come on, Alan, not again," I groaned, still half-asleep in bed.

"I don't give a shit what you want," he shot back, his voice cold. "You've got five minutes. Either get your ass into the woods and hide or lie here like an idiot. Either way, when time is up, I'm shooting."

"When time is up? You don't have an actual watch on your wrist, moron," I muttered, hoping he'd give up his quest.

"Four minutes, thirty-nine, four minutes thirty-eight," he started counting down, his eyes narrowing.

"When Mom and Paul get home, I'm telling!" I threatened, cutting off his countdown.

Dad, our stepfather, Paul DeMeo, had been in our lives since I was two. Even though our relationship with our biological father was strained, Paul made it clear that we needed to call him by his first name out of respect for the man who'd come before him. For years, I obeyed that rule. It wasn't until I grew older and understood what it meant to be a father that I ignored his request and started calling him Dad.

Alan's face twisted, his eyes widening like a young Michael Myers. "Oh, you're going to tell?" he asked mockingly.

BANG.

A BB hit my thigh, sending a sharp shooting pain through me. "Ahhh! You said I had five minutes! Shit!" I yelled, clutching my leg, grateful I had jeans on.

"That was before you told me you were a rat," Alan sneered. "Now, I'm no longer your brother. I'm the exterminator, and this house has a serious rat problem. Sixty seconds," he said, attempting to sound like The Terminator, pumping his gun again with chilling precision.

"That's not fair; you said I had five minutes."

"That was before you made the mistake of opening your mouth, narc. Fifty-nine, fifty-eight . . ."

There was no use arguing. Alan didn't bluff, and I knew it. I scrambled out of bed, dashed to the back door, threw on my shoes, and sprinted toward the woods, but not before grabbing his boots. Fair play wasn't exactly part of the game when the rules were made up by someone holding a BB gun. Later in life, it didn't surprise me at all when Alan joined the Marine Corps.

To buy time, I hurled his shoes over the neighbor's fence as if a snake were inside them and took off down the well-worn trail in the woods behind my house. The last time we played "Adam the hunted," I made the mistake of climbing up a tree to hide, believing it was a brilliant tactical move. It wasn't. When he shot me out of the tree, I fell to the ground, and it knocked the wind out of me. I still carried the small scars from those BBs, and I would not repeat that mistake.

This time, I had a plan. I knew the woods like the back of my hand. I knew Alan would head toward the "Magic Tree," a gnarled ancient thing with a hole big enough to store things, such as a little brother. It looked like something out of a horror film starring the Keebler elf. I knew he would head there first, convinced I was hiding somewhere close by.

There was nothing magical about the tree. It had a massive trunk split into three smaller sections about a quarter of the way up, where large climbable branches shot out from each limb. The name of the tree fit, but I think my dad named it to create a landmark in the woods to remember in case that information was needed in an emergency one day.

Using my head start, I started to loop around, off the beaten path, hoping to sneak back to the house unnoticed. I crept through the underbrush. He was only fifty yards away as I passed him, moving down the path. My nerves buzzed. I couldn't risk another shot; those BBs stung like hell.

Finally, I reached the edge of our yard. There it was, home, salvation. Through the back sliding glass door, our new golden retriever, Harley, was wiggling excitedly, sensing my return home.

"You are aware that those things you were walking on are called leaves, and they make a lot of noise, right?" Alan's voice drifted from behind me.

Damn it.

I ducked behind the closest tree, my heart now racing. "You are aware you shoot like a sissy girl, right?" I taunted him, hoping to distract him.

"I don't think you could have been any louder if you tried," he called back, amusement laced in his voice. "Next time, put on one of my mom's bright dresses and sing show tunes on your way back; you'd probably be less noticeable."

"I made it back to the house without you hitting me. I win," I said, trying to sound more confident than I felt.

"Win?" he laughed. "The house is over there, genius. See, I told Mom not to adopt you. They picked the dumb, broken one."

"Shut up, you ass-face. You're just mad because I beat you, and you suck at this game," I shot back, comebacks clearly not my specialty.

Alan smirked, lifting his BB gun again. "Lost, huh?" He aimed. There was no way for him to hit me. The tree I was crouching behind was much too big. He shot at me anyway. The BB hit the trunk, ricocheted, and shattered the driver-side window of our dad's work truck.

Both of us froze, our jaws dropping in sync. We'd done it now. The game was officially over.

"What do we do?" I asked, my voice barely above a whisper.

The night before, my father had been in pain from a toothache, so today my mother took him to the dentist to have the problem fixed. They had been gone most of the morning and would be home any minute. We didn't have much time.

Alan's brain went into overdrive. "Here's what we do. We go inside, play Nintendo, and act like we've been doing that the whole time. If they notice and ask us anything when they get home, we tell them someone must have tried to break in and broke it."

It wasn't the worst plan, but considering we lived in sleepy Dennis, MA, where the biggest threat to our neighborhood was my brother himself, it wasn't exactly foolproof. But who was I to argue with the guy who had just been shooting at me?

"Okay, but what did they use to break in?" I asked.

"I don't know," Alan said, annoyed.

My eyes landed on a golf ball-sized rock lying in the driveway. I picked it up, marched to the truck, and tossed it through the shattered window.

"There. That'll do," I said, feeling calmer.

Alan nodded. We raced inside, grabbed the Mario Brothers cartridge, blew in it three times so it would work, and started playing.

Alan's game was off. He was distracted and rattled by what had happened, and it showed in his clumsy gameplay. It was as if a guilt-ridden parasite had infected his brain, infringing on his ability to think clearly. I was happy for the distraction, as it meant I was kicking his butt.

Looking back, I imagine my jury saw me as I saw him then. Clumsy and paralyzed, not from feelings of guilt like Alan, but from the fear of having my freedom taken from me.

We hadn't made it through two levels when we heard my mom's car pull into the driveway. We exchanged a quick glance: game time. The silence and prolonged entry into the house told us everything we needed to know. It was obvious they had noticed the truck's window and were now examining it. When the back door finally opened, we did our best to act casual.

"Hey, Mom," Alan said, eyes glued to the TV screen, acting as if the game in front of him was the most important thing on earth.

"Did you bring us anything?" I added without looking up. I don't know what I was thinking. It was a dumb question.

"From the dentist's office?" she asked. "What would I have brought you from the dentist's office?"

Dad walked in behind her, his exhaustion from the dentist and the sleepless night before palpable. "Honey, why don't you go put this stuff away?" he said, handing her a couple of small bags, "and give me a minute with the boys here."

Mom headed toward the kitchen without a word, which was odd to us both. Usually, she'd be in full-blown honey-badger mode at this point.

Dad reached down and unplugged the game, his face unreadable. "You guys mind telling me what happened to my truck?" he asked, almost too calmly.

Alan and I exchanged a look, trying our best to feign shock.

"What happened to your truck?" Alan asked, his voice a terrible attempt at innocence.

Dad smirked, clearly not buying what we were selling. "You mean to tell me that you two have been sitting here, playing this game, and didn't hear my driver-side window being smashed a few feet from the open window next to you?"

Okay, Dad, one, us zero. Clearly, we hadn't thought this through.

"Nope, didn't hear anything," Alan replied while I nodded in silent agreement.

His smirk deepened. "That must be one hell of a game. I did find this in the front seat," he said, holding up the rock I had tossed in.

"Oh, man. Someone must have broken into your truck!" Alan exclaimed, his awful acting skills on full display.

"In broad daylight, someone broke into an empty, unlocked truck in this neighborhood. They must have been the dumbest criminals in the world. Why break a window to steal nothing when they could have opened the door?" Dad asked, sarcasm heavy in his voice.

He had us. The plan had crumbled before it even began.

"So, you're telling me neither of you know anything about this?" he asked, giving us one last chance.

"Nope, nothing," Alan said quickly.

Dad turned to me. "Adam, anything to add?"

I glanced nervously at my brother. "No, there is nothing else."

"Well, alright then. I had hoped maybe you guys knew something, but if you didn't hear anything, then you didn't hear anything," he said, turning to walk away. "Oh, just one more thing," he added, stopping in his tracks. "When I picked up the rock in my front seat, I found this too." He held up a single BB in his hand.

We were completely and utterly busted.

"You have thirty seconds to tell me the truth."

Alan didn't hesitate. "It was me. I did it. Adam had nothing to do with it. I was shooting my BB gun, and it ricocheted off the tree and broke your window. I'm sorry. I didn't mean to do it, and I swear it was an accident."

"Accidents happen, so why didn't you tell me that from the start?" Dad asked.

"Because I didn't want to get into trouble," Alan said.

"And instead of avoiding trouble, you do the one thing that guarantees you'll get into more? You lie to me and develop an elaborate scheme to throw me off the scent?"

"Yes sir, I did," Alan replied, deflated.

"What about the rock? How did that get into my truck?" he asked.

"I threw it in there," Alan shot back, quickly trying to cover for me.

But Dad was staring at me. "Is that true, Adam? Is that how this went down?" I was stuck between a rock and a hard place. We had been caught. Continuing to lie did not seem like a smart idea.

I swallowed hard, guilt weighing heavily. "No, I threw the rock. That was my idea."

"No, he didn't!" Alan jumped in. "Shut up, Adam. I did it, all of it. I threw the rock, I came up with the story, and I shot the BB gun. It's my fault."

"Alright, alright, relax," Dad said, raising a hand to calm the situation. He stood for a moment, clearly deep in thought, his hand on his chin. By now, Mom was standing behind him, fully aware of what had transpired but still silent.

Finally, the silence broke. "No TV or electronics for the rest of the day," he said.

Alan and I stared at him in disbelief. No TV? We were expecting exile in Siberia. The punishment had never not fit the crime before, and the excessive leniency had the honey badger hiss.

"No TV? That's it? They broke your window and then lied to us about it," she said, her voice rising with frustration.

"They did," Dad agreed. "And I am not happy about it. But, when push came to shove, they protected each other. That means I have been doing my job as their father. I will not punish them harshly for it, not this time." He looked back at us both. "Both of you, grab a broom, clean up every piece of glass in that driveway, and then use my shop vac to clean it out. The next time something happens, you tell your mother and me the truth. Understood? This is your ONLY free pass."

"Yes, sir," we both mumbled.

"I want you two to protect each other, but you don't need to protect each other from us. Perhaps I haven't made that clear enough, so I am making it clear now. Okay, go, get out there and clean up the glass."

That night, Alan headed over to David's house, still stewing over the whole thing, mad that I didn't back him. I stayed behind, nursing my bruised leg. I get that he wasn't thrilled with me owning up to my part in the lie, but it isn't like I told them he was shooting at me with the BB gun. Strangely, it felt good that he was mad at me. Despite all the different ways he picked on me, I now knew he would be the first to protect me. That meant something.

Still, my leg ached from the BB shot, and he wasn't going to protect me from himself, so I was going to have to think smarter.

I grabbed a Phillips-head screwdriver from the junk drawer, snuck into Alan's room, and quietly dismantled the trigger mechanism on his BB gun. I removed a few key pieces, reassembled it, good as new, and put it back where he had left it. The trigger no longer worked, and it wouldn't fire again.

That bruise on my leg was the last BB he shot at me.

(Alan, if you're reading this now, I am why your BB gun mysteriously "broke." That's what you get for trying to convince me I was adopted all those times.)

The best way to avoid injury is to be able to defuse the threat before it arrives. This is easier said than done in many cases, but it is a sound theory, nonetheless. Was I going to be able to successfully dismantle future triggers before they fired?

## *Chapter Twenty-Two*

# Dismantling the Trigger

"Recall . . . all inmates return to your housing units in preparation for the 9 p.m. count . . . RECALL."

Like clockwork, the loudspeaker delivered this familiar message every night at 8:30. By 8:45, every inmate was locked away for the night. Most hated it, but for me, it was the only time I could relax, away from the chaos, to be alone with my thoughts. Lying there in the dark, staring at the ceiling, I found a strange peace in the solitude. It was the one reprieve in a place where survival was dependent on constant vigilance. If I was going to make it through the brutal prison politics and middle-school mentality of my fellow inmates, I needed this time to plan, strategize, and figure out how to dismantle the "BB gun triggers" surrounding me daily. Every day was going to bring new challenges, and I knew it.

The tension in the air was pernicious, thick, like smoke you couldn't escape. It hung there, making it hard to breathe, though no one could pinpoint an exact reason for it. The truth was that the tension thrived on ignorance and pettiness that often became magnified into disaster. It was like watching a campfire suddenly consume the entire forest, even though it was pouring rain. It made no sense, defying all you once thought was true about human nature. People like to believe that we have evolved as a species, but when you look inside high-security prisons, you quickly realize that we haven't. We are the most vicious creatures on this planet.

What goes through a man's mind when he decides to secure a lock to his belt and smash another man's face with it over a thirty-five-cent cup of soup? How can another man find justification for stabbing someone in the neck because they were slamming down dominos too loudly outside of their cell? Did they not have the mental faculty to ask the person to stop hitting the dominos?

This raw, animalistic behavior kept me hyper-vigilant and constantly on edge. I found myself studying the body language of everyone around me, watching their interactions, dissecting their motives, and trying to understand their ethos better. It became a full-time job trying to predict what this inimical world of tomorrow would bring to this unpredictable environment.

I wondered how criminologists could ever claim to understand men they have never studied while in their natural habitat. Interviewing criminals after they have been caught and caged only gives a glimpse, an opinion at best. Those so-called experts who spend a lifetime studying killers do so after they have been caught. What insight would have been gained had they been able to study those predators while they were active, in the wild, when they believed no one was watching them? What secrets would we be able to uncover about their decision-making process and true motivations? The true laboratory for understanding criminal behavior isn't in an interview room. It is right here, in prison, where these types of minds and men roam among their kind.

Behind these walls, there is an order to things. A grim structure that even the prison administration silently endorses because it makes the overall population easier to control. Because inmates align themselves with "cars," or groups, divided by race and affiliation. For the white population, you've got the Aryan Brotherhood, Dirty White Boys, Odinists, 1 percenters, Boston, New York, White Independents, Italian or Organized Crime, Russians, you name it. Every day brings new conflict. One day, it could be the Italians beefing with the Muslims: the next, it's the Aryan Brotherhood against the DC car or the 1 percenters clashing with the Tangos.

Whatever problems your car has, they become your problems. And if you don't back them up, you become the problem. When tensions escalated, especially along racial lines, the entire population would split into three major groups: White, Spanish, and Black. The "shot callers" for each car would gather in the yard for a mandatory meeting called to attempt to defuse the tension before it exploded. Watching them attempt diplomacy was like watching a monkey try to fuck a football; awkward, pointless, and doomed to fail. For me, it felt like cleaning a loaded gun with the barrel aimed at my face.

I had committed to always being honest and acting with integrity in every situation, but doing so inside meant walking a fine line between the real world and the artificial prison reality. I had no other option than to learn to compartmentalize my choices, distancing myself from the madness while maintaining enough awareness to survive. The key would be avoiding my reptilian brain as much as possible and using my intelligence, not my instincts, to navigate the landscape. I had seen enough to know that losing control of the ability to choose for myself meant losing what little freedom I had left. Almost all the men surrounding me had no "good time" left in their sentences because they never had control over their behavior. I could not allow that to be me, but for the majority in prison, their choices are dictated by the leaders in their cars, and those so-called leaders were most certainly Neanderthals.

But the dilemma was real: How do you avoid being dragged into conflicts that have nothing to do with you? In prison, leadership often goes to those most willing to resort to violence. Those who dropped out of school in the ninth grade became de facto rulers. It was insane to me. Why do I need to risk being stabbed or being forced to stab someone because some junkie in my car ran up a debt he couldn't pay or because someone else in a rival car failed to settle up?

The caveat was that if I didn't stand with my car when they demanded it, I would be the one they went after next. I spent countless nights dissecting this dilemma from every angle, trying to figure out how to avoid being conscripted into someone else's battle.

I didn't mind standing up for a righteous cause or defending someone who truly needed it, but I wanted to be the person who made that choice. I was already struggling to balance complex emotions from the continuous loss in my life, and I couldn't afford to lose the ability to choose for myself. I've often found that whenever a solution refuses to reveal itself by sitting inside the problem for long enough, ultimately, the answer will find you. I knew that I needed to start being who I was and not who I was supposed to be. This was not a mistake I was going to repeat in my life.

Prison is as dark and bleak as you would expect, but I've always believed that attitudes are contagious. The strongest tool in my tool belt was making my attitude worth catching. I had already spent years perfecting the art of emotional transfer, and here, it was a skill with life-or-death consequences. On the inside, I was hurting, and I prayed my acting skills had improved since the days of trying to weasel out of trouble with my dad. I needed to appear pathologically cheerful, oblivious to the prison politics swirling around me.

I started slowly as if approaching a body of water home to alligators, bonding over humor and common ground with key players from each car. I made it a point to always smile and always remain easygoing. My goal was simple: connect where we are alike. I observed, listened, and learned, using intellect as my shield. I prayed that, with a bit of luck, others would see my social movement as something admirable rather than something suspicious. I wanted my attitude to become the contagion leaving a positive impression on anyone who crossed my path.

I needed a reputation that transcended race and affiliation and would have people speaking well of me when I wasn't present, regardless of which car they were in. It was the only path I could see that would allow me to keep the promise I made to those I loved: that I would stay safe.

Inside, survival isn't just about physical strength. It's about psychological endurance and having people remember your name for the right reasons. This would be the path to making it out in one piece.

# *Chapter Twenty-Three*
# Knight to B4

Sean was a crucial piece in the chess game that led to the path of survival, and I knew I had to move him. He wasn't part of the car I was expected to join, but he liked me, which was enough for me to work with. I could tell he commanded respect from the other "white" cars when we walked the yard; intimidation radiated from him. Years back, the facility had been designated as a "disciplinary yard," collecting all the troublemakers from other institutions, and Sean was one of them. An Odinist from the West Coast, he always managed to find himself in the middle of chaos. In this pagan religion, the hammer worn around the neck had to be earned, and they had to earn it by doing something awful to another person. Sean had a tattoo on his trigger finger that read "Karma," and I often wondered if he could see the irony.

Sean didn't have much money coming in from outside support, but he loved being high on Suboxone, so any funds he did get went straight to that. To supplement his habit, he always had a hustle running for the ticket man or selling off part of his drug stash for the extra cash to buy kitchen food when it would come back to the unit through the workers. Every time I cooked food for myself, I intentionally made too much so I would have extra to offer him.

"Hey man, I made too much. Are you hungry?" I asked, even though I could have eaten every bite myself.

He'd never hesitate. "Fuck yeah, I'm starving," he would say, grabbing it from me like a dog snatching a piece of bacon out of your hand. Seriously, I thought I might lose an arm.

This became routine, and before long, we were working out together, sitting in the chow hall, watching the news, and debating politics. Slowly but surely, he got to know me, my mindset, and my values. With that, his respect for me grew, and we became friends. Phase one was complete.

Meanwhile, through eavesdropping or "ear hustling," I learned that the shot caller for the Muslims had only two years left on his sentence. The stress of returning to the outside world was eating at him. Every week, I'd notice him reading a new book, *Stock Trading for Dummies: How to Invest in Real Estate*, and I could see the fear on his face whenever he talked about returning to the world.

One morning, I stepped out of my cell with my coffee and spotted him sitting alone, watching some bird documentary on the National Geographic channel. It was unusual for someone in his position to be sitting in front of the "black" TV solo. I admit birds are one area of study I lack, but I sensed an opportunity and sat beside him despite the implied racial lines I was now crossing. He shot me a look, clearly confused, but I tried to break the ice by telling an off-color joke:

A man walks into a pet store determined to find a low-maintenance pet to add to the family. Work keeps him busy, so a dog is out of the question. As he is browsing, a voice calls out from across the room.

"Hey, hey buddy, over here! Look at me!" The man walks over, amazed that a parrot is speaking to him.

"Holy shit, a talking parrot. I have only heard of this but never actually seen it. I thought this was something for the movies," he said.

"Nope, not just the movies. I'm real," the parrot replied.

"And you can carry on a conversation with me. WOW! I can't believe how awesome this is." The guy checked the price tag and was shocked by how little the bird cost. "You're not expensive at all. I don't understand. Why so cheap?"

"Promise not to laugh at me?" the parrot asked.

"Yes, I promise."

"It's because I don't have any legs," the parrot confessed.

The man stood puzzled for a moment. "If you don't have any legs, how do you hang onto that swing in your cage?"

"I have to hang onto it with my penis," the parrot said.

By this point, the Muslim shot caller chuckled a bit, and I could feel the tension sliding away, and he stopped looking at me like a raccoon in his trash can. I pressed on.

The man didn't care about the legs, laughed it off, bought the parrot, and loaded him in the car. They talked the entire ride home. When they arrived, he brought everything and set the bird up in the living room, figuring a talking bird might listen to the TV when no one was home.

"Okay, bird, I left the TV on, food, water, and when I get home tonight, we will pick out a name for you, but right now, I am late to work and need to get going," the man said.

He left excited about returning home to hang out with his new friend.

When he returned later that night, the parrot called out for him the second he walked in the door: "Hey buddy, come quick. I need to talk to you."

He walked into the living room excited to see his new parrot. "How was your first day?" he asked.

"Never mind all that, listen, I saw your wife today," the parrot said.

"My wife? She is working a double today. She wasn't supposed to be home until early morning," he replied, a bit confused.

"She wasn't here for very long but wasn't alone. I saw her and your postman, and they were getting . . . intimate," the parrot said.

Devastated, the guy asked, "What do you mean intimate?"

"He started putting his hands up her shirt and down her skirt while kissing her."

"Jesus. What happened?" the man asked.

"I don't know," the parrot says. "I popped a boner and fell off my swing."

The shot-caller laughed.

I breathed.

With the ice now broken, I introduced myself. "I'm Adam," I said, holding out my hand.

"Rashid," he replied, shaking his head. We spent the next half hour talking about life, family, and his concerns about returning to society. I asked him discovery questions, and it was then that I found his biggest stress point at the moment was his credit score.

My previous life afforded me experience in finance and FDCPA law, so I offered to help. The next morning, I went up to his cell with a copy of a credit request form in my hand. I knocked and opened the door. His face was covered in Noxzema.

"Look, man, I know I am your only white friend in this place, but that doesn't mean you have to go all whiteface on me when I stop by. Seems a little racist of you," I joked.

Again, he laughed. I gave him the forms to send out and spent the next few months helping him dispute errors and improve his score. In the end, we got his score up over 100 points. He was thrilled.

"Let me know what I owe you," he'd say.

"Owe me? I don't understand," I played stupid.

"Yeah, money. Let me know how much you want from me for your help or what I can get at the commissary," he said.

I'd just laugh it off. "Send me a thank-you letter when you get your first credit card, and we'll be good."

Building these relationships became the centerpiece of my strategy. I joined a morning handball game with the Boston guys. One of them, Paulie, was shipped to USP Hazelton, where he later became one of the men accused of killing James "Whitey" Bulger. I tutored gang members to get their GEDs and helped some Russian members draft business plans. Slowly, I earned the trust and respect of every group, all while keeping my distance from the politics of their petty feuds. I started to gain more confidence and offered small advice to diffuse conflicts, posing logical alternatives to all-out war. "Do you want to lose good guys over this? Let these two handle their issue with one another one-on-one."

I didn't have a stake in the fight and didn't care if they all ended up killing each other. Still, it made no sense to lose "friends" over trivial disputes, and as the political chains of prison life tried to tighten around me, I was quietly finding ways to break free.

Yet, I still had a long way to go in this fight.

Despite all the time and effort I dedicated to thought, planning, and implementation, some lessons were going to be learned the hard way. The fact is, you don't know what you don't know.

## *Chapter Twenty-Four*

# The Hard Way

Experience gained over time will teach you some of what you don't know, such as cardinal rules. Cardinal rules cannot be broken in prison if one desires to stay alive. One such rule is that one doesn't stay alone in one's cell during the day.

But I couldn't get up.

Morning brought the unlocking of the doors and me lying in bed, doused in pain and drained of strength and will to face the day. In prison, leniency is a luxury, and excuses don't hold weight. Yet, I could not move.

Sean came in to check on me. He told me he would return in an hour, giving me precious time to garner strength without pushing my luck too far. As punctual as ever, he was back in an hour.

"Hey, brother," he greeted me, tossing a white tube onto my bed. "Here, this is for you. Every time you leave the cell, slap some of this on that eye and make sure to smooth it out.

I picked it up, groggy, squinting at the label, trying to make out what it said. "What the hell is this?"

"It's cover-up," Sean replied matter-of-factly, as if handing makeup to a grown man in prison were the most natural thing on earth.

"Where the hell did you get cover-up?" I asked, baffled.

Sean smirked, clearly amused by my naivete. "I forget sometimes you're still green. I sent Jay over to unit 4A this morning to see Trailer Swift, you know, the blond-headed tranny. Whites and Spanish hit him up for stuff like this; the Blacks go to Dickie Minaj in 2B. The way I see it is if the BOP is dumb enough to sell this stuff on a male compound and can't foresee how we are going to use it, that's on them."

"Trailer Swift?" I echoed, stifling a laugh. "That's wrong on so many levels . . . but I'll admit, it's hilarious."

The absurdity hit me. Never in my life did I think I would end up using makeup, much less in a prison setting. If you'd asked me before, I'd have guessed my first encounter with cosmetics would have come during some playful moment with my daughters, them giggling as they smeared lipstick and blush on my face. But life has a way of defying expectations.

The beating, which was meant for my body only, hit my eye, and the bruise was a problem I couldn't ignore. Skipping every meal for the next week wasn't an option, and I needed to prepare for unexpected callouts where an officer might notice the black-and-blue dark shadows encircling my eye. In prison, that would trigger a body check and a one-way ticket to the SHU (solitary confinement—also known as the Box or the Hole), where they would dissect and catalog everything as evidence from a crime scene. The cover-up, crude as it was, worked well enough to keep me under the radar.

Still, the risk remained. I had to survive a week without a body check. I kept my fingers crossed that no other fights would break out near me. My face might pass scrutiny, but the rest of me would not. With any luck, by the time anyone noticed, I would be able to blame the bruises on a game of floor hockey at the gym that was aggressive or on a pickup basketball game that I didn't play. Either way, until then, I would be moving around with my torso looking like a spotted eggplant, praying not to get peeled.

But hiding from the eyes of a corrections officer was not my only problem. For the first time, I would have to lie to Sheva.

We had made a pact: no lies, no matter what. And while we both knew there were some truths I couldn't share, outright lying was something we'd sworn to avoid. But with her scheduled to come for a visit that upcoming weekend, the truth wasn't an option. When I got stripped out in the visiting room, the officers would see the marks on my body and lock me in the SHU.

Visiting required strip searches—one on the way in and one on the way out. The eye was one thing, but there was no way to hide the mottled purple and green splotches on my body from the examining officer, nor could I explain them. And Sheva knew me too well; she'd see through the cover-up instantly.

Those of us on the inside often mask our struggles to spare the ones we love. We groom ourselves, stay in shape, and do everything we can to look healthy so our families can leave visits less worried than when they came in. It's never about us. It's about them. We know our situation has already caused them enough pain, and no one wants them to feel more.

I decided to call and cancel, guilt pressing me with every word. "Hey, I'm not feeling great," I began, opting for a partial truth. "I think I am coming down with something, and the last thing I want to do is get you sick." Her response was immediate. "Oh, please. I don't care about that. I'm coming." Classic Sheva—fierce, loyal, and stubborn. Why didn't I anticipate that?

"Yeah, you're probably right," I replied, forcing a laugh. "But I am not feeling well enough and I don't think risking a visit is a good idea. If I don't rest, I could get sicker and become weaker, and that is never a good thing. I wouldn't be good company, and as much as I hate it, I think it's better if I stay in bed." Another lie.

The universal problem with lying is that to sustain it, you need to continue lying, but like with everything else, in prison, this is underscored—all communication is monitored.

It also highlighted how alone people in prison are; even having loved ones in their life, navigating what is shareable is paramount. I'd lose my cover if I had told Sheva before that staying in bed all day is unsafe. Being fully transparent was a recipe for disaster, so I was not. Still, I found solace in knowing I was lying for the right reasons. We do what we can to protect our loved ones, and I knew that when the time came when I could tell her the truth, she would understand and not be upset by it.

"No, of course," she said finally, her voice softening. "I want you to rest. I can come when you're better, no problem."

* * *

Just 24 hours earlier, Alec, Tee, and Sweeney had followed me into my unit. "Alright, kid," Alec said, his tone leaving no room for negotiation. "The time has come for you to put in your work."

Prison politics never made any sense to me. A white guy in my unit called Mud had screwed up, and a group of selected men was being assigned to "send a message." As a guy who was new to the environment, I was one of the ones being drafted to deliver it.

Mud was a loudmouthed white supremacist covered in swastikas, lightning bolts, and the number 1488. A walking caricature of hate, he had a boar tattooed on the side of his head and a mouth that wouldn't stop running. Men like this of every race are scattered throughout prison. Mud has certainly earned his nickname along the way. I once wanted to ask him if he knew the history behind the term "His name is Mudd," but one look at him clearly showed that he would not know about the assassination of Abraham Lincoln.

Mud's latest offense? He mouthed off a black guy who responded by smacking him across the face. Mud did nothing in response. This was a cardinal sin in his circle and a weakness that didn't fly. The politics of his car demanded retaliation from him, but before anything could be discussed, officers collected them both and brought them to the SHU.

Compounding his sin was word leaked from the SHU that Mud was badmouthing his own "car" for not doing anything on his behalf while he was in the SHU. The whites decided Mud needed to be punished.

"When Mud is let out, we're jumping him," Alec continued. "You will be part of the group waiting for him outside the chow hall when we get him sent up to rec."

"Like hell I will," I shot back. "Not happening. That man's choices and problems have nothing to do with me."

"He is white, and you guys live in the same unit. We need someone from the unit, and you're the new guy. It's that simple," Tee said flatly.

"Is this a joke? This is a dude with swastikas tattooed all over him. I can assure you, nothing about us is the same," I said, holding my ground.

Sweeney stepped closer, his voice lowering. "Nothing personal, but you can either get with the program or become the program. It's your choice."

The threat hung heavily in the air. I knew what was coming. I got in first. "Look, I get how things work, but all of you are off base. You can't fix stupid, which is why I have never bothered with the man. I am not responsible for him, nor have I ever claimed to be. Any responsibility for his actions falls on those who accepted him and called him a brother, but I know I do not have a voice here. I am not directing anything other than myself, so here is what I propose: Sean, Jay, and Smooth are all not required to be a part of this because they have already put in work of some sort during their sentence and are going home soon. So, I'll fight those three in the laundry room off-camera. I'll take my licks, my work will be put in, and all will be settled."

Sean, who'd been eavesdropping, nodded. "That's fair. But it's not going to be a fight. It's a punishment. We'll avoid the face and let you walk out, but we're going to rough you up pretty good."

A deal was struck. I could tell Alec, Tee, and Sweeney weren't happy about it, but they weren't going to argue with Sean, and this did cover all bases. Check, mate. I didn't win anything, but at least I lost on my own terms. I exhaled; a bit relieved I sidestepped the worse fate of the two. I couldn't help but ask. "I don't understand. When a guy willingly calls himself Mud, was that not a red flag? Would anyone be surprised if I introduced myself as a kleptomaniac and started stealing?" Sean leaned in, smirking. "You just won this one. Don't push your luck."

Mud was released from the SHU during the next ten-minute move, storming into the unit like a hurricane, his temper as fierce as his reputation was fragile. With his bag in tow, he came in barking orders and demanding his old cell back, oblivious to how much had changed in his absence. The scene was almost comical. A delusional figure trying to regain the control he never possessed.

Mud identified as an Odinist and, as a member of that car, proudly wore a hammer pendant symbolizing his earned warrior status—or at least he had before he lost it. When he first went to the SHU, his so-called brothers stripped him of the hammer, a symbolic rejection of his failure to act when slapped by an inmate of another race, an action prohibited in their bylaws.

Sean, leaning casually against the wall, always sharp, stepped into the middle of this chaos. “Yo, who the hell do you think you are coming in here barking orders, especially when you showed yourself to be as soft as baby shit. You’re without a hammer, which means you are without a voice. Your guys took it, remember? Until that is sorted, you are nobody. You have no rights and no backing. They’re up at rec waiting to hash this out with you, so that needs to be your only focus right now.”

Mud puffed his chest, but his bravado faltered. “I’m not worried about that; I’ll get it back from them.”

“Good,” Sean shot back. “Because that is priority number one, getting back your hammer. Go handle that before you worry about anything here.”

Mud knew not to challenge Sean. Everyone did.

Still riding the manifested adrenaline that he’d gained through psyching himself up before his SHU release, Mud dropped his green property bag to the floor, muttering under his breath as he stormed back out. Everyone but Mud knew what was coming next. The walkway outside was already a battlefield in waiting. The emergency alarms blared across the compound within minutes of Mud stepping out. Officers scrambled toward the commotion in front of the dining hall, but it was already over when they arrived. Mud lay in the wet grass, beaten and bloodied, ironically smeared with actual mud. The hammerless Odinist had been stomped into submission, his fate sealed by those who once called him brother. Everyone involved was escorted to the SHU.

Sean found me in the unit. “When they call dinner tonight, let’s get this done.” During dinner, the compound was a chaotic sea of movement, and officers were preoccupied with monitoring the flow of foot traffic. It was the perfect window to get it done with the lowest risks of being caught.

When the time came, I didn’t wait for them to summon me. I headed to a room where we hung wet laundry. I went in with laundry as a decoy for the camera, a plausible explanation for entering the room if footage of me doing so was reviewed later. The smell of VO5 Shampoo filled the air, and I sat and waited. Sean, Jay, and Smooth entered together a few minutes later, decoy clothes in hand.

"You ready, kid?" Sean asked, gripping a cylindrical stone from the rec yard like a roll of quarters.

"Go fuck yourself."

Jay and Smooth grinned, clearly enjoying my defiance. Sean swung first, catching me off guard while my focus was on Jay. His punch landed like a sledgehammer against my ribs, knocking the wind out of me. I doubled over, gasping, just as Smooth's fist came flying toward my stomach. I shifted at the last second, and his punch grazed the side of my head instead.

"Hey! Below the neck, dummy! He's a friend of ours," Sean barked toward Smooth.

"My bad, Adam," Smooth said sheepishly. "You bent forward into my punch."

"Did I complain? You hit like a little girl," I lied through clenched teeth. I was reeling, but I wasn't about to give them satisfaction.

Sean chuckled. "Alright, let's finish this shit."

The next sixty seconds felt like an eternity. They delivered calculated blows, aiming for maximum pain with minimal damage. None of them were angry with me or trying to maim me; this was just business, prison politics at work. Still, every punch was deliberate; each hit reminding me that I had willingly agreed to this. They made damn sure I felt every blow. By the time it was over, I was on one knee, gasping for air and regretting every choice I had made that led me to this moment. Adrenaline coursing through me was the only reason I could stand and return to my cell without help, but I knew as soon as it wore off, I'd feel every ounce of their "work."

"Do me a favor," I rasped, "I need to stay in bed tonight. Can you keep an eye on my cell for me?"

"No problem," Sean replied. "Hang a towel over the door to cover the see-through, like you are using the bathroom. People will assume you are getting a tattoo or something with it being up for so long. If I see it come down, I will check on it. No one will bother you, and I will come pull it down when I see an officer about to do a round."

"Thanks," I muttered, hobbling into my cell.

That night, I lay on my back, trying not to move. Every shift, every breath, brought sharp, searing pain. By morning, I still hadn't found relief. It was worse, and I stayed put when the door unlocked, dreading the thought of standing.

Sean came in to check on me. "Hey man, how you feeling?" he asked, a trace of genuine concern in his voice.

"Feeling? I feel like your birth certificate is an apology from the condom factory."

He burst out laughing. "Oh, rub some dirt on it. You'll be fine. It looks like the eye is showing a little, though. Fucking Jay. Hang tight; I'll send him to get something for it."

"I'm not going anywhere," I groaned. "If someone came in here right now to end me, they'd be doing me a favor and putting me out of my misery. I hope you get bird flu!"

"Don't be so dramatic. It's just a little beating. Builds character and puts hair on the chest," Sean quipped. "I will be back in an hour."

I closed my eyes, too exhausted to respond further. He didn't need to know that every word I spoke sent a fresh wave of pain coursing through me. Dramatic or not, I knew one thing for sure: Surviving here wasn't just about strength; it was about knowing when to fight, when to endure, and when to lie low.

Today I had learned all three, but I was just beginning to scratch the surface.

## *Chapter Twenty-Five*
# Stay Clear of Yougots

If you examine the prison population for long enough, it becomes clear that a large portion of the population lives unequipped with basic necessities and envies those who "have." It's ironic because they are the very ones who spend their time bragging about the millions they made on the streets dealing drugs. I would have been able to respect them more if they had told the truth instead of pretending to be Frank Lucas or Pablo Escobar.

When I first arrived at the prison, nobody gave me advice or a heads-up on how to handle "yougots," those inmates who wander around, cup in hand, asking, "You got coffee?" or "You got some creamer?" They'll ask for soap, food, anything. These guys aren't the ones without. They have family members or loved ones who send them money. Instead of using it for necessities like coffee or soap, they blow it on drugs and then beg for their essentials. They also call their families to continually ask them for more money, garnering worry and guilt by implying that if they didn't get more funds, their lives would be in danger. I suppose if they couldn't pay the debts they accumulated to keep their drug habit alive, it could be.

I would watch a "yougot" convince someone to give them a bag of coffee and watch them go to one of the dealers and trade it for more drugs. I learned how to deal with them over time without causing bad blood, but I wished I had listened to the officer at my initial intake interview when he advised me to act indigent and not purchase much at the commissary.

When someone asked for coffee, I would tell them I was low and didn't have much either, but I'd make them a deal: "If you have creamer for me, I can muster up a coffee for you." Of course, they didn't have any, and I had plenty stashed away. But this simple tactic worked, getting them to move along without resentment or second thoughts. It was a great tactic, and I wish I had figured it out sooner.

Buses arrive and depart like clockwork in prison, constantly bringing new inmates. Upon arrival, the newbies have thirty days to produce their paperwork for the prison inmates to prove they are not rats.

Shortly after I arrived, two new arrivals from Texas made an impression: an Aryan Brotherhood Texas (ABT) member and a Dirty Whiteboy (DWB). They arrived together (were transferred from the same prison) and clearly had history with one another. The combination of them being moved so far away and stalling on producing their paperwork made their gangs suspicious. They were thought to have ratted on their gangs at their previous location in order to be moved.

Their property never seemed to arrive, so I initially helped them out. However, as time dragged on with nothing coming, I realized it was not the system but their behavior that was the problem. They had nothing because they messed up with their gang (the gangs send messages this way by keeping their belongings, they convey a loud message to the gang at the incoming prison), but I realized too late. My kindness was seen as a weakness, and their demeanor changed rapidly.

I eventually had to put my foot down, and I did. "Sorry, you guys have been here long enough to hit up the store. I did what I could for you, but my loved ones sent money for me to live, not for you."

"Fuck you just say?" the ABT responded, more of a statement being made than a question being asked.

It annoyed me, and there was no backing down. "Fuck did I just say? Is that your question? I was under the impression you both spoke English. Which part of what I just said confused you?"

His face hardened. "Yo, go get me a scoop of coffee. NOW." The DWB was standing next to him, trying to look tough, but at 5'5", 150 pounds, and with face tattoos, I could only see an idiot who looked ridiculous.

"I'll tell you what, here is what you need to do. First, you must walk about to some other cells in here, asking them for some coffee since I have nothing to give you. Eventually, you will find someone dumb enough to give you one, as I was until today. When you get one, head to the 190 machine and fill up your cup. Since you do not live here, I suggest you head back to your unit to enjoy it. Maybe sit in front of the TV and sip it. Now, if you are anything like me, after you finish the coffee, you might have to use the bathroom, and given how full of shit you both are, I am guessing that is likely. After you have done all this and you are feeling more awake, both of you do me a favor and go fuck yourselves." I was no longer able to remain pathologically cheerful.

"Funny. You think you have all the sense, huh? We'll see you around," the ABT said as they left, a threat hanging in the air like a spider from a single piece of webbing.

A few weeks passed, and I had not seen them anywhere. I figured they were probably lying low, trying to avoid the pressure from their gangs to produce their paperwork.

By then, I had settled into a Saturday morning routine, which consisted of coffee and Torah study from the quiet comfort of my cell while everyone else was out at breakfast or rec. Before coming to prison, I had many questions about life, God, and purpose and was searching for answers; I found my answers in the words of the Torah. I was gifted a subscription to *Chayenu*, a weekly periodical that breaks down teachings, including Rashi commentary, the Haftarah, Tanya, Rambam, and Mishnah, while also offering incredible insight toward living a meaningful life directly from the writings of the Lubavitcher Rebbe, which is brilliant. If you do not know what any of this stuff is, it's totally okay. I didn't either, but I have since come to find all the answers I was searching for within these texts.

The following Saturday, my cell door swung open while I was deep into my studies. The ABT and DWB entered, shutting the door behind them. I noticed the ABT had a razor blade taped to a makeshift handle, just the silver exposed in his left hand.

" 'Sup, Jew, where is the stupid hat for your head?" ABT sneered.

I felt a pit drop in my stomach. This wasn't going to end well for me. "Are you guys serious right now?" I asked, my voice betraying my fear, realizing I was in the middle of this before it started.

I was drenched in disappointment in myself. I had broken two ironclad prison rules: never be alone in your cell during the day, and never take your shoes or boots off. I had broken both. I had made myself comfortable, taken my shoes off, put my feet on the bed, and gone deep into my studies. I was about to pay dearly for those mistakes.

"Of course, we're serious. You want to be a kike?" he said, looking at his comrade before saying, "Let's circumcise this Jew fuck."

I figured that telling them I was already circumcised would have been a futile endeavor.

I don't know why they chose to come for me that day, and I can only speculate. I believe they were trying to gain some favor with other ABs, knowing the walls were closing in around them, and I supposed a man who pissed them off and reads Torah was as good a place as any for them to start.

They launched toward me. I focused on the blade in his left hand, leaving myself vulnerable to a flurry of punches and kicks from the DWB. It happened so quickly. I couldn't control the blade for long. We rolled on the floor, ABT's back on my chest and my arms wrapped around his neck. His left arm didn't have much mobility, but it had some and was flailing around by my waist. He repeatedly hit me in my side, stomach, and head. I knew I wouldn't fare well in this confrontation, and the fear was rising. I was going to be seriously injured, and I could feel it.

The ABT broke free. I had to let him go to protect my head as the blows from the DWB's boot heel were making me dizzy. As the ABT stood up in front of me, I kicked from my position on my back as hard as I could, landing my foot just above his waist and sending him into my sink, creating some distance, but the blows continued. I was saturated in fear now and almost completely out of strength. In a second, I was going to be completely defenseless.

Divine intervention or my dad watching over me (or both) saved me. Just as I was set to fall and just as the ABT picked himself up off the sink, the speaker in the unit crackled to life, and a loud voice came screaming over it.

"RECALL . . . ALL INMATES RETURN TO YOUR HOUSING UNITS IMMEDIATELY. RECALL."

At that moment, a fight had broken out in the yard—a lifesaving miracle for me. The two would-be killers had no choice but to leave and run out of the unit. Neither of them was assigned to my unit, and with everyone returning and a lockdown imminent, they needed to disappear. Like any coward would, DWB kicked me one more time before leaving. I was left dazed, blood soaking my shorts.

Someone in the unit must have heard the commotion because as everyone returned, Sean came racing in from the yard and asked me what had happened.

"Those two scumbags came here and jumped me," I said. He knew exactly who I was referring to. He saw the blood.

"I have gauze in my cell. I'll get it. Where did they get you?" he asked.

"My inner thigh. It is not a big deal, but I need the gauze. Thank you." He ran to get it. They had a lot of people trapped at rec and were video recording each person before they could leave and go back to the unit, so I knew I had time on my side.

But I lied to Sean. I knew they didn't cut my thigh as that was not where I was hurting. When they came into the cell, they mentioned wanting to circumcise me. Coincidently, when I had my hands around his neck on the floor, the only area that was free for him to cut me was from the waist down, and as luck would have it, he had sliced a gash in the side of my penis, which was where all the blood was coming from. I knew gauze wouldn't be enough as the gash was significant.

When Sean returned with it, I took it from him, wrapped a towel around me so the blood could not be seen on camera, grabbed a sewing kit, and went into one of the showers while Sean stood guard out front.

The showers were much different than the Detention Center. Here, there were three large walk-in showers on each tier. When you pulled back the curtain, it split into three large open areas. You put your chair next to a small table outside the shower and pulled back the curtain for privacy. I had an alcohol pad and did the best I could to sterilize the area and the sewing needle and pinched the cut closed with my left hand while sitting in the chair.

For those of you who have not had to get yourself stitched up before, pray that if the time comes, it doesn't have to be where mine had to be. The pain is excruciating, like having a toenail ripped off.

I couldn't go to medical for help because there was no logical way to explain it, and if I had gone, I would have become a rat in the eyes of fellow inmates.

I gave myself seven stitches.

When I finished, I got in the shower and cleaned the wound as best I could. I dried off and loaded the area with antibiotic ointment before wrapping it with gauze.

Word had already spread, and when I got back to my cell, a member from nearly every car was there, angry about what had happened and upset that those two guys were still walking the compound, believing they should have been dealt with weeks before. Tension was building. When they opened the yard back up for dinner, ABT and DWB knew their plan had backfired and ran to the Lieutenant's office to check in to protective custody.

I never saw them again.

That night, I felt like a truck had hit me, and my head was ringing. I was in pain for weeks and constantly on edge about going into my cell for anything I needed. When the wound finally healed, I cut the stitches, leaving only a slight scar behind. I was blessed that the scar was the worst that came from it, but I also knew this event changed me. I wasn't going to be overpowered by anyone physically ever again.

Although no one knew where I got cut, it was not just the Boston car or the white cars that had my back. Members from every group supported me in their own way, which wasn't anything anyone was used to seeing. This highlighted what I was trying to achieve: casting me in the light I wanted to be seen, as an independent with no racial tie limitation.

The next day, Sean sat beside me at the TV and spoke to me: "Every Saturday from here on out, you bring all your stuff next to me, and you do you. I got you," he said.

And that is how it came to be that for every Saturday after that, I'd sit beside a man with a large swastika on his leg, reading the Torah and drinking my coffee, thinking about the irony of it all.

It was also the start of my journey from a 160-pound, lanky athletic frame to the 220-pound, 9 percent body fat, nearly four-hundred-pound bench-pressing man I am today.

## *Chapter Twenty-Six*

# Who Is Free in the World?

I worked out hard and changed my appearance so anyone on the outside looking in would automatically assume that I would be a formidable opponent if they were to try me at some point. Not everyone approved of my decision not to pledge allegiance to any particular car and I hoped to limit any potential pushback from individual interactions. When other inmates questioned my allegiances, the usual response within a group was, "He's just a civilian. He's harmless and doesn't understand our politics." If anyone did feel the need to come at me directly, which became less frequent the bigger I became, I'd play dumb: "I like all of you guys. Why can't I be friends with everyone?" It was hard for anyone to argue in real time since I always did this in a way where others could hear—which, of course, was the whole point.

But I wasn't stupid. I understood the dynamics of control and had no interest in being part of it. Take Walpole prison in Boston, for example. Inside the state prison, every neighborhood in the city was at war with one another, literally killing each other. Charlestown was at odds with Southie, Dorchester against Jamaica Plains, etc. But when those same men entered the federal system, they suddenly united, following the unspoken rules of the place. The same people who were stabbing each other at Walpole became allies overnight, purely based on the system that was housing them. I wanted no part of this sort of madness and left it for the sociopaths.

In my younger years, I started each day focused on the present while keeping an eye on tomorrow. But watching my children grow up in photographs was a constant reminder of the time I was losing, which caused me to broaden my thinking. I had to carve out my path, a path that led me away from the insanity that surrounded me. I had to find a way to do this time and not let the time do me. Walking down this road gave life new questions, keeping me up late at night. What does freedom mean? How could I feel any sense of freedom in a place where every day was a reminder that I had lost mine?

That question haunted me, leading me down a rabbit hole that would consume my thoughts. The more I thought about it, the more I realized that freedom was an illusion and a challenge everyone faced. After all, was anyone genuinely free? Free from debt, loss, addiction, pain, obligation, control?

The days moved differently. Some days were indistinguishable; others stood out, entrenched in my soul. The day I found out that my high school friend Lucy had died is one I'll never forget. I got an email from my brother, and my heart broke while reading it. Lucy and I had been inseparable in high school and never lost touch. Woefully, alcohol took control of her life faster than any of us could have imagined. Looking back, she was always the life of the party and known for consuming more than the rest of us. But we were too young, too naive, to see the future consequences.

Her addiction spiraled, creating conflict and pain in her relationships. We loved her dearly and tried to help in whatever way we could. I would call her a few times a month, skyped often, and when I visited the Cape, I always made it a point to meet her for dinner and catch up. My mother sponsored her for some time in AA, and there were joyful moments in life when Lucy managed to quit. Sadly, those victories were short-lived. In the end, her addiction won. She died at home one night, in her sleep, from alcohol-related complications. Hearing the news pierced my heart. I hurt for her family, her sister, and for Lucy. My prayers for the demon to release its hold on her had not been answered in the manner I had hoped for. Lucy was smart, kind, and beautiful; now the world was much poorer without her.

Being locked away was another punch of guilt because it meant I wasn't around when I was needed most. Guilt spoke loudly, telling me things could have gone differently if I had been more involved. Yes, my situation was tragic, but Lucy hadn't been free either, not for years before her death.

Was I going to sit and feel sorry for myself, or would I use this time to become the best version of myself?

The latter.

I was determined to make the most of my situation, not to let it define me, but to use it as a catalyst for personal growth and self-discovery.

I would not become a product of the environment I was forced into; I would define the environment. I may not have understood the reason I was there at this moment, but my understanding of what it meant to be free was beginning to mature.

# *Chapter Twenty-Seven*
# Remove Your Shackles

How many people do you know who wake up each morning, drive their iron coffins to a job they hate, and perform tasks they don't care about, all to make enough money to survive in a life they do not enjoy? Are they free? Are you? These are questions we all need to ask ourselves in our pursuit of personal freedom and fulfillment.

The more I pondered the prison system I was now a part of, the more I grappled with my journey of self-discovery and the more transparent the world became to me. It isn't just inmates who are trapped; it is all of us.

Some of you might find this difficult to accept because of the emotional response it will trigger, but I want you to remember what you have already learned and apply logic. Prison mimics the world, making all of us convicts in some capacity.

The world is divided into continents. Continents into countries, countries into states or provinces, states into cities, and cities into neighborhoods. Tribalism in ancient times was deeply rooted in human nature. Since prehistoric times, there has always been tribalism, group division, and a natural inclination toward loyalty to one's group or tribe. It gave us identity, belonging, and better chances of survival. We are born in captivity, each accountable to the divisions we've been assigned.

We evolved in small, close-knit groups where cooperation was essential to survival. Maintaining cooperation was important because competition for resources from other groups was inevitable. Over time, it became natural for us to favor members of our group over others, leading to hostility, suspicion, and distrust among those outside of our group.

No wonder a person's self-esteem and identity can easily be tied to membership within a particular group. It's why a person can favor a gang in prison, even at the expense of fairness or equality. Many gangs here in America formed because one group of people was born and raised on a different street than another. They might be blocks away, but because they were competing for the same clientele, blood ended up on the streets, and rivalry became a constant.

Today's powerholders exploit our innate inclination to align with a group. They deepen these divisions to maintain control: white vs. black, rich vs. poor, Democrat vs. Republican, LGBTQ+ vs. straight. The labels of division are endless and constantly growing. Each new label fuels more conflict, and those in control exploit it to consolidate power. Look at the LGBTQ+ community, for instance. The government doesn't value individuality; it sees people as pawns. In the lavender scare of the Cold War, thousands of gay men and women were discharged from the military and government jobs because that was politically popular at the time. In 1950, the United States Senate issued a report titled "Employment of Homosexuals and Other Sex Perverts in Government," which claimed that hiring them constituted a security risk, but the truth was that it was a popular political message.

In 1996, Bill Clinton and the Democratic party, the party that claims to be the champions of the LGBTQ+ community, signed the Defense of Marriage Act into law, defining marriage as something that could only occur between a man and a woman. Many years later, Obama and his administration could have changed this law. They did not. If you are part of the LGBTQ+ community, I must ask, why is it you support them again? The only reason that is not the law of the land today is because of the Supreme Court and their decision in Obergefell v. Hodges, which declared same-sex marriage to be legal in all fifty states.

If you allow someone else to define you, they control you. In this context, it was as simple as assigning a letter to a person within a broader group, making it easier to pit them against each other and the rest of the world. This is achieved through action or simply by manipulating our vocabulary, thereby fostering more conflict. The AIDS epidemic is a stark example. The CDC initially labeled it GRID, Gay-Related Immune Deficiency Disorder, a move that further stigmatized an already marginalized group for political gain.

Division placed between us is nothing more than a form of modern-day slavery, tactics that have been employed since the days of ancient empires. Slave owners during this time in history capitalized on cultural and ethnic differences, mixing them to ensure unity among the slave population would not occur. Joining captives from different backgrounds made it impossible for a collective identity to form, ensuring loyalty to only their masters. The Romans would combine slaves who spoke different languages. The fragmentation made it difficult for slaves to communicate and understand one another and would sow more division.

Modern-day division is not always overt; it can be subtle yet pervasive.

A quick glance at the news will reveal that everything is being labeled as racist, sexist, or propaganda and misinformation. By perpetuating division along ethnic, religious, or socio-economic lines and attacking our language or speech, governments can suppress dissent and reinforce their authority.

Conveniently favoring one group over another will create deep-seated animosities. Once that occurs, the government will intentionally take whomever it is society views as marginalized or a minority and place members of that group into administrative and educational roles. Their only objective is to deepen existing tensions. During the British Colonial Rule in India, the British Empire's strategy involved stoking division between the Hindus and Muslims by promoting Hindus into administrative roles, which not only facilitated British control but was a large contributor to the partition of India and Pakistan in 1947.

The Soviet Union and China often labeled segments of their population as "enemies of the state" to help justify purges, forced relocations, imprisonment, and other repressive measures taken against them, keeping the population in a constant state of fear. This isn't just happening abroad; it's happening here. Does any sane American believe that parents attending a school board meeting because they are concerned about the quality and content of their child's education are "domestic terrorists"? Yet, they are called that on purpose. A war is being waged in the shadows, and we're all prisoners, especially our children. We've allowed this to happen; worse, we've handed a divisive and polarizing world to our kids on a silver platter, packed neatly in their pocket, and labeled as smartphones.

Social media is actively fueling algorithmic polarization, intentionally pushing sensational and emotionally charged posts designed to deepen division between groups. The purpose? To make us more susceptible to manipulation. These algorithms identify our existing beliefs and biases, feeding us a constant stream of content that reinforces our views, trapping us in echo chambers where only one narrative exists, the one they want us to believe.

Whether you realize it or not, the influence a parent is supposed to have over their child is being hijacked by the devices we give them. This device, a seemingly harmless phone, has become as dangerous and addictive as fentanyl. To our children, the act of clicking on what interests them and getting more of the same content is as intoxicating as any drug and comes with the same debilitating side effects. The algorithms are the dealers; Big Tech is the cartel.

This might sound dramatic, especially if you're unaware of the scale of what's happening. But consider this: in just the past twenty years, the suicide rate among children and adolescents has skyrocketed by over 60 percent. While it is true that boys have historically had higher suicide rates, in the last fifteen years, the suicide rates for girls aged ten to fourteen have tripled. These young minds are being poisoned.

It doesn't stop there. Hospitalizations for eating disorders in children under fourteen have increased by over 120 percent in the same time frame. During the COVID-19 pandemic, when children were isolated at home and glued to their screens instead of being in school and socializing with friends, clinics across the country quoted an additional 30–50 percent increase from the already high numbers. This is an actual crisis. It's a ticking time bomb for every parent in America. Yet, it is rarely spoken of.

We are only valuable to those in power if we remain in our assigned group, easily manipulated and controlled. As individuals, standing apart from any group, we're invisible. The ruling class doesn't just not care about us; they make it painfully clear how little we matter to them. Being a part of a car in prison is no different, and you are only valuable if the ones in power can use you and you remain in your assignment. I decided something different for myself, as should every American citizen.

## *Chapter Twenty-Eight*
# Perceived Value

When looking out into the world, we all tend to feel like the center of the universe—because, from our vantage point, we are. Every decision we make feels monumental, like the word hinges on our choice. We're constantly processing our thoughts and emotions through this filter, amplifying the significance of every moment. The way we see the world is, after all, from our unique perspective.

In our early years, this belief is nurtured by our families. Parents, siblings, and those closest to us seem to care as deeply about our lives as we do. Their love and attention fuel the sense that our individuality matters. As we grow older and form new bonds, especially romantic ones, the same dynamic plays out. Our significant others reinforce the importance of our choices and our lives.

But the truth is, we're not the center of the universe. We're grains of sand on a vast beach. In the eyes of those with perceived power, we're often invisible and irrelevant. Their concern for us, if it exists at all, is often superficial. In America, people are lumped into groups, voting blocs, and demographic categories useful only when they serve an agenda. If a group matters to those in power, they'll pretend to care. The moment someone tries to step out of that group to carve out an independent voice, they become a nuisance or, worse, a threat.

When someone becomes too loud or too defiant, the system doesn't view them as an individual with a voice; it sees them as a problem to be dealt with. And yet, most of us remain unaware, swimming circles in a sea of control. We're trapped in an echo chamber, magnifying our importance and meaning of existence, oblivious to the limitations of our reach.

Everyone has had that moment on a customer service call, feeling unimportant and undervalued. You wait on hold, believing you're worth more to the company than you are, only to discover you're just another number. After what feels like an eternity, you are finally connected to someone whose job has been outsourced to the lowest bidder, someone you can barely understand. The frustration mounts, and you realize your time, the most precious commodity we possess, something we cannot get back, isn't worth anything to them. That is the system at work. It's not about satisfaction; it's about keeping your money flowing in their direction.

Our government operates much the same way. Need something? Be ready to be placed on hold. There is nothing more inefficient than organizations run by government bureaucrats, which is why the unofficial slogan of the Federal Bureau of Prisons is "hurry up and wait." On a daily basis, they call inmates so they can sit there for hours and wait to be seen or forgotten about.

As ironic as this is going to sound, given my current situation, crime is abhorrent to me. I detest it almost as much as I detest empty promises of rehabilitation. Prisons aren't designed to rehabilitate; they're designed to warehouse. A drug dealer on the street becomes a drug dealer on the inside. A thief remains a thief, a predator stays a predator, and the hermits that spend their time alone in a room, looking at child porn or worse, acting upon their sickness, couldn't be happier. In prison, they have peers. A community of people they can be around who only amplify their desires and justify their actions. The system isn't built to stop this cycle or change behavioral patterns, it perpetuates it.

I am not a criminal, nor was I one before, and I followed every rule in prison. I stayed true to myself—no disciplinary actions, no trouble. I educated myself, helped others earn their GEDs, and exercised every day. I became invisible to the administration, a ghost because I did everything right. And for years, I thought that mattered. I believed it would be recognized that doing the right thing counted. I was wrong. Despite my efforts to contribute positively and follow the rules, I was not recognized as an individual in the system. Not even when I almost died.

## *Chapter Twenty-Nine*
# On Death's Doorstep

Thursday, January 30, 2020, started like any other day. I woke that morning having never really slept. That day was leg day in the gym, and though I felt a bit off, I pushed through. I convinced my workout partners to go lighter than usual, and we capped out at 275 pounds for squats. Generally, that was not a heavy load for me, but it felt much heavier that day. Something wasn't right, and I could feel it.

When I woke the following morning, my body ached like it shouldn't have—not just sore muscles but a profound, consuming fatigue. My legs, my whole body, felt weak, and it was too early to feel pain in my legs as I did, so I began to worry I was getting sick.

Prison is a filthy place, run by people too incompetent to solve problems and too lazy to care. A month earlier, the administration had decided it would be a good idea to remove all the spray bottles we used for cleaning the unit because a few inmates would use them to disguise the smell of their cigarette smoke in the shower area. They sacrificed hygiene for this, and soon after, the place was hit with a flu outbreak, followed by scabies and chicken pox. Waking up in this weakened state, I feared I was next.

Showering proved difficult, and I dragged myself to the medical department, certain that something was very wrong. After waiting nearly two hours, I was seen for a mere five minutes. I explained my symptoms and my growing concern, but I was brushed off. "You probably overdid it at the gym," they said. "Rest a few days." I wasn't even given the courtesy of being brought into an exam room, nor did I have any vitals checked. Not even a glance beyond the surface. I was disheartened because I had never once visited medical in all the years I had been down, and my arrival was an anomaly—something was truly wrong.

The following day, things got worse for me. A sharp, stabbing pain in my side made it hard to breathe. It felt like a knife lodged behind my heart, twisting with every inhale. I returned to the medical unit, more desperate now. The neglect and the lack of care in the system left me feeling utterly helpless, with no one to turn to for help.

"Sorry," the paramedic said, "it's the weekend. No one is here until Monday, and besides, the Super Bowl is tomorrow, so you have to expect no one is going to be here."

"What am I supposed to do? Something is seriously wrong with me," I protested, anger rising.

"Drink plenty of water. Rest. If you're still feeling bad come Monday, come back," he replied dismissively.

I wanted to scream, to demand help, but I knew better. Making too much noise would only get me thrown in solitary, and I'd rather be sick in the unit than sick in the SHU. I went back to the unit, angry and afraid.

A *Breaking Bad* marathon was airing on AMC until the Super Bowl the following day, and I had never seen the show before. So, I sat and watched, trying to keep my mind off how sick I felt and how with each passing moment my body was worsening. That night, I got very little sleep. The pain intensified, my body was drenched in sweat, and every breath felt like a battle.

On Super Bowl morning, I woke up and went to the TV room to finish the marathon before the start of the game later that evening. It only lasted ten minutes. "Sorry, guys, I am going back to bed. I feel horrible and can't sit here," I mumbled.

That was the last time I could get out of bed alone.

Later, my friend Rich knocked on the side of my bunk. "Yo, man, the game is starting. You're missing it," he said, concern in his voice.

"I can't, man. I can barely move," I replied, my voice weak, my body giving out. It's amazing what sickness can do to a person. The Super Bowl is a big deal every year and something I love watching. It is one of those times you would say, "I wouldn't miss this for the world." But at that moment, I couldn't have cared less about the game.

Rich kept coming back to check on me throughout the night. Each time, he brought whatever he thought might help, such as an 800 mg ibuprofen to dull the pain and a bowl of oatmeal to see if I could keep it down. But I could barely hold down water; the pain was becoming unbearable, only offering short, fleeting breaks. He knew something was seriously wrong.

Eventually, Rich did something he would otherwise never do and went to the unit officer. He told him about my condition, my inability to breathe, and how bad it had gotten.

The officer nodded, called medical, and then came to my bunk. "We called medical, but it's the Super Bowl. No one's there. You'll have to hang tight until morning."

Morning? I wasn't sure I'd make it that far. By 9 p.m., the count came around, and I needed help standing. That night was torture, every breath felt like a knife stabbing behind my heart. The pain had reached a solid ten. Thoughts I never wanted to admit to, thoughts about finding a way to end the agony for good, began creeping in. I was terrified.

The next morning, Rich came back to check on me. "This is bad, Adam," he said, his voice serious. He was a highly trained Marine and knew what he was looking at. You could see in his eyes that he understood how dangerous things had gotten. He ran down the stairs in search of an officer. But no one was there. It was as if the entire prison staff had vanished.

Rich started banging on the unit door as loudly as he could, giving it everything he had. It wasn't long before the Unit Manager opened the door, his face flushed with anger. "Why are you slamming on this door like this?" he demanded.

Rich didn't miss a beat. "My friend Adam is really sick. He can't breathe or get out of bed. He needs help, and he needs it now."

The urgency in his voice was not taken as urgent. Fifteen minutes later, the unit manager and a new lieutenant who had transferred from MDC Brooklyn arrived at my bunk. "You can't breathe, huh?" The LT said, his tone dripping with sarcasm. He wasted no time letting his doubt be known. "What drugs did you take?"

I couldn't believe he was asking me that. "Drugs? Are you kidding me? I don't do drugs. I've never taken anything, but look at my record. I don't even qualify for the year off through the drug program because I have never touched the stuff."

The LT didn't seem to care about anything I said. "So why can't you breathe?"

"How would I know? I'm not a doctor. I know I am sick, and something is seriously wrong," I responded.

He still wasn't convinced. They helped me up, my body barely responding, and started walking me down to medical. Every step was excruciating, like dragging myself through quicksand. But the lieutenant didn't have it. "You look like you're breathing well enough, but I notice you're walking funny."

"I'm walking funny because every breath feels like I am being stabbed," I hissed through clenched teeth. "It hurts."

The walk to the medical was short, but it felt like it lasted a lifetime. When we reached the stairs leading up to the medical, the LT stopped, his voice low. "This is your last chance. I see you holding your side. Tell me, who did you get in a fight with? If you don't tell me now, I can't help you later." My perfect institutional record meant nothing. I was no longer invisible, which meant I was a problem.

"You have got to be one of the dumbest fucking people I have met in my life," I was unable to control my anger.

"Right," he muttered, indifferent to my comment. "Don't say I didn't warn you."

Inside the medical room, the social worker came with a wheelchair. "What seems to be the problem?" she asked the LT as if I didn't exist.

"He says he's sick and can't breathe, but I think he is full of shit. He probably got into a fight or something. Get him an x-ray and call me after in the office and let me know what you find," he said.

"So, you got in a fight, huh? Did you win?" she asked.

"Don't listen to that guy, he's a fucking idiot. I'm sick," I replied, completely depleted.

They parked me in the wheelchair, and I sat there helpless, fading. The pain was debilitating, and I was scared. I begged anyone who would walk by with keys attached to their hip for help. "Please, something is seriously wrong with me. Please, help me."

But no one cared. I was an annoyance to them, another problematic inmate they didn't want to deal with. "You have to wait your turn," they snapped. I felt like some crazy person, a homeless man holding a sign warning that the end was near, ignored by everyone. Every minute that passed brought a new level of fear.

I watched in shock, disbelieving, as a trans inmate who'd been in prison for less than a year, with three disciplinary write-ups already, walked into medical unscheduled. "They" complained of a sore throat, and within minutes, were seen by the Physician Assistant.

An hour and a half later, I was still sitting there, ignored, begging for help. "What the fuck!" I shouted to the social worker who'd walked by again, indifferent to my fleeting state. "He-She, whatever, just walked in with a sore throat and got seen immediately! I've been here for hours, and no one's doing anything for me. Please, I need help!"

She shot me a look of contempt and kept walking. At that point, I wasn't sure if I would make it much longer. I had served almost a decade of my sentence up to this point and remained a model inmate every second of every day. I followed the rules, remained productive, focused on bettering myself, and was now treated like a cockroach running out from underneath the dishwasher. Until today, I had never spoken disrespectfully to anyone working within the prison, but I was running out of options to get the attention I needed.

It didn't matter to me if the other inmates saw themselves as men, women, or grapefruit; I didn't care. My issue was the fact that this was an inmate who continually went out of their way to find trouble, was known for it, and still they went out of their way to help immediately, cutting me, for no other reason than they had breasts installed on their body. It made no sense.

Finally, a woman came to take me for an X-ray. I couldn't stand, so she and the PA had to lift me into place to capture their images. After that, they wheeled me into a small exam room. A PA came in, took my temperature, and strapped a blood pressure monitor to my arm. "How are we feeling today?" she asked, her voice robotic.

"A little better than a dead man," I replied.

"Okay, put this under your tongue," she said, placing the thermometer in my mouth. "103, wow, that's high," she said, her tone still flat. "Let's check your blood pressure."

It was 78 over 36, and finally, I had her full attention. She looked surprised, as if the machine was broken or acting up. Before she could switch arms to confirm the reading, the social worker burst into the room. "We're getting him out of here. They just called 911, and an ambulance is on its way. We must get him to R&D," she said. Urgency finally in someone's voice other than my own.

By the time the paramedic arrived, I was barely conscious. In the ambulance, they put a mask over my face to deliver albuterol sulfate, but it didn't help. When I got to the ER, there was a conversation between the officers who traveled with me and the attending physician. They wanted to know when they could return me, but she was not catching what they were throwing.

Her voice was angry. "This man is incredibly sick, and I am surprised he is still alive. I don't know how you could allow a person to get like this before getting them to us, but he isn't going anywhere. I'm admitting him."

The pain was overwhelming.

She turned to me, her voice soft, "I'm sorry. I can't give you anything for the pain right now. If I do, it will kill you, do you understand?"

I was hooked up to bags of medicine, various machines, and oxygen at the highest level, but nothing seemed to help. My blood pressure wouldn't rise, and my fever wouldn't drop. I don't remember this happening, but at some point, my heart stopped, and I had to be resuscitated. I remember waking up to a group of people around me, one holding a tablet and telling me I needed to sign something that would permit them to bring me back if it happened again. I signed. Later, when I thought about it further, I thought it seemed a bit weird since they had already brought me back, but I let it go because I was grateful they did.

My blood was septic, my lungs black, and my pain unbearable. I was literally on my deathbed. All those hours, they'd treated me like an addict, a liar, someone unworthy of attention. All I had done was follow the rules and be a model inmate, and in my time of need, they put me on hold, leaving me to die. Is this how society is going to see me now?

An hour after the meds hit my bloodstream, I began to cough hard. Each spasm sent blood pouring from my lungs, soaking the vomit bags I clutched to my chest. I could see the LT standing outside my room, horrified, as if my bloody hacking required an exorcist to be on standby. He threw damp cloths through the doorway so I could wipe the blood off my face, keeping his distance as if the sight of me was too much to bear. Every cough felt like it was tearing me apart. The pain wasn't just physical; it clawed at my very will to live.

Eventually, they moved me to the ICU. The flood of machines and tubes around me made me feel like I'd been transformed into some sort of a cyborg. I was tethered to reality by beeping monitors, IV drips, and wires. A nurse would check my vitals every fifteen minutes, adjusting the machine accordingly. It was as if they were fighting to keep me alive in a battle my body had already lost interest in.

By the next day, my condition worsened. The pneumonia had spread to both lungs; I could feel my life slipping away like sand through my fingers. For the first time, I knew how fragile it all was. This wasn't just being sick, this was death creeping in, patient and steady. As the evening wore on, I struggled to keep my eyes open. My body trembled uncontrollably, not out of fear but as some desperate survival instinct trying to keep me conscious. I knew if I let go, I wouldn't come back.

"This is it," I thought. I was going to die here, chained to a hospital bed, faceless corrections officers sitting nearby, more concerned with their phones than the fact that my life was hanging on by a thread. My entire life had been reduced to someone's overtime pay. I thought of my daughters, mother, brother, and Sheva. All the people I loved flashed before me, and the cruel realization that I would never see them again hit me hard. I wasn't leaving anything behind except pain and grief. My death would be another burden, another wound to carry.

And then, the darkness started to talk to me.

"Look at your life," it whispered. "What do you have left? Nothing. You're stuck in hell already, suffering, and it is never going to end. Just let go. It would be so easy. Go be with your father."

I felt the pull, like a tide of despair washing over me. I thought about death, about whether it would finally give me wings to fly away from the agony I was in. But somewhere deep inside, a sliver of light remained. I thought of those I love again. Sheva would kill me if I died. There had to be a light switch camouflaged on this wall of darkness, and I couldn't let the dark win. It was a true miracle I survived the night.

The next evening wasn't much better, but I didn't feel the sand falling through my fingers any longer. My body was no longer shaking. I was still lost in the woods at night, but my sight was beginning to adjust and I could see more clearly. My pain was the same, and because of that, I hadn't slept since I'd been admitted. To underscore just how painful it was, as I sit here now writing this five years later, I can still feel the sharp pain coming from behind my heart when I take a deep breath.

Just after midnight, there was a shift change, and two new COs arrived. One was assigned to the gun and the other to the keys. The one who took the keys looked at me and grimaced, clearly regretting the overtime he had signed up for. He left the room, but not before looking at the seating arrangement and muttering, "This is ridiculous." A few minutes later, he returned with a different chair that was much larger, reclined, and on wheels that he had confiscated from somewhere else in the hospital. I guess he thought he owned the place. He set it up outside the room in the linen closet, blocking the doctors' and nurses' path to me when they entered the room, and he turned on the lights, blinding me.

"Excuse me, sir," I called out weakly. "Could you turn the lights off, please? It's past midnight, and I haven't slept in days."

"No way," he snapped. "I need to be able to see you, and I am not coming into that room. Whatever you got, I am not going to bring it home with me."

"What are you talking about?" I asked, incredulous. "I'm chained to the bed. The man next to me has a gun, and I can't move if I want to. The TV is on, so you can see me. Please, turn the light off."

"Not happening," he said.

I didn't have the strength to argue. It was going to be another long, sleepless night. My cough had gotten worse, violent and relentless. For days, I had been hooked up to multiple liquid antibiotics entering my system through IV, and the hospital staff was still coming in every fifteen minutes to check on the machines. The CO blocking the door made it difficult for them every time they did. He was argumentative and rude, often refusing to move. He was way out of line. He was supposed to sit in the room, not outside blocking their access. Tensions were rising. They needed to be able to monitor me closely, but this guy had decided he was the gatekeeper for my care.

Around 2 a.m., the coughing became unbearable. My body rebelled, and in a humiliating moment, I lost control. The antibiotics they'd been pumping into me overwhelmed my system, and I soiled myself and the bed. Shame flooded me, but there was nothing I could do.

When the nurse returned to check on me, she noticed the smell immediately. I had no choice but to admit what happened. She didn't flinch. She'd seen this kind of thing before and was a professional. Still, I was humiliated.

"Sir," she addressed the contentious CO holding the keys, "we need to unshackle him so we can get him into the shower and change his bedding."

"No," he said flatly. "My job is to watch the prisoner and not accommodate your needs. This is not life-threatening, so he can wait until 7 a.m. when the shift is up. I am not coming in there. Whatever he has, I don't want to risk bringing it home to my family."

"You can't be serious," I said, my voice harsh with frustration. "Why are you even here then? You're not mandated to be. If you're so afraid of me, give the other officer the keys, and you take the gun."

The other CO sat silently, glued to his phone. Clearly, he wasn't about to challenge his partner and decided to stay out of it.

"Because I was assigned the keys, not the gun, and no one is talking to you, so shut it," he said to me, turning his attention back to the nurse. "Bottom line, I am not coming in there, so do what you can without me doing so."

"Sir, this is highly irregular and against hospital policy. I am going to have to notify my superiors," she said. "What you're doing is wrong."

"Do I look like I give a shit what you have to do? I don't work for you people, nor do you have authority over me, my job, or my mandate."

My nurse looked at me, her lips pressed, her face saddened. "I'm so sorry this is what you have to deal with. I'll be back soon." She left.

I thought prison had taught me what it meant to be powerless, but my understanding took on a whole new meaning at this moment. This corrections officer was part of the ten percent who had a vendetta and no other options for employment. He was a former Connecticut Police Officer who got into trouble, lost his job, and was now working for the BOP, where he spent his days treating inmates like trash. Because of this man, I was forced to remain covered in feces for the rest of the night until the following day when a shift change arrived. To his credit, the CO that took over unshackled me immediately so I could be helped into the shower while the nurse changed my bedding.

Twenty minutes after the shift change, a furious head of security stormed into my room. "What the hell is going on with you guys in this room?" he demanded. "The written reports filed by hospital staff are appalling. Corrections officers are harassing my staff and preventing them from providing adequate care to the patient. Do I have to get the actual police up here?"

The COs who had just arrived looked confused. "We just got here," one of them said. "We know nothing about what you're talking about."

"Well, I am telling you now," the security officer continued, "if I hear anything like what is being said again, I will have no choice but to call the police. Am I being clear here?" he asked.

"Yes, not a problem. Again, we weren't here at the time in question, and this is all new to us," they replied.

I was now clean and being helped back into the bed. The security officer turned his attention toward me. "Have you been being treated properly?" he asked bluntly.

All eyes were on me, and the room was silent. I wouldn't be in this hospital forever and knew the cardinal rule: "You can't beat the guys with keys." Retaliation would be a given if I got out of line, and besides, COs were protected with qualified immunity, so what could I really do?

"Everything is fine, sir," I said. "Your hospital staff is great."

"You sure?" he asked.

"Yes, sir." I had no other option but to lie.

After everyone left the room, the COs questioned me. "What the fuck went on here last night?"

I gave them one word: "Nothing." But this experience changed something in me. I saw everything differently from this moment on.

# *Chapter Thirty*
# From Sheva's View

This book is not my story. But it is part of the story of change that needs to happen on a national level.

At a young age, my love for books led to reading about the Holocaust. Mainly memoirs, these personal accounts seeped into my being. I reflected strongly on the journey of unbearable pain, suffering, and loss despite the triumph of the author's individual survival.

Throughout my reading, questions reverberated strongly in my young mind, especially: "How did loved ones remain in existence while those they loved were tortured?" How could families go about their daily lives knowing the devastation that their own people were experiencing?

It was unfathomable to me, utterly incomprehensible. And then, as life has its way about it, I experienced a form of this myself. I had to exist and choose to live while the man I love navigated hell, and I could do absolutely nothing about it.

We all have defining moments in life; Adam features in a significant number of mine.

It was February 3, 2020, when the name ADAM flashed across the screen of my phone, and like always, I eagerly answered it. But what came across the other line was nothing like I had ever heard before, and my heart froze in terror. Adam was wheezing—he could barely speak, and with great effort, he finally said, "Sheva, I can't breathe." This was a moment of sheer panic, a stark realization of the physical strain of the hell that is prison. He had hidden that part well, and despite knowing that he did, the gap between knowing things are hidden and witnessing them is illimitable. Adam had emailed me the night before saying he wasn't feeling well, but nothing prepared me for the voice that came through the phone line that day.

Instinct took over, and I firmly told him to go to medical and make a fuss. This was no joke. He did not have the strength to stand and talk to me for over half a minute and had to hang up. I begged him to take care. I begged him to get help. I hung up, panic-stricken.

Up until this day, I had kept my connection with Adam private, shared only with a few in my inner circle. But in that moment, everything changed. I called every organization I could. I called every family member that could possibly assist. No one could help. I called the prison ad nauseam. I knew in my gut this was dire. I knew about all the medical interventions he performed on himself over the years; excruciating procedures, like ripping a diseased toenail off or healing his tooth with self-inflicted oral surgery—but this was not the same. He needed essential medical care now, and despite me knowing how flawed the prison system was, it was beyond my mind's grasp that Adam might die due to lack of care. I could not accept that reality, and I refused to allow it. I was determined to fight and ensure he received the care he needed.

The week that followed was dark, there was no news to any of his family—including his mom—that he was admitted to the hospital, and I turned lethal. I don't remember much of what I said or who I said it to, but my voice and message in my relentless calls to the prison were persistent and unyielding. I finally scared someone enough. They gave Adam a phone in the hospital bed he was chained to and allowed me to speak to him. He mustered something painful, but I was able to talk to him. I told him to survive. I told him he was loved. I reminded him that he was the strongest man I ever met, and he was not allowed to die. It was a brief minute or two but a lifeline. He was in the hospital. He was alive. He knew we cared.

The following Monday was a visiting day at the prison. I went. I wanted to know if Adam was still at the hospital, and I could not get that information from anyone. I was shaken by fear that the road had reached an end, that two physical beings' journey together on this earth was over. As I made the almost two-hour drive, I listened to one song on repeat. A song in Hebrew about being surrounded by the guardian angels Gabriel, Michael,

Uriel, Rafael, and mostly God: I imagined angels surrounding Adam and surrounding me and getting us through this, to be whole again.

Adam was in the prison; they confirmed when I entered, but he was not available for a visit. My heart sank, the time in hospital had been too brief. What sort of medical attention would he get here? I demanded to know why he couldn't come to visit. They refused to tell me and would not confirm or deny anything more than that. In all the years of visits, I had never questioned anything, regardless of the issue or who was in the right, quite against my nature, but essential to ensure zero retaliation against Adam. Now, I quietly but forcefully demanded to speak to a supervisor. They looked at me like I was raving mad but could hardly refuse this request; I was directed to the waiting room.

It was a visiting day, so the room was packed with people. I sat waiting, my heart thumping apprehensively. I wanted him to be okay so badly, the line between life and death is exceedingly thin. Shortly after, I heard a voice bellow with outrage: "Who demanded to speak with ME?" A very tall, very broad, and large woman stormed into the room, fury radiating out of her pores. "ME," I replied emphatically as I slowly raised myself out of the chair. I stood super straight, defiant, silently daring her to challenge me and simultaneously aiming to appeal to her humanity, quite a rare feat within these walls, where my race worked against me. She stared me down. I looked straight back, unwilling to bend. I explained that Adam was hospitalized, that something was severely wrong with him. I did not know anything, and I was there to see him and ensure he had adequate medical care. I had been told that I could not visit, and as it was visiting day, I deserved to know why. I spoke confidently, but inside I was praying for God's kindness to reveal itself. This sort of thing didn't usually end well. She was staring at me but listening, a small win in itself. When I stopped speaking, I saw her demeanor melt ever so slightly.

She, shockingly and thankfully, responded to me like a human and explained that Adam had an issue with his lungs and was very weak. He couldn't make it to visit because he was getting oxygen treatments at the prison.

I later learned that he died at the hospital. Twice. He was revived. Twice. He was also forced to leave the hospital too soon. There was an actual treatment that day I came to visit, probably promoted by the visit, but the treatments ended prematurely a few days later. Till today, Adam has pain when he breathes. The wall he slept next to for years was covered in black mold. The absolute horror and neglect of the prison system is endless. It is unconscionable.

* * *

For many years, every week that I was able to, I visited Adam. The prisons shifted, each with its own specific experience, with some overlapping similarities. Having visited these institutions for over a decade now, I am qualified to objectively state that how the inmates are treated is abominable, but perhaps warranted in many cases. It is prison, after all, and many who are there belong there for a reason. However, visitors are not prisoners. Why are they treated poorly?

While waiting to enter the antechamber to one visiting room, there was a slideshow of imposing photos of those "in charge." These stern professional photos feature the Director of the Federal Bureau of Prison, the acting warden, and the employee of the month. Every week, the same thought crossed my mind: "Who on earth would be proud to own that they run this mess?" This is the stark reality that this is what the FBOP currently is.

Studies have repeatedly shown that maintaining strong connections with loved ones significantly reduces the likelihood of reoffending post-release. Isn't that the whole point of prison? To hinder crime and rehabilitate? Yet, instead of promoting policies that encourage visitation as a tool for rehabilitation, the system appears to do everything in its power to make the process as difficult and degrading as possible.

There are many changes that need to be instituted in the FBOP, mainly the separation of inmates. Violent and nonviolent offenders should never be housed together. That would uncomplicate so many of the underlying tensions and problems for inmates and their families. Regardless of your opinion of prison and the treatment of inmates respective to the crime, their families are not liable. They are not criminals. They are usually forced into this situation, one they did nothing to create.

Over the years, I have met many bearing the burden. The mother who must fly in from Alaska to see her autistic son, the mom with twin infants strapped to her belly and the toddler held in hand, and the fiancée who just had her wedding canceled. The men they visit may very well belong in prison; I do not know their story. But the people I spoke to carry the struggle of having to pick up the pieces of their lives alone. They prepare to visit with a financial, emotional, and energetic burden. In turn, almost every single visitor experiences a range of panic and anxiety from the moment they walk into the facility until they drive off the property. Visiting a loved one in prison should offer a glimmer of hope—a humanizing connection in an otherwise bleak environment. Instead, it has become an exercise in frustration, indignity, and bureaucratic chaos, exposing the gross incompetence of a system that prioritizes ego, control, and inefficiency over humanity and basic competency.

Approval for a visit is a messy, lengthy process. Families may wait for months to get approved to see their loved one. The needless red tape exacerbates painful isolation and creates a harsh separation between inmates and their families.

When visitation is granted, the experience is marred by indignity and an air of suspicion.

Security measures, though necessary to maintain safety, are excessive and poorly executed. Visitors are subjected to invasive searches, demeaning questioning, and arbitrary rules. The dress code violations change depending on who is on duty and their mood. I have experienced and witnessed so many of these instances, such as wearing the same pants for eight years and being told one day that they are unacceptable. Women with bras that set off the metal detector are sent away. Jeans that elicit a "beep" will result in the wearer being sent away. I have seen children denied entry. Anything that is decided by the intake officer that day as being unacceptable clothing is rejected. If you argue, say, because your sweater is not a hoodie because there is no hood, but it doesn't make the cut because the officer says it is, you are at risk of never being allowed to visit again. It's a panic-inducing, horrible experience. Visitors are shouted at, spoken down to, and often leered at. In the many years I have visited, the officers on rotation would shift, and an incompetent and harsh group of officers would create months on end with a rare day that someone was not targeted and turned away—mostly as a result of ego and power trips.

In one facility, visits used to be offered from Thursday to Monday. The facility decided to delete the Monday option. If you read their handbook, the option to visit on Monday is still available. Yet, it is not. This forces families with the option to visit only on Monday to come on the other days. There is never enough room, so people are asked to leave early, decreasing the worth of the investment to visit. I was once privy to watching a family member who flew in from India be asked to leave early because there was no room. In addition, visits can be canceled at the last minute, usually under the guise of "fog," despite not a cloud in sight, with zero regard for the time and resources visitors have invested in travel and preparation.

And there is the utterly disrespectful wait. Arrival is 8:30, and you can be made to sit until 10:00 or later to enter. There is no way to make up the time with your loved one, and there is usually no reason for this apart from gross incompetence (the officers are chatting) and an utter lack of regard for those visiting. There are some well-meaning officers who are efficient, but it's a mixed bag, and you never know what you are going to walk into.

The visits are set up to be as impersonal as possible and the threat of a visit being revoked hangs heavily in the air. This is a reckless attitude, as visits are not privileges to be taken away—they are a right. They are essential times of connection for families and inmates to facilitate the relationships necessary for rehabilitation and a healthy future. Despite being treated as if they are an extension of the problem, families and friends are actually part of the solution. The harshness of the experience pushes visitors away, which alienates inmates from their support networks. By doing so, we are perpetuating higher rates of recidivism, and the cycle of crime and punishment keeps churning.

Subjecting one's family to this horrid extension of prison needs to shift into a more positive experience and an absolute overhaul of the way we, as a country, penalize crime is in order. Reducing gross negligence of taxpayer resources, fortifying national safety and upholding justice are American values that will contribute to the collective strength of our nation as a whole.

# *Chapter Thirty-One*
# Ideology

Clarity—about ourselves, the world, and where we fit in often emerges after a long, painful journey. I've gained that perspective, truly seeing things now. But I feel alone, as though everyone else is blind to these truths. Why was a model inmate with nearly a decade of clean conduct treated like trash and left to die in a hallway? In contrast, problematic inmates received premium care simply because they were men identifying as women. It was clear to me that the priorities of my government were totally out of whack.

Why did the prison pharmacy neglect my antibiotic prescription upon my return? Three weeks of "lack of oversight" allowed my infection to come back. No one cared. No apology was given. Yet, no effort or expense was spared during this same time period to provide gender-affirming care and medication. Inmates enrolled in the MAP program never missed their daily dose of Suboxone. I mean, God forbid they weren't high out of their minds for a day. For reasons I choose to not accept, the system went out of its way to help inmates change their sex or keep them high all day, but when it comes to providing antibiotics prescribed by my doctor at the hospital, who just spent ten days treating me in the ICU, helping me to battle an infection that almost took my life, it is easily overlooked. This is a problem and not one that is limited to the inside of prisons.

Whether or not you challenge essentialist views of womanhood or argue that gender is a social construct, there is a virus spreading in our society, a kind of ideological cancer eroding logic with emotional manipulation, undermining the very foundation of society. The implications of this erosion are dire, and we must recognize and address it.

The history of the feminist movement in the US is remarkable, with pivotal victories for women, including the right to vote, access to education, suffrage, and property ownership. These achievements were essential, not just for women, but for the strength of society; women deserve equality as much as the enslaved deserved freedom. However, the powerful always control the strings, often twisting even the best intentions, and the unintended consequences will always exist at every stage. We, the people, are supposed to be the balance of power. This is our country, not a rental we occupy temporarily. We must remind our leaders that they serve us, not their interests. And to do that, we need to see clearly, not be swayed by raw emotion.

The 19th Amendment, passed in 1920, was a giant leap forward, empowering women with the right to vote. Yet, this victory shifted how the ruling class viewed women as a voting bloc, a tool to be mobilized and influenced. Women, once merely objects of the male gaze, were now viewed as pawns in a political game.

Then came men like Saul Alinsky, author of *Rules for Radicals*, a brilliant communist organizer in the 1930s who watched as women fought and won their rights. He saw the feminist movement as a way for the ruling class to seize more control. By organizing marginalized groups, helping them realize their collective power, and using that strength to push power toward specific causes, the ruling class could consolidate influence while appearing to champion the people.

Alinsky's model emphasized achievable goals and incremental progress over utopian ideals, using agitation and confrontation to spotlight issues. His manipulation strategy became deeply embedded in American politics by pressuring those in power. Just look to the unrest in burning cities demanding for the police to be defunded, or Ivy League campuses being overrun with pro-Palestinian protestors demanding a cease-fire and calling for the destruction of Israel in the same breath. The legacy of his work can be seen in young Americans rallying for causes they don't understand, guided by emotion instead of logic or intellect. It's the same infection that directs prison officials to cater to a trans inmate over one who is dying, and none of it is by mistake. It had been implanted; a corrosive pathogen released upon the people by those we elected. A powerful tool used to keep us divided.

Former President Obama embraced Alinsky's methods and supported his work. He applied Alinsky's principles in the late eighties when he was a community organizer in Chicago. Hillary Clinton was also an Alinsky admirer, following the principles of his communist thinking, and met with him many times in her life. While attending Wellesley College, her thesis was titled "There is Only One Fight: An Analysis of the Alinsky Model." Both these Democrat Party Politicians know how to wield the power dynamic, often using radical methods to achieve their ends. Ironically, they label those with differing views as radicals, but who truly fits that description? When you see cities burning, campuses being seized, and officials refusing to maintain order, look closely to see which political party is endorsing the behavior. You will see who the true radicals are.

This ideology doesn't stop with politics. It reaches into the relationship between men and women, skewing it with mistrust. Look at today's feminist movement and where it has led. Are women happier and more respected? Because what I see is women cutting off all their hair and going on sex and relationship strikes because their candidate lost. Sixty years ago, when a woman walked into a room, a man would stand, remove his hat, pull out her chair, and insist on paying. He would offer his arm and escort her if she desired to go somewhere, opening all doors. Why was this wrong, and what did women gain from suppressing this gesture?

I was raised to believe that women are to be cherished. If I were ever in the situation I saw on the news where I arrived at the same time at an electric bike station as a pregnant nurse and there was only one bike remaining, not only would I offer her the last bike, but I'd be happy to pay for it. But the woman I saw on TV faced indifference and mockery, and the bike was forcefully taken from her. What is happening worldwide, and how is it better for women?

What is this movement teaching my daughters? Strip away the language of empowerment and blow away the smoke, and the message becomes clear: You're not good enough as you are. Only if you become "independent" from men, find a better job, and delay motherhood do you stand a chance at being so.

The Obamas and Clintons of the world have hijacked the women's movement, weaponizing it for control. They perpetuate a narrative that encourages women to view men as oppressors, to distrust and even resent them. This continual friction damages relationships and attacks the core of our society, marriage, and the nuclear family. Dividing families into isolated, oppressed individuals gives those in power greater control over the population.

There was a time when men understood the immense value of women more than they valued their own lives. When the *Titanic* sank, "women and children first" was a rule accepted and understood. Men could have forced their way onto the lifeboats, but they didn't. Why? Because they knew women were the future, the heart of our humanity. Women are closer to God than men. There doesn't need to be a fight for equality because we were never meant to be equal. More is required of men because, in many areas, we are lacking and further disconnected from God; thus, we need to compensate for where we are lacking.

Society has already come across that sweet spot. There will always be room for improvement, but this delicate equilibrium between men and women has been deliberately disturbed by those in power. Ladies, when was the last time a man stood when you entered the room or removed their hat for you out of a sign of respect? When did he last offer you his arm to escort you somewhere? Men's gestures of honor weren't born out of viewing women as weak but by recognizing that women were more valuable than themselves.

The relentless pursuit of equality is eroding the hard-won rights of women that it claims to protect and has strained the relationship between men and women. An atmosphere of distrust has replaced the space of cooperation and mutual understanding that once reigned supreme, attacking the very core of our nation. We can only regain control if we recognize this divide-and-conquer strategy and refuse to be manipulated. Our strength lies in cooperation and mutual respect, not in endless divisiveness and conflict. Life on the inside allowed me to see this more clearly than most. If there is one thing that prison officials never want the inmate population to have it is cooperation and mutual respect for one another, because that would allow them to obtain more power over their existence. Power that they currently wield and the world outside of those walls is no different. The question we need to ask ourselves is, how do we change the status quo?

# *Chapter Thirty-Two*
# United or Separated?

The strength of any nation, owned by its people, is deeply rooted in its foundation: the nuclear family. This historical success story, where men and women stood as partners, is a tried-and-true road bound for personal advancement. Those who seek to shift power from the people to the government understand this well and know that to gain control they must undermine the family structure, creating new categories of the marginalized and further dividing society. Today, instead of men and women supporting one another, they are pushed to distrust. The rise of single mothers, the labeling of fathers with "toxic masculinity," and children facing a barrage of negative self-images via social media, all while parents grow more divided and less connected, is by design, not chance.

Thirty years ago, no parent in America would have believed their children's school might transition them to another gender without their knowledge or consent. But this madness has invaded our lives and stems from an overreach that grew out of the feminist movement, which, unfortunately, is now harming women more than it is helping them. This realization should evoke a sense of concern and empathy in all of us.

The United States rose to power on the unity of family, with men and women standing side by side as partners. This unity was, and remains, the foundation of America. But as division and mistrust rise, the country falters and slowly loses its way, its identity. My home state of Massachusetts was once the beacon of family values, where communities thrived on family strength and unity. Historical records indicate that from 1692 until 1786, only thirty-eight divorces were recorded, each due to adultery or desertion.

Compare that to today, where 60 percent of American marriages end in divorce, a result partly fueled by policies and ideologies encouraging separation, with radical feminists contributing to this outcome, going too far with the notion of sexual liberation and pushing unrealistic notions of "freedom." There is a reason we are now seen as a nation in decline.

The publication of *The Feminine Mystique* by Betty Friedan in 1963 came toward the end of a successful era in the fight for women's equality, such as the passing of the Equal Rights Act of 1963 and Title VII of the Civil Rights Act of 1964, which opened endless professional opportunities for women. Friedan adopted the same ideology as Alinsky, Obama, and Clinton. Friedan argues that women were oppressed, confined to the home, and stifled intellectually. Yet, women like Estee Lauder, Mary Kay Ash, Katherine Graham, Brownie Wise, Lillian Vernon, and Beatrice Fox Auerbach did not see themselves this way. These women were business juggernauts of that same era, rising above their male counterparts and paving the way for future young women to succeed in business.

These women did not conform to the Feminine Mystique "think." They credited their achievements to the love and support of their families and husbands, and all emphasized their mothers who stayed home and raised them. It can be argued that without their mothers, they might never have been able to achieve what they did. No job on earth is more important than that of a mother, and everyone today seems to be missing the point. The most significant "hard-fought win" for women was the ability to choose the life they wanted for themselves. Whether that choice was to be a full-time mother and wife or to become a CEO, that was the freedom of choice women wanted. Yet, the movement moved away from equal opportunity to bastardizing motherhood. Now they want to strip mothers of this very title and label them a birthing parent. This is insane, but they aren't stopping there.

Issues are focused on with intentional blinders and then amplified. For instance, the "wage gap" rhetoric intentionally paints an incomplete picture. Men and women often choose different career paths, with women tending more toward nurturing roles such as teachers or social work, which often pay less because nurturing is in their nature. Many women also prioritize family, willingly reducing hours or taking time off. When these nuances are ignored, women are made to feel more oppressed and not empowered, but when this data is applied, the wage gap narrows significantly.

Ironically, if a man stays home to support his wife's career, he is seen as a hero. But a woman doing the same is told she is stifling her potential. Why did Mom stop being a hero in this country? This double standard has led to an epidemic of burnout and misery as women are pressured to meet impossible expectations: to excel in a high-powered career, be a perfect mother and wife, and achieve personal fulfillment all without compromise or trade-off. The truth is that life cannot be lived without trade-offs, and true equality means having the freedom to make different choices for your life without judgment. An unrealistic standard is being pushed on women, causing them to feel inadequate and bitter instead of loved and supported, and those negative emotions are being targeted toward men under the presumption that they derive from "toxic masculinity."

The emphasis on sexual autonomy has only added fuel to the fire. Women today are told to express sexuality as empowerment, but this only leads to objectification, reversing hard-won gains. The popularity of pornography, OnlyFans, and similar industries promoted as "empowering" choices signals a troubling shift. When girls as young as fifteen express a willingness and desire to post a sex tape if it meant they could be "like Kim Kardashian," it's clear something is wrong. True empowerment for women will never include commodifying oneself; it comes from living authentically. I want my daughters to be empowered, not reduced to a commodity.

Women aren't being empowered; they are under attack. Once women are labeled as marginalized and oppressed, they can be grouped with others in similar categories, fostering division and making all groups easier to control. It's a tactic that's been used to subjugate others for centuries. When you become an inmate you gain a unique understanding of what it means to be marginalized and oppressed because you are the very definition of it. In the beginning it hurts, but that same hurt ended up driving me to want to change what I see as wrong in the world and I have never seen things more clearly.

I support the rights of trans people to live freely without discrimination as I am an American, and that is the value Americans hold dear. But the inclusion of biological men in women's spaces such as sports, restrooms, and shelters does not advance a woman's rights; it erodes them. This, too, is a tactic to stoke division, presenting a false front of "progress" while undermining hard-won rights. Rights are stripped away by politicians who later claim to "fight" to restore them, fooling the public repeatedly.

Look at what they accomplished with Megan Rapinoe, a champion of the LGBTQ+ community, USA soccer star, gold medalist, and a fierce advocate for her beliefs, supporting the policies of a political party that showcased her as a figurehead. Yet, the same party supports policies that want to replace her, filling her place on the field with biological men identifying as female, those with whom she cannot compete. They manipulated her to fight for her own extinction. I don't resent Rapinoe for her beliefs; I respect her right to fight for what she thinks is best for the country, but this is a perfect example of the insanity occurring and an example that illustrates how division is sown even among those advocating for unity.

Women are powerful, but some are being misled into self-doubt, objectification, and confusion. This movement isn't about empowerment at all; it's about control. The only way we can move forward is to reject the manufactured divides and embrace genuine, respectful choices—ones that honor both men and women, their nature, authentic roles, and opportunities. This will strengthen rather than weaken the foundation of our society. I have spent years existing in the Penumbra, looking out, watching society slowly lose itself, too wrapped up in all the noise. This is not how we are supposed to be living our lives, and it is not freedom.

# *Chapter Thirty-Three*
# Knowledge Is Power

You now understand how emotional decision-making can be and how often it is weaponized against you. Currently, the weapon of choice is abortion and women's rights, as it is the strongest emotional background for political debate. This issue has been used to divide Americans more than race or gender and creates a complex web of influence. The only way to avoid being trapped in the web is to look at it purely logically.

Consider the African American community's support of the Democratic Party over the past seventy years. It's puzzling to see such loyalty given to the same party that historically supported slavery and Jim Crow laws. The KKK was a wing of the Democratic Party, composed of Democratic members.

How were they then able to secure the trust of that same community?

While history may fade from view, it isn't erased. It isn't by mistake that Martin Luther King Jr. was a lifelong, loyal Republican, and simultaneously, that most in the African American community are unaware of this fact. How easily the world forgets that Abraham Lincoln, the President who ended slavery in America and was murdered for it, was also a Republican. Understanding this historical context is crucial in making informed political decisions, yet the majority of Black Americans still support a party with a troubling history while referring to the party of Lincoln and MLK Jr. as Nazis.

Would the community's loyalty remain if information was shared freely? During the last four years of his term, President Obama, a Democrat and Alinsky follower, enacted policies that had wages drop significantly for Black Americans while wages for the white middle class rose. You don't have to take my word for it. The facts and data aren't hidden. But you need to look; as mentioned, they don't want you to focus on certain facts. Politicians like Obama, Biden, and Clinton operate beyond the framework of oppression and privilege imposed on the public. Their allegiance isn't to any specific community but to maintaining power and influence. Everything else they do is pandering. Examining the facts, Obama's policies didn't close the racial gap as much as they reinforced the economic divide. The proof is in the pudding, as they say. Obama was a wolf in sheep's clothing, loyal to power and crafting policy that helped his party maintain that power.

Look at Joe Biden, the author of the 1994 crime bill that President Clinton signed into law. This bill disproportionately incarcerated Black and Hispanic men, devastating families and communities. Yet, these same communities overwhelmingly elected him as president years later, helping him complete his overall plan for control. Control over the population is obtained by weakening the nuclear family, lowering wages while elevating costs, increasing citizens' dependence upon government assistance, pitting men and women against each other, and enabling high abortion rates.

Speaking of abortion, if we set aside emotion, the raw data reveals a troubling truth. The wayward feminist movement has been fighting for the rights of women to have an abortion by claiming they are giving them more access to health care. The Democratic party has inserted itself into this fight and uses it for political currency, manipulating the population. Still, we must all look behind the castle gates because it's clear there is always a greater agenda at work, and caring about the people is not it. Remember, we are put on hold. Critical thinking is not just important; it's essential when advocating for social issues and political actions because you need to know what you are fighting for. It's our responsibility to critically evaluate the information presented to us and make informed decisions.

Do you believe it is a coincidence that there is a Planned Parenthood close to every African American community in this country? Today, over 60 percent of US abortions are performed on Black and Hispanic women, with Black women accounting for 40 percent of them. This is wildly disproportionate to their population size. Coincidence? I'll leave the conclusion to you, but again, if you are going to fight for something, you need to look at what it is you are fighting for.

Abortion divides Americans across all demographics, much like economic policies. Some believe life begins at conception; others believe in unrestricted choice. Most Americans fall somewhere in between, as I do, supporting limited abortion rights with exceptions for health, rape, or incest. But all these views are emotionally charged equally.

The repeal of Roe v. Wade has become a politically charged issue saturated in false statements meant to deceive the public of its true meaning while angering women. The repeal shifted the rights from the federal level to that of the voters in each state—democracy at its very best and as intended. Yet, political messaging has made it seem otherwise, igniting public outcry. The federal government should not be deciding for the people; the people should be deciding for themselves, and now those who believe life begins at conception have the right to vote on laws that reflect their view, just as those who believe in unrestricted abortion rights have the right to fight for and vote on theirs. This democratic process empowers us to be part of the decision-making process and respect the rights of our fellow citizens to hold differing beliefs.

Besides, a government mandating questionable vaccines has quite the audacity to push "My Body, My Choice." However, as we know, you cannot trust leaders when their messages are rife with contradictions.

To restore harmony, we must respect each other's rights and find common ground even in disagreement. This is how we take back control of our country, by respecting each other's rights and living the values we believe in. When you are given a voice and the ability to articulate what you believe, what is best for you and your country, that is what it means to live in a free country. Without that, you are nothing more than the incarcerated.

# *Chapter Thirty-Four*
# My Body, My Choice

When we first met, my children's mother and I were young. Though we initially shared moments as a romantic couple, we were fire and water, clashing at every turn. We parted ways long past the expiration date of our relationship but remain connected because of our beautiful, shared children.

When I was still in my early twenties, the endless cycle of casual encounters, the chase, the detachment, and the dating experience all felt hollow. I longed for stability, a home filled with laughter, and holidays with family. I met a single mother and got married, but what initially felt like love and possibility begat the clarity that what bound us was convenience, not connection or genuine love.

In retrospect, it is easy to see why two twenty-somethings like us would flounder. She was more attracted to the life I could provide for her and her daughter than me. Our marriage was a calculated step for her as much as it was for me, more anchored in ambition than affection. I was a rising star when we met, scaling corporate heights, turning heads, and commanding rooms. Looking at me, she saw a sturdy rafter to cling to, a means to navigate her storms in life. It was a truth she managed to keep shrouded for some time, but time, as we all know, is not kind to masks. Eventually, everything comes to the surface. Still, I don't fault her. I was complicit, checking a life goal off my list without conviction. Carpe diem, I often thought.

The truth is, I was young and had views on marriage that lacked depth, maturity, and wisdom, but I held steadfast to my role as a father and stepfather; it was and will always be the pride I have in life. But as husband and wife, we lacked the soil for nurturing roots, and the fragile peace we managed to live with easily collapsed under the pressure of the relentless pursuit of the FBI.

It came to light that my wife had not been loyal or honest in the relationship, making me certain that she didn't love me, but it was also clear she didn't despise me either. I was a good husband and good to her daughter. When the FBI could not convince her to fabricate lies about me to suit their narrative, they went after her too, and still, she wouldn't cave and lie about me for them.

Our marriage was riddled with fissures, and the blame was distributed evenly between us. I should have noticed the layers of deception and paid closer attention, but apathy is blinding.

When the marriage ended, I found myself questioning when my indifference had begun, when I had stayed not out of love but out of a sense of duty to honor my commitment to her. I had reduced the marriage to a business transaction of calculated loyalty. When I tried to pinpoint which moment in our lives shifted the relationship, only one memory surfaced.

After being together for about a year, she approached me one afternoon with an air of detachment. "I need you to sign a check for the doctor. I have an appointment today and don't know how much it will cost."

I handed her a signed check without hesitation. "Is everything okay?"

"Yeah, everything's good. I also need you to drive me as they said it would be unsafe for me to drive home afterward."

An uneasy silence settled between us, buzzing with tension. My instincts were telling me that something was off.

"Alright, let me call into work and let them know I won't be in today," I replied.

The silence grew heavier in the car as she entered the destination into the GPS. Finally, I couldn't stand the silence anymore. It felt like I was allowing a green fly to bite my leg without swatting it away. "This doesn't feel right. What's going on?"

"It's not a big deal," she said, her voice unnervingly calm. "I'm pregnant."

Her words fell like a grenade. "You're what?" I said, the disbelief slicing through me like a knife. I was shocked. Not because I didn't want more children, but because, at the beginning of our relationship, she had shared with me that she wasn't capable of pregnancy, complications stemming from her daughter's birth, and subsequent endometriosis sealing her fate.

"I don't understand. Pregnant? How, when you told me that was impossible for us?"

"I don't know, but it doesn't matter. I am having an abortion. That is where you are taking me."

"Like hell I am," I responded, my mind reeling. "What the fuck?"

"Adam, I didn't lie to you or anything. I am not supposed to be able to get pregnant, and it may become complicated. As I told you, I have already been to the doctor and decided what I will do," she said.

The air stilled, the world narrowing to the thumping in my chest. "Wait, what? Why am I only hearing about all this now? Why have I yet to be included? Shouldn't we get different opinions, see specialists, and explore all options before making a final decision?" I asked.

"No, we shouldn't. This is not something up for discussion. This is my choice, not yours. Your job is to support me."

My hands tightened around the wheel. "Support you? How do you expect me to do that when you make me a bystander? You didn't even think it was necessary to mention this to me? It's bizarre and illogical. Everything feels wrong about how you have gone about this. What? Is this not my baby?" I regretted the words as soon as they left my mouth, but a wound had been exposed that I couldn't ignore. It was the only thing that made sense as to why she would choose to go about everything this way.

"You're an asshole," she muttered.

The drive continued in strained silence, my mind racing between anger, confusion, and a dawning realization. "Okay, I am turning around. We're going home, and we're going to talk about this first," I said, trying to steady myself a bit.

"Do that, and I'll have a friend waiting in the driveway to take me before you make it back. Your choice."

I relented to the robotic voice of the GPS, tension suffocating the car.

"Why didn't you say anything to me before now?" I asked.

"I am saying something now. Look, I could have done this without you, but I didn't," she said.

"Is there nothing I can do to change your mind so we can at least discuss this first?"

"No, I made my decision."

I had already gone through the complex process of accepting that I would not have any more children before we married. Having two beautiful daughters from a previous relationship and now a stepdaughter made that easier for me to swallow, but it was a decision I had to make and not one that I took lightly. This news shook my world.

When we arrived at the clinic, she told me to wait in the car, but I followed her inside, unwilling to abandon her entirely at that moment. When she emerged from the procedural room, she looked diminished, eyes hollow but defiant. The ride back was thick with everything unsaid and remained heavier than any prison transport I have dealt with since.

At home, I offered to take care of dinner.

"I can cook; we can order out or go out. Up to you," I said.

"Let's just order something," she replied. She disappeared to the shower, leaving me with my thoughts and the job of burying the events of the day six feet under, where they were to remain, despite haunting me. I clung to the idea that maybe she was right and that was the best decision for us, but I couldn't silence my wondering, the alternate endings playing in my mind. I didn't need veto power, only the right to stand on even ground.

Weeks later, a bank statement arrived with a copy of the deposited check—$500. I kept it, tucking it away in my nightstand, where it lingered—a wisp of something profound and unresolved. It didn't seem like a normal item a person would save, but for some reason, I did.

I don't claim to have untangled the fierce knots of the abortion debate, and in fact, I may be adding a knot of my own. I know the spectrum is vast and nuanced, but what became clear from my experience is the absence of one vital piece: the right for the dad to be seen as part of the story.

When it comes to the issue of abortion, society has come to accept the position that men have little to no say. This is a deeply unjust situation. How can it be that I, as a father-to-be, had no right or recourse to at least delay the process for discussion? The asymmetry in these situations is glaring because if, on the way to that appointment to kill it, I caused an accident that injured or terminated that unborn child, I would have been held legally responsible as legal precedents state that an unborn child represents a potential life worthy of compensation or criminal liability if harmed.

The irony is astounding. Why is it that men can be legally obligated for the welfare of an unborn child in certain cases but have no recognized standing in the decision of whether that life continues or not? It's an unsettling contradiction in our understanding and claims of equality under the law.

To be clear, I am not advocating for men to have ultimate veto power over a woman's right to choose. This is not about overriding women's autonomy but recognizing that men deserve a voice. For decades, women have fought for equality under the law, and rightly so. Does this make men less equal? It is time for men to claim their right to be part of this life-altering conversation.

If a man wants to become a father and is willing to take full responsibility for raising the child as a couple or on his own, provide for the mother, and cover all related costs, should that man not have a say in the future of his unborn child?

In relationships where two consenting adults engage in sex, they enter into a tacit understanding of the potential outcomes. It seems unreasonable that one partner holds all the legal power while the other remains only bound by financial and moral obligations. Baby-making is shared, as must be the decision-making process, especially when life and responsibility are at stake. A woman cannot expect to have it both ways, leaving a man at the mercy of her choices. The need for shared responsibility in such crucial decisions cannot be overstated.

Politically, the varying stances of political candidates on abortion and the dramatic contrast between their voiced opinions and legal rulings that have occurred within their states are illuminating. Their policies often reflect the dissonance between what they preach and the laws where they reside.

In Ohio, for example, courts have determined many men to have been liable for prenatal expenses, acknowledging a shared obligation to the unborn child. Yet, these same men have no say in whether that life will continue. In one case, a woman had an affair, which led to an unknown pregnancy. Before becoming aware of her pregnancy, the affair ended. When her husband found out that his wife was pregnant and the child was not his, he left her. Her former lover wanted nothing to do with her, nor did he want to have a child with her. Despite this, she chose to continue the pregnancy and sued for prenatal expenses as well as child support. She was successful in doing so. Thus, despite the father not wanting the child before it was born, he is now financially obligated to it for life.

Similarly, in Florida, there are many cases where men have been compelled to provide financial support for a child during pregnancy without being involved in the conversation at all. In one case, a man, upon hearing the news via the courts that he was to be a father, excitedly and immediately began providing assistance over and above what the court had ordered. In the third month of pregnancy, the mother aborted the child without any forewarning, and he was left devastated when he found out. Should a man fully committed to fatherhood be left powerless in such a scenario? Is it okay that she told him only after it was done?

In New York, one of the bluest states in the nation, the state has gone after fathers-to-be and ordered them to repay the state Medicaid costs for prenatal care using the same reasoning as some of the other states while giving the father no rights in relation to abortion. In California, much of the same hypocrisy exists. The state has issued many temporary child support orders that have begun before birth. Financial obligations have been made clear, but the corresponding rights are missing from this equation.

I understand the "my body, my choice" principle. However, it has lost its weight as it is pushed by the very same people who demanded the government force untested, unsafe vaccines into the bodies of all. "Your body; no choice" was their argument then.

However, neither side answers the question that burns inside me: What about a father's love? Is this not his child as well? Consider the love your father has for you; do you not value that connection? Dismissing a father's emotional investment overlooks a significant aspect of sharing in creating life. Fathers' emotional investment in their unborn children is a crucial aspect that should not be overlooked.

The idea of toxic masculinity falls relatively short when looking at the statistics of children without fathers in their homes. Children from father-absent homes are statistically more likely to face challenges such as higher rates of juvenile delinquency, substance abuse, and incarceration. Eighty-five percent of youth in prison reportedly come from fatherless homes. Fathers matter.

If a man with firm convictions on parenting and opposing views on abortion enters a relationship that leads to pregnancy, I believe he has an inherent right to decide a life equal to that of the mother. The abortion debate has become so polarizing that the complexity of shared responsibility between men and women is often ignored. Meanwhile, governmental interference in these personal issues divides families further and edges into controlling aspects of our private lives.

A conversation about abortion should start between the mother and father. When paternity is clear, and a man is willing to assume responsibility, perhaps under oath if needed, both parties should have an equal say in the decision about the unborn child. In such cases, mutual consent should be required, with the government stepping in only when an agreement cannot be reached. Mediation in family court could help facilitate these decisions, allowing input from both families if the parents agree.

Fathers also have the right to be informed about a pregnancy within a reasonable time frame. Once aware, a paternity test can confirm the father's identity, paving the way for shared decision-making. Suppose a mother is unable to identify the father. In that case, she must be able to prove that she has made a reasonable attempt to do so before seeking an abortion without the father's consent, signing under oath as well.

I do not believe abortion is an issue for the government at any level beyond what is necessary. This is a shared responsibility between two adults who created that life together. The healthiest path for society lies in fostering accountability and communication between parents. Families, not legislation, should shape the future of our children.

A father's love, commitment, and voice should not be trivialized. They are just as essential to the conversation as a mother's choice. Perhaps we stand a better chance of finding solutions if we listen more and try to understand one another.

# *Chapter Thirty-Five*
# See What Isn't Shown

Mike Tyson said it best, "Everyone has a plan until they get punched in the face."

The first morning I was locked away clarified that any survival plan would be fruitless. Chaos reigned, and the only certainty was the unexpected.

I don't believe anyone could have predicted that Mike Tyson would emerge in society as a cultural hero while Bill Cosby would fall from grace as a symbol of betrayal. Did you see that coming from "America's Dad"? What about "America's Athlete"? Never did anyone think that the champion featured on the Wheaties box would one day be a trans woman leading the fight against biological men in women's sports. But perhaps if we paid closer attention, we wouldn't have been surprised at all.

In prison, everything is exceptionally amplified, raw, and twisted. The men on the inside are far more ruthless, their cruelty sharpened by desperation. To claim to have figured them out would be akin to learning that Hitler was Jewish and then claiming that you saw that coming. The behavioral patterns of these men exist in a world outside the logical realm, and understanding them is not for the faint of heart.

The stakes were as high as life itself, and I knew the key to survival was identifying the hidden darkness in the man sitting next to me long before it usually came to light. I may have been at the other end of the spectrum, but I was not an exception to this rule. Outwardly, I was the guy who was sentenced to twenty-seven years, but inwardly, I was nothing like them. Whispers started: Why is this guy here? It didn't take long for the truth to surface that I wasn't supposed to be.

But for my survival, I was in a constant mode of observation, listening to the conversations happening between other inmates, telling stories of their hardened lives, trying to figure out who the "real" them was.

There was this one older gangster type who had been locked up for a long time. He was always complaining about the length of his sentence, which I could empathize with. "All they were able to prove in my case was the gambling and gun charges," he'd vent. "How come these scumbags benefit from the changes in the law and are going home early, but not me?" You might feel for him if you were not privy to other conversations. For on the same day, I listened to him boasting to officers about how he would "build rape cages and train dogs to fuck a guy in the ass." It was a warped theater where in one moment, he would glorify his brutality, and in the next paint himself as someone wronged. The truth is he was now two different people. The man he used to be, and the better version he had become were at odds with one another, fighting for control of his identity.

Meanwhile, I, a nobody who had never committed a crime in my life, not from the streets, raised by a good family, afforded a proper education, was given the same sentence as the rape cage man. But did I complain to anyone, ever? No. I believed myself to be more wronged by the system than any of them, but I was also aware that other people around me were never going home again.

Singh, a friend of mine, is a perfect example of this. Every Thursday, I shared a meal with this man serving five life sentences, one for each person he killed. But Singh was unlike anyone I'd met; he was wise, generous, and surprisingly calm. He had built his wealth in a brutal world, from gas stations to skyscrapers in New York. To most, he was just another lifer, but to me, he was a study in contradictions. "When a dog bites you, you have to put him down. I was dealing with animals out there in the world, and that was how I had to treat them if I was going to survive them," he once said, explaining his past violence with chilling simplicity. Ironically, out of all the people there, he was the last one I would have feared introducing my family to until someone made the mistake of trying to steal something from him when he wasn't in his cell. Then, with knives taped to his hands, he became a warning no one needed twice.

Being among them, I started to piece together what truly separated me from most of these men. It wasn't just our backgrounds but a more bottomless chasm: their pursuit for more, materialism at its most venomous. Outside of prison and inside, they were the same. They chased the same shallow high they did in their lives before prison, from exclusive items to fast money, only this time within the tight circle of prison life. Everything was ego, greed, and envy, the currency of many, especially the criminal and the incarcerated.

If the goal of the prison system in America is rehabilitation, it is failing spectacularly. Nothing about prison is correctional. Prison is a finishing school for criminals where lessons aren't learned as much as they are refined. Daily life teaches inmates to be a sharper, more elusive version of the man who walked in. Inside, they gain a better understanding of the law, which only helps them break it more successfully.

Prison is filled with the worst people in society on their best behavior. It is nothing more than a town of 1200 people behind a fence and gun towers. Like the world outside, they go to jail if they get caught breaking the law. The jail I speak of is the SHU (solitary housing unit). The more they go to jail, the more likely they will be shipped to a different town. The high-security prison I was at was designated a "disciplinary yard," meaning my town housed all the miscreants from around the country. Violence was the weapon of discipline.

One afternoon, I returned to my unit from the gym when I saw a guy paralyzed, stuck in front of the officer's station, high out of his mind on duce. Duce or K2 is a synthetic drug that is rampant in the prison system, laced with who knows what. This was far from his first time being like this. Months before this, there was an incident where he had stripped down naked and started dancing in front of the chow hall. No music was playing. Watching the officers attempt to tackle him while also showing discomfort with the fact that he was naked was quite hilarious. They dragged him to solitary, but because of their incompetence, they forgot to have him evaluated by medical in time. Therefore, his disciplinary infraction was dropped, and he returned to the unit weeks later.

This time was different, though. This time, his car saw him as a liability to the criminal activity in their cells, and they did not want any extra attention on them. The officer catching him would have done just that. The next time he was noticeably high in a public space, a group of them grabbed him, pulled him into one of the cells, and punished him with brutal finality. While he was still stuck in his frozen state, they each started beating him, weakening him before turning a broomstick into an instrument of terror, silencing him with a pillow stuffed over his face. They raped him with the handle, and I can still hear the monstrous sounds of muffled screams. You desperately want to help, but in this world, that is a death wish.

When they finished, they brought him back to his cell and put him in his bunk, leaving the blood-stained broom by the doorway as a reminder. Perhaps they could have stopped selling him the very drug that made him act like this, but nope, they were selling him more drugs starting the next day as if the nightmare hadn't happened. It was insane. If they didn't want him to act like that, all they had to do was stop selling it to him.

I wasn't surprised when another incident occurred a few weeks later. This time, the officers took notice and were not patient. When they passed his cell at the 4 p.m. count, he wasn't standing as everyone was required to. He was stuck frozen underneath the sink, high on Duce. They shouted for him to stand but quickly realized they were wasting their time and moved along. When they finished, their announcement to the unit was blunt. "Interference with the count is a hundred series shot," the CO warned, raising the stakes for everyone.

A one-hundred-series shot is the most severe and the same category as stabbing someone. His car knew the officers would write up and deliver a shot to the LT's officer when they were done counting. So, the moment the doors were unlocked after the count cleared, they ran into his cell and inserted a bunch of drugs into his prison wallet to be sold for them in the SHU, where they fetched triple the price. Moments later, the summons for him came crackling over the speaker to report to the LT's officer, and within minutes, the "secure compound" indicated that they were taking him to the SHU, drugs in tow.

His time in solitary did little to help him; it only magnified desperation. When he returned a couple of months later, he only had half the money he was supposed to. He reported a shake-down that confiscated the drugs. His car didn't believe it, and within minutes, lockdown resumed. Guards led him out, bleeding from stab wounds. He never came back. Nor did the guys who stabbed him.

When we finally opened back up a few days later, the politics simmered. Other cars claimed that he had owed them money, too, which was supposed to be worked out when he got out of the SHU. They held his car liable for payment. His car did not agree. Tension crackled in the air like static.

I was on the computer while all this was occurring, emailing a loved one who hadn't heard from me in a couple of days, undoubtedly worried. While typing, I heard Sean's voice cut through the air like a knife. "Adam, yo, Adam, get off the computer and get over here," he said, sharp and insistent. I looked up, annoyed at being interrupted.

"Hold on, I am sending this off real quick," I replied, hoping to delay a bit. The look in his eyes told me I was making a mistake.

"Look around, you idiot," he snapped.

I did. Standing ten feet from my left was a Blood gang member with a lock-laden belt, swinging it around in a slow arch, surrounded by three members of the Paisas gang. I logged off and moved quickly in the opposite direction, and right as I did, the fight exploded. The belt snapped against a jaw, scattering a tooth before blades started to find their mark. Within moments, an army of COs came rushing into the unit; the air choked with the sting of mace from the grenade they set off. We scattered to the cells, using wet shirts to breathe as the acrid fog burned our throats and eyes.

This was life on the inside, where even the air could become poison, and survival meant knowing when to hold your breath.

## *Chapter Thirty-Six*
# Easy to Miss

A few days later, when the cell doors rattled open, I stepped out into the morning haze, feeling the familiar throb of confined monotony. Sean was waiting with a half-smile, the bitter scent of instant coffee hanging in the space between us.

"Let's get our workout in early today. You never know what will happen in this place and we've been missing a lot," Sean said, his voice firm with anticipation.

"Cardio or weights?" I asked, trying to muster the energy.

"The weather is trash today, so let's hit the weight shack. We can step outside between sets and do some burpee pullups," he said.

"Sounds exhausting," I said, shrugging.

"You could always ask for a transfer to the women's facility and work there. I'm sure they don't train as hard. You'd fit right in," he said, a spark of mischief in his eyes.

"Ha-ha," I snorted. "I'm sure over there they're smart enough not to have swastikas inked on their legs, either."

Sean's face darkened a bit with embarrassment. "I was eighteen," he muttered, with a hint of regret.

By 7:30 a.m., the compound was alive with movement as inmates streamed out, eager to shed the restless tension built up over days of lockdown. A simmering aggression was in the air, heavy and sharp as a blade edge. I ignored it. It wasn't my business, nor was I a part of anything happening. Earbuds in, I cranked the volume up and let the beat drown out the world, focusing on the thrum of music pounding. The repetitive clang of weights and muted grunts faded into the background noise as we began our routine.

I was now practicing, having spent countless hours examining my surroundings, paying attention to every detail, and mapping out a plan for the following day, so, ironically, I would still be blindsided and miss what was occurring right in front of me. When the air gets tight, it's common sense to stay alert and never let your guard down. You need to make it a point to catch every whisper, every side glance that could signal the start of something, yet there I was, earbuds jammed in, volume cranked, living as if I were at some suburban gym, oblivious to the crackling storm around me. I was about to learn that lesson again the hard way.

I finished my set on the sled and stepped out from the weight shack, ready for the pullup bars just as shouts sliced through the air. Fists were already flying, a cluster of Serranoes and New York guys locked in a violent brawl. Before I could register it, I was caught in the crossfire, bodies slamming into mine like a wave.

"Hey, I am not in this!" I shouted, trapped in the maelstrom. My voice vanished inside the roar, panic surging as elbows and fists covered me like a swarm of angry bees.

Adrenalin hit me like a hammer, and I felt my pulse in my teeth. Out of the blur, Sean emerged, eyes wild, grabbing the back of my shirt and pulling me from the fray. I stumbled, taking a few more hits to the shoulder and head that sent sparks through my vision. It was only after we broke free that I felt a sharp, burning pain searing through my ribs from what felt like behind my heart. It was the white-hot sting of a hornet, getting worse with each heartbeat. Blood seeped through my fingers, and I spotted the crude weapon in one of the guy's hands: a thin PVC pipe, a nail driven through its end glinting with fresh red. In a frenzy, he had landed a strike.

"Shit, we gotta go. They're going to call a move soon, and if they notice this fight before and lock it down, then we are screwed. They'll do body checks," Sean said, urgency thumping in his voice.

We returned to the housing unit just as the officers stormed the rec yard. "Secure Compound!" blared through all the speakers. I slipped into my cell, heart thundering, and peeled off my sweatshirt and T-shirt. The fabric was stuck to the wound, and each movement felt like a bite. Sean pressed gauze to my side and taped it down, but the pain was setting in now, sharp and insistent. Anxiety coiled in my gut. Was the wound deep? Rusty nail? The questions spun in my head, but there was no going to medical. Not here. Not without consequences that would have been worse than my current state.

The bleak reality gnawed deeply. In what twisted version of the world did anyone call this "rehabilitation"? I'd just taken a shiv to the side for daring to walk to a pullup bar. The irony wasn't lost on me how all my meticulous attention to detail could fail me when it mattered most.

Later that afternoon, SIS summoned me to their office because they saw me on camera near the fight that broke out. I walked into their office, pulse spiking, trying to seem unfazed, my side aching.

"What can you tell us about what happened out there?" he said, his voice detached, but his eyes bored into me.

I kept my tone measured. "I don't know anything. I was working out, but I don't know what those guys were beefing over. Whatever was going on wasn't my business."

The officer studied me. "You're not in any trouble here. We're just trying to get a handle on what's happening," he said, fishing.

"I get it, but like I said, I wasn't involved."

Sean was called down after me, probably to compare stories, but I knew he would say the same thing. We were just collateral, pawns on a board we weren't trying to play on. We genuinely didn't know what sparked the brawl.

* * *

That night, pain anchored me to my bunk while I turned everything over in my head. Missing that tension, the danger brewing before me was eating away at my pride. I reminded myself that everyone misses things at times and let my mind drift back to a college memory of an argument I had with one of my professors. It was here that I realized something that has been missed by every sharp eye that has studied the Constitution since our nation's founding. I had to think of something to help my bruised ego.

One of my high school teachers sparked a love of history in me, especially the discussion on the Constitution and the philosophical duels that birthed it. College deepened that fascination, as did the Federalist papers and discovering Alexander Hamilton's razor-sharp mind. There was something almost divine about peering into the thoughts of those who shaped our nation, to see the passion of men who feared tyranny but still respected the order that power and strong governance could bring. Hamilton was especially important in crafting the constitution, with his paradoxical admiration for the British model and a lifetime presidency, if only to maintain stability. It was easy to label him a monarchist, and perhaps he slightly was.

Article I Section 8 of the Constitution stood out to me, which I do not believe had stood out to anyone else, which reflected Hamilton's genius. Was it possible that he could have foreseen the flaws that would emerge in a system designed to guard against tyranny yet be vulnerable to human ambition? Was it possible that he could plant an obscure safeguard, a "parachute" within the Constitution, meant to be discovered at a time when we were desperate as a nation? Is it possible that everyone missed it?

With some of the greatest minds in our nation having studied this doctrine, you would assume that it would have been found by now, but as I reminded myself in this painful moment, even the most watchful can miss what is right in front of them.

In this section, the Constitution gave Congress the power to regulate time and "fix the standard of weights and measure." On the surface, regulating measurements for trade and science seems mundane.

Congress was given this power with the understanding that definitions need to be updated. Time itself has evolved from being measured by sundials to atomic vibrations, and in a world where seconds are defined by cesium vibrations and years by planetary orbits, definitions matter. In truth, our current description of time is inaccurate because no planet orbits the Sun directly as we currently define; they all orbit the shifting center of mass of the solar system. What if Hamilton knew that, at some point, the very fabric of timekeeping could be twisted and manipulated and gave the power to Congress to do so?

Currently, we define a year as the Earth's revolution around the Sun, which takes, on average, 365.25 days, and the average term in office is four years or 1,461 days. What would stop Congress in a time of desperation from changing the legal definition of a year to the Earth orbiting the Sun ten times? This could be done with a pen stroke, making four-year terms equal to 14,610 days in the office, giving most a lifetime appointment. If unchecked materialism could erode a nation, then what about unchecked ambition? Could such an oversight have been intentional in bringing about the lifetime reign Hamilton lectured on? An elegant mechanism left hidden in plain sight, overlooked for generations? Perhaps.

Thinking about this that night in my bunk did make me feel better. It dawned on me that it's human nature to miss what's right in front of us, whether in moments of survival or the intricate web of governance. That thought, mixed with the throbbing in my side, was a wake-up call. I vowed I would not be caught unaware again. Too much had already slipped past me. I was done paying the price. I couldn't sleep. My mind raced for hours, thinking about the answer to the question pressing on my mind. What is the root cause behind most of the violence in prison? What did I need to pay more attention to?

## *Chapter Thirty-Seven*
# Evil's Dessert

Locusts devour all in their path but are only noticed when the return to harvest reveals only a barren wasteland. We have a unique chance to halt the destructive forces spreading across our society, but we must remain vigilant.

In their brilliance, the founders of this nation recognized the frailties of human nature and the potential ruin that could follow unchecked ambition or corruption. They crafted the Constitution as a safeguard against such collapse. Yet even their foresight could not predict the rise of materialism in America.

Materialism has woven itself into the fabric of our culture like an aggressive cancer, not unlike the ideology that compels a portion of society to believe in the necessity of medicating and performing irreversible surgeries on children under the pretense of gender-affirming care. It spreads insidiously, unnoticed at first until it reaches its fatal stage. To grasp the endgame of this unchecked materialism, you only need to peer, as I did, into the realities of life behind prison walls.

Inmates are the ultimate product of a society intoxicated by material excess. Before they were incarcerated, the insatiable desire for possessions gnawed at them until it tore loose, ravaging everything in its path. This bottomless hunger for goods suffocated any inclination toward personal growth, genuine relationships, or community core elements of true happiness. The corrosive effects of this obsession are evident at every moment within prison walls.

When everything you own can fit into a single locker, you learn just how little is necessary. Yet most inmates don't. They remain trapped by the phantom promise of happiness through material gain, spending most of their time chasing stamps. The prison hierarchy revolves around controlling the limited resources within the compound. The location of your cell near the TV, the quality of your mattress, the placement of your chair, your clothing, the watch on your wrist, and the access you have to the kitchen and its bounty become the new measures of status. Drugs, alcohol, contraband cell phones, and black-market power define influence. The desire to accumulate more of these items echoes the lives most led outside, driven by false ideals of fulfillment. In prison, anything of value is at risk of being stolen because someone always believes that having more will elevate them.

It is not uncommon for an inmate to slip a weapon into a particular cell and tip off the administration, ensuring those within are sent to solitary confinement, so the cell is now available. This is why I once paid others to watch my cell when I wasn't around. Every rare or exclusive item becomes a target, turning possessions into burdens. This reflects the toxic trajectory our society faces if materialism remains unbridled, fostering a "prison mentality" obsessed with possessions and disintegrating the bonds that keep communities together.

The architects of America envisioned a land where the pursuit of freedom and opportunity was the true dream. But as the economy boomed and boundaries of progress expanded, the purity of that pursuit became muddied. The American Dream mutated, transforming into a relentless chase for wealth and material comfort. Corporate giants capitalized on this shift, marketing a deceptive path to happiness and status through goods. It wasn't long before credit cards emerged, seducing Americans with the illusion of instant gratification. "Buy now, pay later" became a mantra that whispered promises of fulfillment and fostered entitlement. In prison, 50 percent of the violent acts that occur are a direct result of the "buy now, don't pay later" mentality because often, when later arrives, they can't pay.

Before long, the bonds between corporations and government strengthened, each feeding off the other. This unchecked rise allowed the government to wield control with greater ease. A society consumed by individual gain and wealth accumulation loses its empathy and sense of civic duty. When personal success trumps community, cooperation erodes, isolation increases, and people become more susceptible to manipulation. It becomes a playground for policy engineered to control rather than serve.

Lobbyists from powerful corporations molded laws, deregulated industries, influenced tax policies and filled campaign coffers to deeply root consumer culture. Social media took the reins, recasting materialism in a subtler yet more insidious form. Our feeds are saturated with curated lives that incite comparisons and breed discontent, urging us to buy more to keep up. Have you ever turned to "retail therapy"? It is not healing; it is a dose of dopamine as fleeting as a shot of heroin.

The unending chase for more is not the American Dream but America's nightmare. It drives anxiety, depression, and a chronic sense of emptiness. No matter how many objects we accumulate, they can never fill the void they promise to. The pursuit itself is hollow, fraying the threads of our communities and replacing authentic connections with superficial interactions.

The evidence is all around us. Churches once at the heart of neighborhoods now stand empty or repurposed. Civic groups dissolve, leaving behind an increasingly disconnected and divided nation. This suits the ruling class perfectly. A populace absorbed in personal gain rather than collective strength becomes easier to govern. They want a nation not under God or united by shared values but one fragmented, devoted to material gain, and oblivious to the loss of family ties and real fulfillment. The fallout is evident: family structures crumbling, birth rates plummeting, gender divisions deepening, and an atmosphere of alienation seeping into everyday life.

Unchecked materialism is a perfidious disease that spreads before you notice it, sapping the humanity of everyone it touches. The antidote is purpose and meaning in life and in prison, where men struggle to grasp any meaning in their existence, this truth is highlighted and starkly underscored, as materialism is king in the cell block, and the most dangerous material sought by a large portion of the population is drugs.

# *Chapter Thirty-Eight*
# Close to Home

If life teaches you anything, it will show you that it has a way of upending itself, like a tornado upending trees along a quiet stretch of midwestern road. Everything seems familiar and safe one minute, and the world has been turned upside down the next.

When I was in the fourth grade, life showed my family its destructive power. It started as a scheduled appointment for a simple, routine surgery for my mother at a reputable hospital in Boston. The low-risk kind of surgery you do not need to worry about, so we didn't. None of us knew that an E5 tornado was quietly picking up speed around the bend, about to tear through our lives, leaving behind an unrecognizable world.

The surgeon, perhaps more human than we'd like to admit, made a life-altering mistake. At first, no one realized what had happened, but as hours passed, instead of Mom waking up, her condition worsened. The supposed routine procedure turned into the very real and horrifying possibility that we were going to lose my mother.

The simple operation spiraled into a nightmarish two-year ordeal and left my mother hospitalized for many months, fighting for her life. My father, who I thought of as a superhero, had to stretch himself now to become not only Dad, husband, and provider but also the man who hoped and prayed that his nearly two-hour daily drive (each way) to the hospital would not be his last.

Dad stayed at the hospital as much as he could, and my brother and I moved into my grandmother's house. I don't know what would have become of our family without our grandmother, but I know she saved us. Without hesitation, she stepped in and became our rock. She cooked, cleaned, drove us to school, and ensured that two boys who viewed parents as the bones on which they sharpen their teeth never strayed too far from the rules. Alan and I were challenging to manage. We were wild and rebellious, but Gram kept us in line with her quiet authority. We tested her constantly, wrestling loudly upstairs and arguing over nothing, but she always managed to ground us.

Gram always made a point to make us feel included in what was happening with our mother and emphasized how our parents wanted nothing more than to be with us. She was masterful in her approach, and her wisdom and strength made all the difference. Gram was the glue that held our fractured family together. I often say that if anyone in our family had been a wizard in their past life, it would have been her because only a person of magic could alchemize the darkest period in our family's life into one filled with memories of gratitude and fondness.

After many months away, my mother was finally released home but would require constant medical care for the next two years. It took just as long for home to feel like before we left. The previous warmth and love that once pervaded seemed to have evaporated in our absence. I was in sixth grade by the time we were back in the normal swing of things, a teenager in the making. I had my first girlfriend and an awkward kiss at a school dance, and my voice was cracking.

The road of recovery was not easy for Mom and alcohol took hold of her. More than half of American families have members suffering from alcoholism or some form of addiction, making it likely that you understand how the following years played out. It was a tough time and when I was eighteen years old, my mom hit rock bottom. Rock bottom is a double-edged sword; it's the hardest moment but from which upward is now possible. Finally, my mother was admitted into a rehab facility, and I began to navigate the complexities of her illness; I sought solace in understanding. I gathered as much material as I could from the Betty Ford Clinic, spoke with her counselors at her treatment center, and read a few books, eager to learn as much as I could about the disease that consumed her. I mustered the courage to attend an AA meeting at a church near my old preschool, and when I did, each person introduced themselves and acknowledged their affliction. When it was my turn, I bared my soul: "Hi everyone. I am sorry to invade your meeting, and regretfully, I do not know the protocol. I am not an alcoholic. I am not even old enough to drink, but I am here today because my mother is. Right now, she is away in a rehab facility, and I am trying to do my part to understand and help her in her sobriety. I want to understand this addiction. I want to understand the disease, and I want to know what I can do to help her overcome it when she finally comes home."

The group was incredible, and I recognized the intense passion in participation that night. I had nothing to compare it to, but I knew that using their experience to educate and help someone save their family gave the attendees a different purpose. The impact of this night never left me, and through this experience, I was able to gradually let go of my anger and resentment. I came to understand that addiction was not a choice but a cruel disease that had taken hold of her. I no longer saw her as weak or selfish but as a woman challenged with overcoming a demon.

When my mother returned home, the weight of addiction had lifted, revealing the woman she once was. I recognized her, and it made me emotional. Despite the disease that had control of her, she always still managed to be a good mom, but her healing brought her to another level of mom. It was someone I had not seen in a long time, and I hadn't realized how much I missed her. We reconnected on a deeper level, sharing stories and secrets that had been long buried. She spoke openly about her struggles, fears, and hopes for the future, and we cried, laughed, and reunited in forgiveness.

I realize that through my mother's journey, I had touched the depths of empathy, compassion, and forgiveness. I also learned that a person who has succumbed to their addiction still exists somewhere inside, trapped. Addiction is like a parasite attaching itself to your soul, and I could see now that the only way to rid yourself of a disease is to make the host stronger than the parasite.

I decided then that I, as the host, would always be stronger than the parasite attempting to attach to me. I lost any desire to get drunk or try drugs. It would have been so easy for me to turn to drugs and alcohol in my time of despair, and I was able to avoid that path of destruction.

I don't believe in coincidence. We are meant to use our times of suffering as a lesson, as a transformative power to improve our world. When an E5 hit my life, I was able to determine that I was the host, and although the parasites may look different—they could not be allowed to latch on.

# *Chapter Thirty-Nine*
# Society's Anchor

The anchor of addiction is an invisible parasite attaching itself to the souls of our citizens, draining away the people they once were. The only way for our nation to overcome this affliction is to empower each host, providing them with tools to grow more potent than the parasite while cutting off the fuel that feeds it.

Drug and alcohol abuse weave through American neighborhoods like an intricate web, the threads of addiction stretching out in every direction, entangling our people at random without bias. The problems this creates are endless, perpetually multiplying and entangling everything in addiction's path. If you turn the microscope on society's most devastating crisis and zoom in, the nucleus of it all is perfectly displayed inside the prison system, swollen with inmates who are often products of this very epidemic. The actual scope of the opioid crisis in America is not only an issue of addiction but a massive, deep-seated industry, one that feeds off the pain and suffering of its victims. Shockingly, it becomes increasingly evident that the government has little incentive to solve the problem. Why would they? The opioid crisis in this country is a cash cow of epic proportions. If the crisis were solved, the livelihood of countless bottom-feeding bureaucrats, law enforcement agencies, health care providers, and many criminal justice system employees would be jeopardized. If we woke up tomorrow and the problem was gone, about a million people would suddenly be out of work.

The economic toll of the opioid crisis is staggering, roughly one trillion dollars a year. That's a trillion with a "T," with hundreds of billions of your hard-earned tax dollars being directly spent on it. When you look at how the crisis reverberates through our society through the healthcare system, lost productivity, the criminal justice system, and social services, it becomes impossible to ignore how deeply it has become embedded in our nation's economic and social infrastructure. Much of that trillion-dollar price tag can be tied to the bloated government bureaucracy that profits and survives from its very existence. The deeper you look, the clearer it becomes; the more significant the problem, the greater the profit, which is why those vested in it want to keep the crisis alive. In this way, the government expansion spanning from the bureaucratic complex to the prison industrial complex is symbiotic with the rise of addiction. They are bound together in a way that, for many, would be unthinkable to untangle.

Data from The Council of Economic Advisers (CEA) estimates that the economic costs of opioid-related mortality and morbidity were around 700 billion annually, which includes lost wages and lost economic output. While taxpayers do not directly pay this, the social safety net and public health systems that absorb the consequences of overdose deaths are dependent upon funding from taxpayers.

According to a 2023 report from the CDC, an estimated 80 billion per year in economic burden comes from prescription opioid misuse. The US Department of Health and Human Services allocates billions annually through SAMHSA to fund prevention and treatment programs. According to the Congressional Budget Office (CBO), the federal government spends between 15 and 20 billion annually on drug-related law enforcement efforts. At the same time, programs like Medicare and Medicaid play a critical role in financing treatment for opioid use disorder (OUD) while also covering around 45 percent of all opioid-related treatment services in the United States (KFF, 2022). I could go on and on.

Consider the stark growth of government employment: In 1940, there were roughly 2.6 million government employees. Today, that number has surged to over 22 million. The Trump administration has made bold moves in establishing the Department of Government Efficiency, tasked with cutting waste within the government. I wonder if this agency is looking at the one trillion annually the opioid crisis is wasting. Are they willing to confront it? Will they understand that the real solution to the opioid epidemic is much deeper than simply stopping the flow of drugs into the country, but confronting the deep structural issues within the system that survive on it?

Thus far, in all my conversations with politicians, I've yet to meet one who truly grasps the scope of the crisis or has the foresight to reverse the economic and social damage it causes. This is why the problem has never gotten anything but worse. The political class always finds a way to bypass the heart of the issue. Prison is similar, except that in prison, the solution is far simpler to implement, and yet, they do nothing.

It is clear that personal and upfront experience changes perspective. Politicians, as informed and moral as they may be, have not lived within the addiction crisis in the way someone like me had, or many others have.

Standard solutions dominate the mainstream discourse: secure the border, shut down the cartels, stop the flow of drugs, and pressure China to stop sending fentanyl into the country, all by sheer force. While I agree that doing these things is part of the equation and helps to cut down the fuel that feeds the parasite, it is only a tiny piece of a much larger puzzle. Without a more nuanced, multifaceted approach, any progress made will be short-lived.

If the government takes action to reduce the influx of drugs coming into the country, there are profound economic realities that must be acknowledged. The basic laws of supply and demand dictate that as drugs become scarcer, their street value skyrockets. When addicts are unable to get their fix, they will do whatever it takes to get it, even if that means committing a crime or resorting to violence. The bottom line is that crime will rise exponentially on the streets. Drug dealers will fight for control over the market and remaining supply, escalating the violence, and none of this does anything to solve the problem of addiction. All it does is intensify suffering. So, what is the answer? Do we continue to pump more money into a system that feeds off the misery of addiction, or is it time to reevaluate how we approach this crisis?

The answer is not as simple as blocking the supply of drugs. If history has taught us anything, it's that the "War on Drugs" was an utter failure. The trillions of taxpayer dollars that have been poured into the criminal justice system, prisons, law enforcement, and the pharmaceutical industry have done little to curtail addiction and, in many cases, have only made things worse. Many of you still remember when the big pharmaceutical companies sold the public on opiates, making the claims that they were NOT addictive. Did any of them go to jail for that?

The time has come to acknowledge that our current system isn't working, and it's time for a fundamental shift in addressing this problem. Addicts aren't faceless criminals. They are our fellow citizens trapped in a cycle of pain, self-loathing, and desperation. Addiction does not discriminate. Whether the addiction is born out of trauma, injury, or simple curiosity, an addict's road to usage often starts the same way. At first, they may only use casually, which usually goes unnoticed by those around them. But addiction works quickly. With each hit, their brain releases a rush of dopamine, the neurochemical that creates a feeling of pleasure and reward. Over time, the brain's natural dopamine production starts to decrease, and the addict finds themselves needing more of the substance to feel "normal." During this process, the body adapts, becoming more efficient at metabolizing the drug, requiring more and more to achieve the same level of high the user is looking for.

This is where the brain's reward system hijacks the person, altering the prefrontal cortex, the part of the brain responsible for decision-making, impulse control, and emotional regulation. As these changes take root, it becomes harder and harder for the addict to make rational choices or break the cycle of usage. Their neural pathways become rewired in a way that makes relapse almost inevitable, even after long periods of abstinence. This is the exact reason why an addict is often misunderstood. It isn't simply a matter of willpower. The person's brain has changed, making the disease incredibly hard to overcome.

Society does not understand addiction, which is a large part of why, up to this point, there has been no real solution. How can you solve what you do not truly understand? Friends and family start to give up, trust is lost, and bridges are burned. Employers fire them, and the self-worth of the individual plummets into the gutter, leaving them nothing but their addiction.

My mother taught me a valuable lesson through her journey: No matter how bad it seems, there is still a person underneath it all, a person trapped by their own biology and brain chemistry. The problem isn't the person at all; it's the disease they have succumbed to. But how do we get them out? How do we free them from this cycle? The cure to addiction and the opioid crisis in America isn't going to be achieved through attacking the supply but by curing the user. It doesn't matter how many drugs are around if the addict isn't taking them.

During my time in prison, I've spent years working with some of the worst addicts society breeds, working with them on modifying behaviors, teaching them to be accountable, and helping them to understand how they make choices. I saw it as an opportunity to occupy my time and gain a new understanding of addiction. I watched them destroy themselves further from the inside out. Rock bottom is a myth. After years of trial and error, I saw a different path forward. I was having success after success with these young men, often hardened by their environment, making incredible transformations.

It was not easy, but I discovered that recovery is possible at a level never before seen, and "getting clean" is just the beginning. Both society and the addicted require a fundamental shift. We need to see it not as a moral failure but as a disease, and we must be willing to make a long-term commitment to healing both the addict and society. Otherwise, nothing will change, and we will keep wasting trillions chasing our tails while people and families crumble and the real solutions remain out of reach.[1]

Addiction is the bureaucracy's fountain of youth and society's Achilles' heel, sucking the life out of the people while feeding on their corrupted souls. Across the country, there are countless facilities and programs designed to

---

1 Sources: US Department of Health and Human Services (HHS): "The opioid crisis in America." 2021.

Congressional Budget Office (CBO): "The Federal Budget and the Role of Opioid Spending." 2018.

Council of Economic Advisers (CEA): "The Economic Cost of the Opioid Crisis." 2019.

Kaiser Family Foundation (KFF): "Medicaid and Substance Use Disorder."

address addiction. Yet, their long-term success rates are frustratingly low, and I believe that is because they are trying to bring forth a solution from the outside instead of seeking the solution from within. While many methods and interventions can lead a person toward sobriety, very few are sustained long-term. It's easy to assume that a person hitting "rock bottom" would be enough to inspire them to break free from the chains of addiction. Yet, even in the direst of circumstances, such as landing in prison, the addicts still find themselves returning to old habits, to the same behavioral patterns that brought them down in the first place. As we said, their brain is wired differently now, and the high is its gas.

The urgency of the opioid crisis cannot be overstated. In just the past four years, more Americans have died from opioid overdoses than in World War II. This is a staggering statistic that demands our immediate attention and action. We are not just dealing with numbers here, but with the lives of our nation's children.

Through a long and tedious discovery process extending longer than two decades, I have learned of four pillars of recovery that have the inherent strength to temporarily overpower an addict's desire to use, albeit for a short period of time—Fear, Incentive, Respect, and Existence/Purpose.

When a person faces going to prison or ends up in the hospital, often they feel fear. Fear is a powerful emotion. It allows them to see that they are testing their mortality. Incentive and desire also hold behavior altering power. When someone has potential advancement on the line, i.e., up for a job or promotion that requires them to pass a drug test, often, the user can overcome their addiction just long enough to pass the test.

When a person is respected and admired by their peers, failing to meet that expectation can create a level of guilt, which can lead to second-guessing their choice to use. Last but certainly not least, when a person has purpose in life that gives their existence on this earth meaning, it often has the power to overcome choices that impede that purpose and can motivate someone to stay the course. These pillars can keep a person sober but are mainly short-term changes. To obtain success in the long term, we must find a way to combine all of these pillars: Fear, Incentive,

Respect, and Existence in a comprehensive solution, a proposal I refer to as the F.I.R.E. Initiative. Now I admit, one thing the government does very well is acronyms and if they take this up I am sure they will do better than I on this front, but for now this will suffice.

When a user hits their lowest point ends up in a hospital because of an overdose, or is imprisoned, this acts as a temporary stop, forcing the addict to detox from the substance that has dominated their lives. For a while, many find the motivation to be clean, to prove to themselves they can break free. But within months, the same old cycle repeats itself, sobriety slips through their fingers. The reason this happens is because addiction is a symptom of deeper wounds that are consistently left unaddressed. Once the immediate physical craving is gone, there's nothing to combat the emotional and psychological pain that drove their addiction in the first place. This is the exact area where initiative needs to be taken because without a robust framework for long-term healing, without combating the root cause, relapse is inevitable.

Bluntly put, to fix the opioid crisis in America, we must focus on rebuilding the person, the individual, that addiction has all but destroyed. By the time someone enters the criminal justice system because of their addiction, they have often lost everything that once gave their life meaning. Their relationships have fractured. They can't hold down a job, let alone maintain a career. Their family has lost hope, their friends have walked away, and every penny they've earned has been spent fueling their addiction. With no income, sense of purpose, or support system, their lives have devolved into a never-ending cycle of desperation. There is nothing left for them to fight for.

The current government approach is locking addicts up, subjecting them to the judicial system, and incarcerating them with the hope that "prison will change them," which has proven to be ineffective and costly. I understand the saying that if something isn't broken, don't fix it, but this is beyond broken. It costs the US taxpayer an average of $44,000 per year to incarcerate an individual for crimes committed due to addiction, but that's just the cost of keeping them in prison. On average, it costs $250,000 to prosecute and process an individual through the legal system. This is an astronomical amount of taxpayer dollars spent—only for the addict to be released back into the same environment, doing the same thing they were doing before. As this cycle persists, the cost of addiction continues to climb, affecting healthcare, the economy, and public safety. If we step back for a moment and ask ourselves if this is working and if we are making the best use of our resources, the answer is clear: No, we are not.

There's a better way to solve the problem and dramatically save taxpayer dollars. Instead of releasing an addict from the hospital untreated and without a plan or throwing them in prison, we can provide meaningful rehabilitation and give individuals the tools they need to rebuild their lives. The solution is not just about getting sober; it's about creating a life worth living, a life that is built on purpose, accountability, and the opportunity to contribute to society.

My proposed initiative is a comprehensive model that offers a clear path to recovery. It is a compassionate and pragmatic program that can be applied to anyone struggling with addiction, whether court-ordered or entering voluntarily. The solution is possible with the four essential steps of Fear, Incentive, Respect, and Existence/Purpose. By combining these four pillars, we can create an all-inclusive solution that supports long-term recovery.

The first step is for the individual to enter into a contractual agreement with the government. This agreement holds the participant accountable, and in exchange, they receive both support and structure. The best time to get a participant to enter into such an agreement is when fear is at its highest. When they are looking at jail time or in the hospital from an overdose or even as a solution put forth during a family's intervention, anyone can voluntarily sign up, but it's crucial to have hospitals and courts ready to enroll new participants when they will be most agreeable.

One requirement under this agreement is for the participant to agree to bi-weekly injections of naltrexone or a comparable opiate blocker, which generally lasts up to four weeks. Naltrexone is a powerful medication that binds to opioid receptors in the brain, blocking the effects of opioids and drastically reducing cravings. It's a forced stop. For as long as the participant continues their treatment, never misses their shot, and passes regular drug tests, the drug will do nothing for them if they try to use it. This is an effective way to break the reward center of the brain and break the physical cycle of addiction. What would be the point of using an opioid if you feel nothing from it any longer? However, stopping the use of opioids is only part of the solution.

To truly transform their lives, we must focus on rebuilding the individual, their self-worth, and their sense of purpose. Support will be given to individuals that need a job to secure one, suited for their stage and skillset at the time. Once a participant is enrolled in the program and successfully completes their first month (naltrexone + work), the "incentive" element comes in, and participants will receive a $1,500 monthly stipend from the government, provided they remain drug-free, pass monthly drug tests, both scheduled and random, and maintain steady employment. This amount may seem modest, but it's transformative for someone who has been going downhill and doing without. Combined with a participant's employment earnings, it adds up to a steady and significant income. With this, individuals will slowly regain things previously lost, starting with dignity and stability. Maintaining a steady job and earning a legitimate weekly paycheck will help them rebuild many parts of their lives. Family members and employers will take notice of their progress, and before long, trust, once broken, will begin to be restored. They will start to feel pride in their achievements, creating a virtuous growth cycle. A participant will begin to feel emotions they have forgotten they could feel.

Respect given and received is the binding agent that holds recovery together. It's the glue that helps addicts maintain their sobriety and build a life beyond just "not using." After six months in the program, participants will be required to donate their time to causes that will help others and reinforce their recovery. This can include mentoring youth struggling with addiction, visiting schools and sharing their personal story, participating in Narcotics Anonymous (NA) or Alcoholics Anonymous (AA) meetings, and much more. There is a proven psychological principle at play here: Sponsors in the 12-step program, for instance, are 90 percent less likely to relapse than the participants they help, and that is because they are part of something greater than themselves. This sense of purpose is vital to long-term success, and mixing sobriety with becoming a contributing member of society and re-establishing one's place in the world is a dish we can digest. It will lead to a better existence, filling the voids in their life with purpose.

Throughout a three-year period, a participant will continue to receive regular drug tests and receive support from the program. Once they reach the third year, their position in the program is elevated, and from there, they will be mentoring new members who have joined the F.I.R.E. initiative. Their obligation to receive naltrexone injections will be removed, and the monthly stipend will be lowered to $750. At this point, there will no longer be monthly drug testing; only random drug tests will be required at the discretion of the program. By this time, the participant will have developed a stable routine and a job, mended broken relationships, and maintained continued access to the internal resources necessary to stay sober. At the end of five years, a F.I.R.E. participant will have graduated from the program and may choose for themselves how to move forward. Studies have shown that after five years of sobriety, the chance of relapse significantly drops each year following.

The alternative to this, what we do now, is a broken system. It's inefficient and costly. Currently, low level drug offenses fill the federal prison system. It costs taxpayers roughly $250,000 to arrest and process these offenders through the system, and another $44,090 per year to house them in the BOP. Changing the status quo and investing $18,000 a year for the first three years with an additional $8,400 for the next two will dramatically change a person's life trajectory and save taxpayers billions of dollars. By making this investment, we save money and remove a person from the category of economic loss into that of a productive and contributing member of society: a citizen who is sober, employed, pays taxes, and helps others in need. This is a far cry from the same person who would have otherwise remained in the criminal justice system, perpetuating their addiction and costing taxpayers even more.

As a key element is the forced stop, the same program can be done with alcohol, and the forced stop would be antabuse. Instead of naltrexone, individuals battling alcohol addiction can be injected, voluntarily or because they are incentivized, with antabuse, a drug that causes extreme illness when alcohol is consumed.

The only question that needs to be asked is simple: Why not try a better way? Do we not owe it to ourselves, our communities, and those suffering from addiction to change our current approach? The current system has failed. It is time for something new—something that can work.

As an added benefit, we can lower the cost of the program further by dealing with the insurance companies that already cover the cost of rehab. That money can be reimbursed to the government through the insurer rather than being sent to a facility that has a high fail rate, saving taxpayers even more money. Full-on wins all around. But I never would have been able to identify a different way of looking at addiction that could help the country and its citizens if not for my time behind bars. I have achieved clarity in my life and that is a far cry from where I started.

## *Chapter Forty*

# This Is Who Is in Charge?

A great thinker once said: "If you want to see the dregs of society, go to a prison in America during a shift change."

A federal holdover spot is very different from the long-term joints where prison politics is learned, enforced, and ossified. But it's still its own kind of hell, filled with fresh catches plucked straight off the street. Young, reckless, loud. They arrive carrying the arrogance of freedom. They don't know the rules that existed long before they got there and will exist long after they leave, and as a result, many of them will not make it through the years in front of them.

On paper, these facilities are supposed to teach restraint—what not to do, what behaviors to leave behind, what mistakes not to repeat. In reality, they sharpen bad habits into weapons. The lessons don't teach; they maim. And the consequences come back later to carve people open. One of those consequences arrives in the form of a mass shakedown of a unit by officers and staff, because the general rule of thumb is simple: Punish everyone for the actions of a few.

On this particular day, the unit was under siege. That meant we were all herded from our cells into what they had the nerve to call a "recreation area." Calling it that was an insult. It was a hollow gray box of concrete—lifeless—with a thick steel mesh cage forty feet above, open just enough to give you a vague sense of outside city air. A hoop clung to the wall like an afterthought, and some half-faded paint hinted at a handball court that once was. Over a hundred bodies were packed inside, shoulder to shoulder, in this bleak gray coffin, under a single shaft of sunlight cutting through the cage. To me, that beam wasn't hope; it was a reminder of the world outside passing by, always out of reach.

You can always tell who's worried during a shakedown—the ones with something to lose. They're the guys darting to the windows, eyes glued to the officers tearing apart cells, trying to guess where the sweep will land, whispering emergency plans for when the worst hits. The irony is perfect: If you're the one with contraband, the last thing you should do is act like you're guilty. But they can't help themselves. They turn into human billboards advertising their own fear.

All it takes is one CO to glance at the camera, push a button, mutter one word over the radio—and thirty officers are on you in seconds, digging through your cell. Criminals they may be, but stupid ones, and if they hadn't learned the lesson by the time they got to prison, they never would. I could see their past lives in their eyes: hustlers flashing pistols for selfies, kids fanning out stacks of hundreds on social media like it meant something. Dealers, robbers, wannabe gangsters—advertising their own downfall long before prison swallowed them.

I stayed calm. I knew officers were going to trash my cell, toss my property around like confetti, and enjoy every minute of it. It would give them something to brag about to their significant others over dinner, puffing up small acts of destruction into tales of bravery. Small and petty men masquerading as heroes. I leaned against the wall and waited it out, detached. Which is why the shock hit harder when the recreation door swung open and a CO's voice barked:

"Lacerda. Cell 614. Lacerda—six-one-four."

Heads turned. Eyes followed me as I stepped forward. I could feel their thoughts echoing my own: *Why him? What did he have? What did he do?*

I reached the rec door and saw the kid who'd called my name. He looked about nineteen, like he only needed to shave once a month.

"What's your ID number?" he asked.

It took me a second to process the question. "Six-four-four, zero-nine, zero-five-zero."

He motioned me out into the hallway, which was saturated with COs, and shut the door behind me. Within seconds, a much larger officer—his stomach spilling out over the waist of his pants, hiding his utility belt—stormed toward me. His beard was patchy and his cheeks were swollen, like a lugubrious clown. He grabbed my arm and shoulder, spun me around, and slammed me face-first into the wall. My cheekbone screamed with pain, and the taste of copper filled my mouth.

"What the hell?" I snapped, my agitation unmistakable.

"Shut the fuck up and put your hands behind your back," he roared. His breath smelled like rancid beef jerky. The tremor in his voice gave him away. This man wasn't tough—he was thrilled. This was his moment. Finally, he wasn't the bullied kid at recess; he was the big man with power. I held my breath and complied. He cuffed my wrists, wrenching my arms just high enough to hurt, but not enough to break me.

"I know for a fact I haven't done anything wrong, so what gives?" I asked, genuinely confused.

"You'll find out soon enough," he replied, his smug grin making it clear that in his mind, this story already had a heroic ending—with him as the star.

My mind churned. What could this be about? Did someone on the outside grease palms to make my hell a little hotter? He dragged me down a few floors like a dog on a leash, dumped me in front of a steel-mesh holding cage, and shoved me inside with so much force that my teeth split the inside of my mouth again. Blood pooled slowly on my tongue.

"You're a real piece of work," I muttered, tasting iron.

"Need tissues?" he sneered. "Enjoy your new accommodations."

I sat there for hours, confusion thickening with each passing minute. I started to wonder if I had done something wrong without realizing it. Why else would they be treating me this way? Eventually, the door to the office across the hall from the cage creaked open and I realized where I was: outside the lieutenant's office. That, at least, clarified things. This wasn't casual. This was deliberate.

The LT unlocked the cage, beckoned me inside his office, and gestured for me to sit. His dark eyes scanned me like prey. His pants were tucked into his boots, but he didn't carry himself with the tidiness of someone who'd actually worn a real military uniform. I got the sense he had watched too many movies.

"What happened to your face?" he asked, nodding at my lip and taking a seat.

"Bit it. One of those days," I answered robotically.

He didn't press. If anything, he seemed relieved, as if my answer had saved him paperwork. Instead, he went straight to the point and tossed a Ziploc bag across the desk. Inside was a small mound of white powder. His movements in his chair betrayed his excitement. He looked like a guy who thought he'd finally caught his big fish.

He licked his lips while he waited for my reaction, reminding me of a child waiting to open a birthday present. I met his eyes and said nothing, a slight sense of pity rising in me.

"Well?" he pushed.

My eyes shifted from his to the bag. That's when it clicked. He thought this was Pablo Escobar's lost stash. I could practically see the barbecue stories forming in his head—how he and his staff took down the big, dangerous inmate in a major drug bust: burgers, beers, and high-fives over their "once-in-a-lifetime" moment of real law enforcement glory.

"Well, what? What do you want me to say?" I asked, calm but irritated. *They busted my face for this?*

"First, I want to know how you got this into my facility." He leaned forward, palms on his desk, trying to appear intimidating. All I noticed were his long fingernails, with dirt under them. Messy.

"I ordered it. It was delivered. Pretty basic stuff, actually."

"Don't be coy with me, asshole. You're in a lot of trouble."

"Coy?"

A smirk crept across his face. "What, too stupid to know what that means?"

There are always a few ways you can play a situation like this, but my frustration narrowed me to one.

"No, I know what it means," I said. "I just wouldn't describe my conduct as 'coy.' I'd say I'm being sardonic. There's a difference."

He blinked. He didn't know the word.

"What, not smart enough to know that one?" I added. I knew I was inviting more trouble, but at that point, I didn't care. "Look, if you have a problem with the bag in front of me, maybe you should stop your officers from selling it to us."

The smirk vanished. So did the fake interrogation stance. His face went white—anger turning to nerves.

"What?" he muttered.

He grabbed his phone before I could answer. "I need you down here. Now," he said, then hung up. Seconds later, Buzz Cut from SIS walked in. Sharp blue eyes. Ex-military written all over his posture. He didn't waste time. "Which one of my officers sold this to you?" he asked.

"Not sure," I said. "I'm not good at remembering all your names yet. I haven't been here long."

His jaw tightened. "Could you identify him from a picture?"

"Probably."

"How much did you pay him?" By then, he was seated, taking notes in a small notebook. Playtime was over—for him, at least. For me, I was just done. Done with their incompetence, done with the throbbing pain in my mouth.

"I'm not one hundred percent sure," I said, "but I think it was two dollars and fifteen cents."

They both stared at me, blankly.

"What did you expect me to say?" I continued. "The lavender baby powder on commissary isn't exactly wholesale cocaine."

Their expressions turned to confusion. I went on.

"Go ahead. Smell it. You never have playing cards in stock, but when we finally get them, they get old and start to stick. So we throw them in a bag with baby powder, shake it up, and it keeps them from sticking for a while."

Buzz Cut looked over at the now-embarrassed LT, then cracked open the bag, sniffed, and tossed it back down. Baby powder. Exactly like I said. Whatever barbecue-story fantasy they had going evaporated on the spot.

"Take him back," the LT ordered, voice flat.

The walk back to the elevator with SIS was silent until we got inside, and then he tried to save face.

"You know, you're lucky you're not in trouble. You can't be doing that," he said.

"What? Using baby powder on cards?"

"Putting it in a bag like that. It can only be used in its containers."

A million responses ran through my head. I settled for the one I didn't say out loud: Next time I'll sprinkle it directly onto the cards so none of your officers get confused.

Back on the unit, the door clanged shut behind me. *I can't believe that just happened,* I thought. And yet in prison, "believable" has no place. These are the people running institutions. These are the people investigating serious matters. Why should anyone trust what they say? Most of them have trouble getting dressed in the morning.

This is why the American people don't trust the institutions surrounding our leaders. It's why so many didn't believe it when they told us Jeffrey Epstein killed himself in the Brooklyn detention center. The people I was dealing with here were the ones in charge of investigating what happened. Think about that for a moment—and remember that they are part of the entrenched power structure that impeached President Trump twice, tried to cancel his presidency, tried to kill him, bankrupt him, put him in their cells, and are still working day and night to remove him from the Oval Office.

What should scare you is not the idea that our president is hiding something from us, but that the deep state is hiding something from him. You should be terrified that the BOP was the first entity to "investigate" Epstein's death.

When news broke that Epstein had been found dead in his cell, neither I nor the public recoiled in shock. We nodded with grim recognition. It was an ending most of us expected—and that, too, should terrify you. The odds of that happening to an anonymous inmate are 1 in 10,000. This wasn't just some anonymous inmate. He was a man believed to hold damning secrets about some of the most powerful people in the world, who somehow ended up dead in one of the most secure jails in America, housed in the most protected, watched, and surveilled area.

Because of that, and because I have no confidence in BOP staff, I decided to do a deep dive into the records, eyewitness accounts, toxicology reports, and apparent procedural failures. I am uniquely positioned to view the situation from the inside looking out, which gives me a level of understanding the public doesn't have.

Let's start with the days leading up to his death. At the onset of his incarceration, Epstein complained of lower back pain, insomnia, and fear of living among the general population. Epstein—brilliant, manipulative, calculating—knew exactly how to game the system, just as he'd done years earlier in his Florida case. The first step in his plan (which is the plan of many who enter prison) was to secure medication that would help him sleep most of the days away. Those medications also ensure that you receive a bottom bunk pass and do not have to climb up to the top bunk. Epstein's complaints weren't casual; they were strategic. He was a billionaire pedophile surrounded by people who saw him as prey, and to solve this "problem," he did what manipulators do best: he gamed the system.

He started with psychology, convincing them to prescribe medications to help him sleep. He was given Mirtazapine (Remeron) and Trazodone, both heavy sedatives that would knock a man out for most of the day. Any inmate will tell you: a single dose of Remeron can put a grown man down like a tranquilized animal. Combined with Trazodone, even an elephant wouldn't wake until the afternoon. It's a potent combination. Once that first issue was "resolved," the red flags began to pile up.

On July 23, 2019, Epstein was found semi-conscious in his cell with minor injuries to his neck. The ambiguous nature and minor severity of those injuries made it highly unlikely that a serious suicide attempt was the cause. Still, out of "an abundance of caution," he was placed on suicide watch while officials tried to figure out what happened.

At first, investigators suspected that maybe he'd been assaulted by his cellmate, Nicholas Tartaglione, a former police officer facing multiple homicide charges. Tartaglione denied it and, through his lawyer, claimed he had tried to help Epstein after finding him like that. Video evidence seemed to support his version: he was seen entering and leaving the cell, and to this day, no one can say with certainty what really happened.

But insiders knew this wasn't a man trying to die. If a mind like Epstein's genuinely wanted to kill himself, he would have taken a razor blade from commissary, gone to the shower, pulled the curtain closed, sat in a chair, slit his wrists with the water running, and gone unnoticed for hours. No, what he did was resolve his second problem—removing himself from threats in the general population by staging an "incident."

While on suicide watch for six days, Epstein showed no signs of suicidal ideation. After each interaction, the psychology staff recorded, "No apparent suicidal ideation present." He was then moved to protective custody in the SHU with a cellmate, and that remained his situation until Friday, August 9, 2019. That evening, Epstein's cellmate was suddenly removed from the cell—arguably the most significant event of all. SHU meetings are held early in the week when staff decide who will be released back to the general population. Everyone knows that if you're not out of SHU before 2 p.m. on Thursday, you're not getting out that week. No one gets released from SHU on a Friday evening unless something significant happens. Ever.

There was no altercation between Epstein and his cellmate. No hospital runs. No significant incident occurred in the population that required urgent bed space for a wave of incoming inmates. No riots. No massive fights nor any event requiring large-scale movement. None of that happened.

Once again, Epstein's cellmate being removed on a Friday night is another 1-in-10,000 scenario. So I ask: What are the odds of all these "coincidences" stacking on top of each other?

To make it worse, we're told the two guards on shift "fell asleep" and falsified their logs. The security camera failed, and footage was lost right around the time Epstein died. It's hard to find another example of that happening with any inmate, much less the most high-profile inmate in federal custody at the time.

We're supposed to believe this is all coincidence?

When the autopsy was completed, Dr. Michael Baden, a seasoned forensic pathologist, stated that Epstein's broken hyoid bone was consistent with manual strangulation—not hanging. That's not speculation; that's medical observation. The type of neck fractures Epstein had is rarely seen in suicidal hangings. That's why I focus so much on the word "hanging."

This isn't *The Shawshank Redemption*, where Brooks carves his name into a beam, ties a rope, and kicks the chair away. Epstein was roughly six feet tall. He could touch the ceiling of his cell with his hands. From where exactly was he supposed to hang himself in a way that produced the necessary drop and force to snap those bones? From a bunk that only reached his chest? He would have had to hang himself in a position where his legs still touched the floor. Wouldn't the body's natural fight-or-flight reflex kick in? Are we expected to believe he calmly waited for his own strangulation to complete?

Many conservative commentators now argue that Epstein probably committed suicide, asking, "Why would they want to kill him? They arrested him for a reason." But that's the wrong question. The right question is: Who stood to lose the most if Epstein talked?

Epstein wasn't just a predator. He was a gatekeeper. He had names, photos, videos. He had an island. The kind of evidence that could take down billionaires, politicians, royals, celebrities, and intelligence operators across continents. That's why the story that he simply "gave up" never passed the smell test. The math doesn't work.

What does make sense—cold, chilling sense—is this: Once Epstein handed his enemies the perfect cover story of a "depressed man on suicide watch," their window began to close. At some point, someone got into his cell, in the perfect window of time, while the cameras were "down," and strangled him. Under the influence of Remeron and Trazodone, he wouldn't have put up much of a fight. The whole act could've taken under a minute.

Unless, of course, we are to believe Epstein was the one inmate in existence who could shrug off that pharmaceutical cocktail, stay awake for hours, and then somehow engineer his own hanging under those conditions.

The love for President Trump is real, which is why the Epstein story isn't hurting his popularity. But it has lit a slow-burning fuse beneath American political life—a wick winding its way toward something unpredictable, possibly explosive.

This is why MAGA supporters won't let it go. It's not because they're aligning with the Left's narrative—far from it. It's because they remember the lies, the setups, the dossiers, the leaks, the betrayals. And now, as Trump battles again for the soul of the nation, his supporters are scanning the battlefield for traps, and Epstein feels like one of the biggest. They care just as much about protecting the man they elected as he cares about protecting the American people.

Having gone through what I have, I understand better than most: The truth does not always get its day in the sun. If you want it, you have to dig. You have to be willing to go deeper than the official story, to question the institutions and the people running them, because if you don't, they will happily bury the truth—and you along with it.

# *Chapter Forty-One*
# Divided We Fall

Nothing can prepare you for the first time entering a federal detention center, where you are in the Penumbra of existence. You might try to imagine it, perhaps inspired by media reports, movies, or infamous cases like Jeffery Epstein or Sean "Diddy" Combs, but you would epically fail.

I was transported from trial to FDC Philadelphia with my ankles bleeding from being shackled too tightly and found myself standing in an elevator, heading to the unknown. The doors opened to the Receiving and Discharge department, a preposterous name for what it is.

"Welcome to Telladelphia. Don't talk about your case," barked the correctional officer (CO) as he herded me into a changing room.

"What does that mean?" I asked, green as the grass outside.

"Most people here are cooperating with the government, trying to reduce their sentence. Keep your mouth shut if you don't want someone jumping on your case and ratting you out to the feds."

"Got it, thank you," I replied, trying to mask my unease.

"Good. Now strip and place all your belongings in the box next to you."

The demand came with an irritation reserved for dealing with rookies. I hesitated, removing my clothes piece by piece and placing them in the cardboard box provided. When I stopped at my boxers, the CO's voice snapped again. "Socks and underwear, too. Let's go! I don't have all day."

Awkwardly, I obeyed, feeling exposed in every sense of the word. There's something uniquely degrading about being completely naked in front of a stranger who is inspecting you like livestock.

The CO was annoyed that I didn't know the procedure, and the instructions worsened. "Come on, moron, ears, let's see behind them. Mouth. Tongue up. Arms up, I need to see your armpits. And your junk, go ahead and lift it so I can see under." The humiliation was nearly unbearable, but I complied, gritting my teeth through the barrage of commands. This was his job? I wanted to ask him: Is this the dream you had as a kid? Looking at penis after penis all day? But I held my tongue. Nothing good would come from it.

"Turn around. Bend over. Cough and stay bent," he continued. The indignity peaked as he shined a flashlight into a place I'd rather not acknowledge, checking for contraband in what I later learned inmates call "the prison wallet." It was both surreal and sobering.

Once I was stripped of every shred of dignity, blood still trickling from my ankles, I was handed an institution uniform and instructed to bring my personal belongings to the front desk so the officer could ship them home. The noise from the holding tanks behind me was deafening, sounding like competing packs of wolves fighting over a freshly killed carcass. In the mix, I heard laughter. Guys were having fun?

"Put him in that tank over there with the other whites," the property officer said without hesitation, gesturing to a smaller cell with fewer than ten inside. The statement hit me hard. It was the first time in my life I encountered racial segregation. Up until that moment, I believed the Equal Protection Clause of the Fourteenth Amendment was immutable, a shield against this being possible or allowed. But here, clearly, the rules were going to be different.

In theory, racial segregation shouldn't happen. In practice, it's a grim necessity and an area where the law allows an exemption. As Chief Justice Roberts once observed, "In the context of racial violence in prison, courts can ask whether temporary racial segregation of inmates will prevent harm." This isn't just policy; it is survival. This exemption to the law has become standard practice. I quickly recognized that every behavioral pattern that seemed backward to my world directly results from what is occurring in society on the outside, despite the world choosing to be willfully blind.

Prison, I would learn, is a magnifying glass, exposing the ugliest rot in our society, that which is being intentionally camouflaged by the ruling class in America. I, too, wore blinders.

The tank was frigid, like a meat locker. Like a piece of meat hanging in that locker, I sat there for hours, waiting for Rocky Balboa to come in and beat on me. Conversations hummed around me, and I sat, raw with shock. I tucked my arms into my shirt for warmth. Was the staff freezing us on purpose? It certainly felt that way. I tried to pass the time by listening to the other men swap stories. Their words hinted at a world I didn't know yet.

The intake officers finally decided where to house each of us. It was a calculated process, factoring in gang affiliations, known disputes, and the ever-present specter of informants. They could not risk placing someone in a lion's den, where enemies awaited. It was a game of human chess, and I was the newest pawn.

FDC Philly is eight stories high and has two separate housing units on each floor. After six hours in the tank, I was assigned to 6 South. Entering the housing unit late at night was another whirlwind of discomfort. All eyes turned to me as I walked in, their gaze stripping me bare once again. Per standard practice, my ID card pointed me toward a cell already occupied by another white inmate.

When I found my cell, I was bombarded by questions from other inmates. Each wanted to know who I was and why I had been locked up. They became more intrigued when they discovered that I had been locked up in the middle of my trial. Many now offered me things, wanting to be my best friend. "Welcome to Telladelphia," I remembered.

I was physically and mentally drained. My new cellmate was surprisingly kind, recognizing my exhaustion. "Hey man," he said, "I have to ask you this before you get settled."

"What's up?" I asked.

"Are you a Chomo?"

"What is a Chomo?" I asked, confused.

"It's a sex offender. You know, a child molester—hence, Chomo."

"Oh, okay. Sorry. I didn't know what the hell you were talking about. No, I am fighting bogus mail fraud and wire fraud charges and clearly not doing a very good job," I responded.

"No one does. I know today has been rough, and I'm not going to lie, it doesn't get easier, but go ahead and put your stuff away, shut down the lights, and get some sleep. We'll be locked in for the night soon anyway."

Despite his reassurance, sleep didn't come easily. The mattress felt like a slab of stone; the floor of my house would be more comfortable. I had not been provided with a blanket or bedroll, and the air conditioning was pumping in the cell—another meat locker. I lay awake for hours, tossing and turning until finally exhaustion took over. I fell into a disturbed sleep and dreamt a dream that rocked me to my core.

I was out walking my dog down a dimly lit, eerie street. Other dog owners walked alongside me, each in their own world. The air was thick with unease. My dog, usually leashed, was not, but stayed close to me. It was as if no one was aware of anyone else, and the dogs ignored each other, sniffing their own patches of grass, mine wagging his tail in innocent curiosity.

Out of nowhere, a voice shouted, "Everyone line up on the side of the road now, and don't move."

We obeyed, forming a silent line. My dog ran to my side excitedly, looking back up at me, waiting for me to give him his next command. A group of menacing figures, accompanied by monstrous white pit bulls, came down the road. These dogs were unnatural, their rage bleeding through their eyes, making Cujo look like an innocent pup.

A voice rang out again when they started to pass us. "Nobody moves."

We stood frozen, hoping they would pass by without conflict. Each one of us breathed a sigh of relief as they passed. As they approached, the fact that my dog was without a leash came to mind. Anxiety filled my heart. I looked down at him with worry, while he still looked back up at me with excitement, awaiting orders. As soon as our eyes met, he became aware of what was approaching, and his curiosity betrayed him. Ignoring my commands to heel, he approached the group, tail wagging. The pits attacked.

Sensing the danger, my dog tried to run away, but they were all over him, biting viciously. My dog's cries shattered me, but I knew it was too dangerous for me to interfere. I was powerless. Blood stained the streets as the pits tore into him, and the owners laughed. Finally, they called their beasts off, continuing as if nothing had happened, leaving me to gather the broken pieces of my companion. I was heartbroken and lost. All I could think was that I had to get him to the vet.

I helped him up, and we started walking, but I had no idea where I was or where I was going. We were all trapped on this dark street without an end or beginning. I was leading him nowhere.

I noticed he was having a difficult time walking. His limp was dramatic, so I walked around him to examine his other side, and that was when I saw he was missing a leg. The pits had chewed it off. Guilt consumed me, and I didn't want him to have to suffer through the pain of walking anymore, so I leaned down to pick him up in my arms. As I did, he yelped in pain and defensively bit my arm.

The bite jolted me awake. My cell was still cold, but I was drenched in sweat. I lay there, haunted by the vividness of the dream. I'd never been one to analyze dreams, but this one felt significant, a metaphor for the trials ahead. I then knew the road I was walking had no end or beginning. The dread within reverberated.

## *Chapter Forty-Two*

# A Better Way

The pervasive racial divide inside prison walls is not just a reflection of individual prejudice but the magnified product of policies enacted in society. It serves as an unfiltered lens, exposing tribalism that our government perpetuates to consolidate its power. I seek to help you understand all this because I aim to enlist you in the fight to dismantle it.

Why haven't we, as a people, demanded policies that foster unity rather than division? Our collective failure to do so has only allowed stereotypes to grow stronger, sowing distrust, resulting in a society that views individuals through a narrow lens of race rather than a broad spectrum of merit. If our nation's leaders genuinely cared about "equity," they wouldn't focus on racial distinction. Their goal would be to move beyond it and prioritize building a future where success is determined by ability, effort, and opportunity.

When was the last time you consumed news that wasn't drenched in discussions of race, gender, and identity? We need to detach ourselves from this divisive framework. The fight for equality, I believe, has already been won on paper. What remains is for the American people to enforce that victory, paving the way for a more harmonious, stable, and inspiring society.

In the previous chapter, I cited parts of an opinion by Chief Justice Roberts.[1] This case is important because it provides the framework for why I believe we have already won the fight.

---

1 The case I was referring to was Students for Fair Admissions, Inc. v. President and Fellows of Harvard College 600 us 181;143S. Ct. 2141; 216L. Ed. 2d857; 2023 Nos. 20-1199 and 21-707.

The court's opinion reaffirms that discrimination violates the Equal Protection Clause of the Fourteenth Amendment, and when that act is committed by an institution that accepts federal funds, it also constitutes a violation of Title VI of the Civil Rights Act of 1964. This is important because the Constitution of the United States is not a suggestion. It is the law. And yet, look around. Our society does not reflect this ideal. Instead, it consistently draws lines between people, reducing them to categories.

Our government thrives on these divisions, wielding them as tools to maintain control, but to a free people, a distinction based solely on ancestry is anathema to liberty and, by its very nature, odious to the institutions founded on the doctrine of equality. Racial balancing is patently unconstitutional, and our government is required under the law to treat everyone as individuals, not as simple components of a racial, religious, or social class.

The implications of this ruling are vast and hold the whole government bound to it. Do not all our government institutions exist with federal funding? Is it not our tax dollars that pay for the entire party? In my view, the Supreme Court has made it abundantly clear. "Given the Constitution, in the eyes of the law, there is no superior, dominant, ruling class of citizens in this country. There is no caste. The Constitution is color-blind and neither knows nor tolerates classes among citizens." Thus, our government and institutions, funded by our hard-earned tax dollars, must also be color-blind.

Our government must be stripped of its wandering eyes to see only two distinctions among its people: citizen and non-citizen. It must be a government that neither knows nor cares about your race, gender, religion, or sexual orientation. A government that is incapable of bias because it sees only the person, not the category. This is not some utopian fantasy; no, it is a legal obligation waiting to be enforced.

It's not a secret that many who work in government are easily corrupted, and racial biases within the workforce are inherent in the decision-making processes, which always leads to resentment and polarization rather than the cooperative spirit needed to tackle common challenges. If we want our elected officials' choices to focus on our shared humanity, we must force them to be color-blind. Otherwise, they will continue to enact policies that favor one group over another, maintain control of your lives, and perpetuate the cycle of division and resentment. This is the same cycle amplified in prison, making the possibility of rehabilitating impossible.

Enforcing this change would dismantle systematic barriers that hinder individuals of all races, paving the way for a more equitable society. Is this not the change their propaganda claims to want? I say we go ahead and give it to them because it is within the people's power to make it a reality.

A color-blind government would be handcuffed into prioritizing equality, meritocracy, and unity, which will unite America. Any government focusing on shared human values and individual ability generally serves the people's best interest. Who do you know in your life that would object to such an approach? Every decade since 1776, our country has continually become more racially and ethnically diverse. There is only one way to address the needs of an evolving population fairly: to DEMAND that its government is color-blind. The path to an equitable society is not through forced balancing but by removing artificial barriers.

The census, for example, should ask only one question: Are you a citizen? Why does the government need to know anything more? By now, I trust you can answer this question. The fact is the data collected in past censuses has been taken and used in terrible ways. It has been weaponized for political gain against the people it claims to serve. Is it not unconstitutional to classify citizens based on race when the purpose of doing so is directly to undermine the principle of equality?

During a recent political conversation, someone attempted to challenge this idea and my thinking. "Well, what about black neighborhoods with high crime? Without knowing it is a black neighborhood, how would anyone know the type of help that neighborhood needs?" he questioned. "This," I said, "is exactly the problem. Why is this a 'black' neighborhood? Why is it not an American neighborhood? I believe it needs to be seen through a totally different lens. Suppose crime is seen as too high in any *American* neighborhood. In that case, the government needs to look at the surrounding areas with a higher budget and lower crime statistics and reallocate funding, providing those resources to law enforcement in the area where it is needed so they can work to lower the crime rate. The ethnicity of the people residing in that neighborhood should not matter, nor should the potential exist where racial bias could enter the decision-making process regarding those resources. Bias makes it possible for someone to ignore the problem."

I was able to watch in real time as his opinion changed. This sort of reframing is crucial. By transcending racial lines, we strip the government of its ability to manipulate and control us through an amorphous concept of injury. We cannot allow them to continue to justify racial classifications on our citizens and impose disadvantages on people who bear no responsibility for whatever harm the beneficiaries of their policies have suffered. We must fight for a government that serves humanity over division because together, we have the power to create a society worthy of the ideals on which it was founded. Call me a radical, but I think what would best serve the nation would be for us to do things differently than an inmate population.

# *Chapter Forty-Three*
# And So, I Changed

In all my years of suffering, one thing always remained clear. Love was the thread that held me together in the moments I felt I was going to fall apart, and it is because of this that I spent many nights contemplating love and its complexities. I understood so little about it, yet knew that it was why I was still moving forward in this life.

Given that love and relationships significantly impact health and success, the urgency of teaching about love as rigorously as we teach math and science cannot be overstated. Imagine the potential of challenging our children's minds by contrasting Gandhi's belief in nonviolent love with Nietzsche's idea of loving with your whole heart and killing anything that tried to hurt what you love. This could open discussions and lessons that are currently overlooked. Exploring love through science could provide profound insights into neurobiology, attachment theory, and conflict resolution and teach essential communication techniques. Enhancing our understanding of human behavior and emotions and fostering self-awareness is crucial at a time when relationships in America are faltering, and infidelity and isolation are rampant.

Unfortunately, our public education system falls short of providing meaningful guidance on this crucial aspect of life. Some schools still dissect *Romeo and Juliet* in an archaic manner, not to understand love but to serve as a cautionary tale of love's potential to inspire destruction and tragedy. This is a far cry from the proper roadmap our youth deserve.

Many of the greatest philosophical minds in history have gone to great lengths to explain love in a way that deepens our ability to comprehend different cultural interpretations. Developing our children's ability to delve within and aspire to self-growth and self-development to inspire wonderful human connections and relationships is a lofty cause. These lessons would strengthen their analytical and reflective skills, sharpen their reasoning, and increase their ability to make more accurately calculated decisions in their lives and relationships, an area social media has hijacked and is destroying.

Much like the examination of God, the greatest minds in human history have contemplated the complexities of love. Plato, Aristotle, Erich Fromm, Rainer Maria Rilke, Sigmund Freud, C. S. Lewis, Carl Jung, and Alfred Adler all spent a lifetime attempting to understand and explain love, sharing what they learned with the world, offering incredible insight but, in many cases, leaving behind more questions than answers. Why are we not passing down their work to our children so they can fill these missing pieces on attachment and its evolution? Our ability to feel for another is intertwined with our desire, our consciousness, early childhood experience, and sexual instincts.

Prominent anthropologist and researcher on love Helen Fisher says, "Romantic love is a powerful force in human life, but one that we do not fully understand yet." Love is not something we have control over, and every attempt to explain it logically highlights it as a paradoxical force coated with endless wisdom and learning potential. Why are we not teaching it? Without understanding, we are nothing more than the blind in the woods—navigating by our other senses, unable to see the road ahead. The interplay of biological impulses, personal history, and emotional fulfillment becomes too much to balance, making successful integration nearly impossible. Learning that love is a choice you're willing to make and that it requires effort, discipline, education, and a willingness to grow is imperative for the survival of our nation. Yet, as a society, we've relegated love to the realm of the abstract, failing to equip ourselves or our children with the tools to understand and nurture it, when doing so is of great importance. Yes, there is still so much we do not know which begs the question, why would we teach children about something we know so little about? We teach children what we know about the universe, something we know even less about, but it inspires future generations to want to explore the stars, learning more than the generation before.

Love is not just a personal endeavor; it is a societal necessity. When we educate ourselves about love, we strengthen the foundation of our humanity. Fostering real, meaningful love has the potential to create a more connected, compassionate, and whole world, offering a hopeful vision for the future.

For much of my life, love felt like an enigma, a more poetic than practical concept. I felt an emotional risk, choosing to guard my heart instead because I didn't realize love requires feelings, effort, discipline, and self-awareness. Without these, it's easy to mistake the thrill of infatuation for the depths of connection, leaving us floundering when the waters get rough.

Deep within, intellectually, I sought growth. As a result, I understood that love, as a form of social interest, is built on mutual respect, a sense of belonging, and cooperation, ultimately leading to a greater connection. Plato once said, "At the touch of love, everyone becomes a poet." Beautiful, yes, but an emotion I had yet to understand. The idea of one soul existing within two bodies seemed like a fantasy. I could not see how a person could balance personal autonomy while experiencing a deep emotional connection with another. This had not been a topic of conversation in my whole life.

One of my favorite and once famously profound examples of love has been lost in the pages of history: the love between President John Adams and his wife, Abigail. Despite years of separation due to the revolution and his work in diplomacy, their love always found a way to endure, captured in over 1,100 letters they sent to one another. Those letters revealed that their love was rooted in mutual respect and affection. Abigail was not only his wife but also his confidante, counselor, and equal. In John Adams's words, Abigail was his "ballast and solace." Their enduring and steadfast love reassures us that love can weather any storm. John Adams could never have achieved what he did for himself or the fledgling United States without her love, steadfast support, and wisdom. Their partnership, captured in those letters, is a testament to love's capacity to inspire greatness not through grand gestures but through quiet, unwavering commitment. Their relationship sets a standard for marriages in America, blending personal affection with a shared sense of purpose.

Love's unpredictability and timing are among its most perplexing traits. A single person can walk into your life and change everything about it, carrying that transformative power across even the most substantial roadblocks; we must know how to receive it when it comes. This is why we must start teaching our society, especially our children, how to recognize, nurture, and cherish love. It is fragile, yet there is nothing more precious. Alfred Adler once said, "To love and to be loved is to feel the sun from both sides," so let's prepare our children to embrace it. Let's prepare them so that entrance into their life doesn't end with a sunburn.

# *Chapter Forty-Four*
# I Love You All

Over the years, people who have witnessed my journey in any capacity are often perplexed, wondering how I have maintained my sense of self. How did I not lose my mind? How is it that I did not change to become either mad or jaded?

There is no formula for resilience, and change is inevitable. It's impossible to witness endless acts of brutality day in and day out and not be changed by it. It's thoroughly challenging to watch a man remove cooking oil from a microwave and throw it on another man's face, melting the skin off like wax. It's gut-wrenching to see a man chat on the phone with his wife and moments later slit his own throat (she was leaving him for another man). Witnessing many horrific events, I knew change was unavoidable. The unknown I sat with was: How will it change me?

I was determined to control the change—as best as I was able—and my journey of digging deep, exposing my genuine self, and dedicating myself to what I hold true, saved me. I demanded everything of myself. I asked myself hard questions, converted the stumbles into challenges, and explored tirelessly in search of meaning. I stopped comparing myself to my fellow man and led the comparison against my former self. I shifted my perspective from continuing to navigate difficulties to becoming the solution. Meaning and purpose entered my life because I ushered them in. In the darkest places, I was able to find some light, and that light became the compass that guided me through the darkest storms, helping me rise above the swell instead of being sucked down in the undertow. Meaning and purpose became the engine that propelled me forward.

As every engine needs fuel, mine did, as well.

Love, being profound and mysterious, is one of the most influential and enigmatic forces of the human experience. It can inspire extraordinary selflessness and overcome even the most unimaginable hardships. Love transcends time, space, and reason, offering both joy and pain, and is the force that connects humanity to something greater than us. It is the thread that ties us together, stretching beyond logic and explanation. Having kept poets in business for thousands of years, love is not a human invention but a divine bestowal. The longing to be with those we love is the essence of our humanity, the fuel that can ignite an engine like nothing else can, as it did mine.

The fuel for my engine was love, an emotion that would have remained a mystery for me if not for my time incarcerated, which forced me to feel the entire human spectrum of emotions.

The love a parent has for a child is perhaps the most selfless form of love. It drives countless sacrifices. Parents will give up comfort, dreams, and even life itself to ensure the safety and happiness of their children. If you are a parent, like I am, you already know this intimate instinct that awakens within, the one that would have you step in front of a bullet without hesitation. I've been blessed with a family that embodies unconditional love and unwavering support. They have stood by me through every trial (literally and figuratively) and every triumph.

My father, before losing his battle with cancer, was my unshakable foundation. There wasn't a moment when I couldn't rely on his wisdom or guidance. One unassuming afternoon the month before his illness showed its presence, he came to see me at FDC Philly. Having witnessed the injustice of my trial for himself, he carried the unbearable weight of knowing he couldn't protect me from what had happened. It broke his heart. Still, he resolved to be there for me in every way he could. At that time, I was drowning in the emotional torment of knowing my children would grow up without me. The pain was consuming me. On this visit, he told me, "You're going to have to turn everything off, son. You must go deep inside and shut it all down to survive this. Don't let yourself feel the pain." He never spoke of it directly, but I knew that the wisdom he was passing on to me at that moment came from his experience surviving his service in Vietnam. Those words kept me from breaking completely.

My mother has been a pillar of love and resilience, loving me unconditionally and remaining the cornerstone of my support system. Despite her struggles, she never wavered in her devotion to my brother and me. We were never forgotten. Never was an event in our lives missed. Never did we not have what we needed. I know I inherited my strength to survive from her. The same unconditional love and strength defined my grandmother as well.

Like many siblings, my brother and I had a complicated relationship growing up, but as we matured, so did our relationship, and we became best friends. When my world started to fall apart, he didn't hesitate. He sacrificed everything, even his career and home, to step in and help manage my life and business when they locked me away during my trial. Piece by piece, he worked to keep things from collapsing entirely, even knowing it would be impossible to sustain it all without me. His love for me was boundless. When the chips were down, he put my needs above his own, even at a significant personal cost, because that's what love demands: sacrifice. Over the years, I leaned on his strength and wisdom when I needed to, sharpened by his battles and the horrors of war. He would share his insight freely, never judging my request for it.

But the love and support from your family come with a unique sort of pain. Their sorrow mirrors your own, and their lives are disrupted by the chaos you bring into theirs. The shared anguish becomes a reminder of how deeply joy and suffering are intertwined. I was dragging my family into my hell, and I was being pulled into theirs. I felt myself falling into the abyss, darkness taking over my existence, but then fate put my very own Abigail Adams in my path.

I don't believe it is a coincidence that love broke through my defenses when I expected it least and needed it most. It came as a balm, healing wounds and illuminating parts of me I didn't know existed. For the first time, I understood what poets and philosophers have been describing for centuries: love's power to transform and connect us to something divine.

Shortly after my father was hospitalized and well before my sentencing, I met Sheva. At the time, I was at my lowest, grieving and directionless. She, too, was navigating a significant transitional phase in her life. The odds of us entering one another's life felt as unlikely as being struck by lightning, and the practical connection was just as rare. Through mutual acquaintances, Sheva was exposed to an idea of mine. Sheva's intellectual curiosity was piqued and she wanted to meet "the man with that brain."

And so, one day, I emailed her. I applied radical transparency, and her response matched. Little did we know that this would be the start of our exchange of 1,100(+) letters to each other.

Ranier Maria Rilke once wrote, "Love consists of this: two solitudes that meet, protect, and greet each other." That was us two distinct souls finding unity in trust and shared purpose. I made her a stronger person, and she made me a better one. In *The Symposium*, Plato discussed a profound longing for the divine, the ideal, and intellectual growth, and this was the journey Sheva and I embarked on together. Our never-ending conversations began with emails, followed by phone conversations, and then visits. We talked deeply about everything—life, business, philosophy, politics, and theology—one soul, mind, and vision being shared. We built a bond rooted in mutual respect, understanding, honesty, and transparency, no matter how uncomfortable. It was a radical experiment for both of us, but it became the foundation of a connection unlike any I or she have ever known.

In his book *The Four Loves*, C. S. Lewis discusses love in its various forms: affection, romance, friendship, and selflessness, which Sheva and I experienced simultaneously, transforming us both. She became my anchor in the storm, the calm voice in my chaos, and the driving force when I felt like giving up. Even when the hardship of my journey, at times, separated us, our connection never faded. It could always transcend time and space, teaching us both the meaning of unconditional love. I know I would not have survived what I have without it, and no matter where life takes me, I know that love and its impact will forever be etched into my heart.

For myself, love changed what I wanted out of life and became a goal I believe every person can adopt for themselves if they strive to make their life meaningful. I no longer desire material gain or think that path carries meaning. What I desire now and what I will spend my life trying to achieve is this: I hope to one day walk into a theater and stand on stage while everyone else is standing in ovation, cheering, acknowledging not me, but something great I have done that has made the world a better place. This day may never come, but the lifelong quest to accomplish it will ensure my most meaningful life. Like all of you, I have no clue what the future has in store for me. Life always has a plan of its own and never shows you what's just around the bend. What I do know, what I am sure of, is that I am finally able to face the future and will be doing so as the best version of myself. I hope you all join me.

# Epilogue

For over twelve long years, I have waited. Twelve years of dragging myself through the jagged edges of a broken judicial system, one that the BOP mirrors with a cold and unyielding face. It's a machine that runs on the cruel philosophy of hurry up and wait—grinding men down until even their patience becomes another form of punishment. That it has taken over a decade to reach the end of a fight that began before my trial even started is itself the clearest testament that justice in America is not only delayed but deliberately deformed. And as though fate hadn't already dealt me a heavy hand, my case was transferred from Judge Hillman to a newly appointed Biden judge, sealing the sense that the deck was stacked against me from the start.

I struggle to name a single thing Biden, or his administration, has done right. Their sole achievement was to open the doors for a Trump resurgence. The judges Biden appointed—clueless, arrogant, detached from reality—brought the overflow of ineptitude to the courts. I fought tooth and nail to avoid being dragged back to FDC Philadelphia, the very dungeon where it all began. The prosecutor wanted me to marinate in misery for as long as possible, but mostly he wanted me on the stand so he could try to butcher my character in public. The judge denied my request, fully aware that I didn't have to be present and that I would suffer the hell of transit in getting there.

Once again, there was no law to be seen in the courtroom. The scales weren't brought out to determine the strength of the argument or the weight of the law. Instead, I sat there on the stand listening to a prosecutor, who, twelve years later, was still frothing at the mouth at the chance to deface me.

Among the accused, there is an unspoken truth: guilt and innocence no longer matter. The facts don't matter. Once the federal government decides it wants you, it will get you. Simple as that. And so countless men accept plea deals—not because they are guilty, but because they know fighting is futile. They trade their dignity for a smaller sentence, not justice.

I never got that choice; the option of a plea, to consider at least, was not offered. The only map I was given had one destination stamped in bold letters: trial. Something that I then didn't question. I was innocent, and I intended to prove it to them, or so I thought.

After a hellish week shackled in transit, I was dumped back at FDC Philadelphia, the birthplace of my nightmare. I sat there for another month, stewing in the purgatory of waiting for my court date. When I was first placed back into the holding tank of R&D, it was as if time itself had folded in on me. The air smelled the same. The walls hummed with the same lifelessness. But the man sitting there was no longer the same. I was no longer a "green" first-timer. I have scars, both visible and invisible. I am hardened, shaped by a decade of battles most men wouldn't survive. Among the younger inmates, they now call me "old G" (which somehow translates to Original Gangster).

The first time you endure intake, it breaks you. You are stripped, searched, poked, and prodded, your dignity peeled away layer by layer. It feels like being processed as an object, not a human being. But this time, I hardly flinched. Once cleared, I was marched back to the sixth floor—the very unit where all this misery had first begun. The second I stepped onto that tier, everything stopped. Conversations froze. Dozens of eyes turned. In FDC, white faces are scarce; every new one sparks suspicion. But I now knew precisely what those stares meant.

The green intake jumpers were baggy, swallowing my frame, designed to erase body language and strip individuality. To anyone sizing me up, all they could see were my forearms and a disheveled mess of a man—dirty, drained, and unshaven from weeks of transport. And yet, as is always the case here, the assumption from many of the Black inmates was immediate: chomo. In this twisted microcosm, white skin often bore that stigma, and now it clung to me.

I hadn't been on the unit for five minutes before a parasite appeared. "Ah yo man, let me holla at you a minute," he sneered. He was a Yougot.

Everything about him reeked of bottom-feeder—the teardrop tattoo beneath his eye, a grin so wooden his smile gave you splinters. It was the kind of smile men wear when they think they've spotted prey. "Imma need some of your phone minutes each month, so we need to work something out," he demanded, his tone arrogant.

I was exhausted, raw from transit, and so without a word, I unbuttoned my jumper and rolled it down to my waist, freeing my arms and revealing a fitted brown t-shirt beneath. The fabric clung to my frame, muscles honed over years of forced survival, sending a silent message: push me and I will break you. I hated what this world forced me to become—but survival gave me no choice.

"Step inside the cell for a minute," I told him flatly. Reluctantly, he followed. I turned on him. "Boy, I don't know what game you're playing or who the fuck you think I am, but if you ever come at me like that again, you'll leave here in a stretcher. I'm not some fool fresh off the bus. I'm twelve years in, on a thirty-year bid, and I'm back here fighting to overturn my conviction."

The look in his eyes shifted. His bravado cracked. He realized I wasn't a target—I was an "old G."

"Shit, sorry man, I didn't know," he said.

"Didn't know what? You don't ask, you can't know. That's basic. And from the looks of you, I doubt you know how to tie your shoes, let alone read a man. News flash—you're a piece of shit. So, here's the deal: either we get it in right now, or you get the fuck out of my cell and never speak to me again."

This wasn't the street. He had no gun. No backup. Just me staring him down. He backed off.

"Good ol' Philly," I muttered under my breath.

A month crawled by in that place. I spent my days helping some kids gain perspective and understanding of their cases and their best options forward. Then, on the morning of June 10th, déjà vu struck me like a hammer: "Lacerda, court." Exact words, same ritual. Down to R&D. Shackled and chained like some monster. Loaded onto a US Marshals transport as though I were Hannibal Lecter himself.

At the courthouse, they shoved me into a holding cell. Alone. Cold. Hungry. Forgotten. I sat there from 8 a.m. until 2 p.m., hours dragging by in silence, my stomach hollow and my mind screaming. The walls radiated despair; every crack soaked with the ghosts of men who once prayed in vain. The stench was not just sweat—it was broken hearts, shattered families, dreams crushed into dust.

By the time the marshals finally came for me, I was exhausted, frayed at the edges—this is by design. They want you beaten down before you ever set foot in front of the judge. The moment I was led into the courtroom, the memory of my sentencing surged back. And there they were again—my loved ones—watching as I shuffled in, shackled like an animal on display. My chest burned, my throat tightened, but I fought to hold it together. Seconds later, the hearing began.

And the government unleashed hell.

Of course, my first lawyer was never going to advise me that it would be in my best interest to take a plea and cooperate against him as the government was arguing. No lawyer would do that. No lawyer would advocate for you to try to put them in jail. It's stupid to suggest anything else, which is why a plea was never explored at any point in my case. Hindsight is always 20/20, but the tragic irony is this: had he done so, I could at the very least have cooperated by firing him on the spot, thereby solving the very problem they claimed existed. Just that choice alone could have saved me years of torment. It would have given me a lawyer who worked for me, worked for my life and my future, instead of one paralyzed by self-preservation. A new lawyer could have explored a plea option rather than leaving me chained to a man fighting for himself instead of his client. During those critical months, who was working for me? No one. In the end, you already know the outcome: I went to trial with a lawyer who was woefully unprepared and had no clue how to defend me because the previous months before were spent representing his friend, not learning anything about the case.

But that is the point: none of this was revealed to me at the time. I was kept in the dark. This concealment—this sabotage—was at the very heart of my ineffective assistance of counsel claim, the very issue I now found myself testifying about at this hearing.

And yet, in a twist that could only happen in the circus of federal court, at my hearing, the government was now arguing the opposite position from the one they had once relied upon. The Assistant United States Attorneys (AUSA) brought in his former partner, now in private practice, to testify that she never opened a criminal investigation against him, and that the government would not have accepted cooperation from me on the matter in any event. I sat there stunned, confused. For over twelve years, I have immersed myself in the law, poring over it daily, committing cases to memory, learning how arguments shift and twist. And still, this felt different. This felt like the government was playing fast and loose, saying whatever they needed to say in the moment, rules and consistency be damned. How could they argue one position, win on it, and then turn around and argue the opposite side later? Would any judge allow such duplicity? Would a Biden judge?

You would think, given the circumstances, that the government's cross-examination of me would focus on this glaring issue—the heart of the hearing itself. But no. Instead, for over an hour, I was subjected to pure character assassination. Ad hominem attacks. Not a single question about the law. Not a single question about the actual issue. Just venom, projection, and an attempt to paint me as inherently corrupt. The prosecutor didn't focus on what I had ever been charged with. He didn't touch on the crimes brought before a jury. He avoided anything I might have had a chance to confront or cross-examine. Instead, he dredged up collateral allegations—uncharged, unproven—and twisted them into some grotesque caricature of obstruction. This was the playbook: if you can't win on the facts, destroy the man.

It was contentious. I refused to bow, refused to give legitimacy to lies. And that defiance became their weapon. Predictably, the judge ruled against me, writing that I had "not presented any evidence to show that counsel was motivated by his conflict when he did not discuss or explore an option to plea," and that my "assumptions and speculation about counsel's motives are not enough to warrant relief."

Pause for a moment. Judge Hillman, years earlier, had said the exact opposite. Quoting precedent, he ruled: "the government need not provide direct evidence so long as a reasonable factfinder could infer on his client's defense." But he had inferred exactly that when ruling in the government's favor, "given the mere possibility that he may face criminal or professional misconduct charges, it is certainly plausible that he could be consumed by his own self-preservation in proceeding forward as counsel rather than focusing on the client's defense." But now, this Biden judge rejected that standard entirely, saying inference was not enough. Two judges. Two polar opposite rulings. One man destroyed in the crossfire.

Let's be plain. Is it not reasonable to infer—as Hillman himself once did—that my lawyer, accused of potential criminal liability, might have avoided exploring a plea out of sheer self-preservation until the disqualification motion was resolved? Of course it is. But under this new judge, that reasoning was swept aside. Why? Because the outcome was predetermined.

Here is the truth, every word of which can be examined and verified:

The government's first line of attack was an accusation that one of my customer service representatives contacted a government witness—a supposed "victim" named EC. At the time, my company had five offices across multiple states, hundreds of employees, and thousands of calls each day. Our customer service team's job was simple: stay in contact with clients, guide them through the process, and follow up to ensure they weren't tricked again by the same predatory developers. EC was in our system as a successfully completed client. We had helped her get out of over $70,000 in debt and into a smaller, mortgage-free ownership. She was, by all accounts, someone we had helped.

One day, a rep came into my office and said, "Mr. Lacerda, I just got off the phone with a client listed as successful, but she's saying we failed to get her canceled out of debt, and she wants a refund. I told her I'd look into it and call her back."

"Did you upload the call into her file and task me?" I asked.

"No, I called from the office line, not the dialer," he admitted.

I was swamped, so I said, "Look, call her back. Verify everything she said before. Upload it. Task me. I'll review tonight."

He did. That night, I listened to the call. It was short, just two minutes of verification.

"When we first spoke, you said you were lied to by your developer and ended up in massive debt you couldn't afford. Is that correct?"

"Yes."

"You said you paid us to do a debt reduction deed replacement program, and that we promised to get you out of debt and into a smaller, fully paid ownership. Correct?"

"Yes."

"And you said earlier that we failed, and now you want a refund. Is that accurate?"

"Yes. I had to go to a debt consolidation company."

"Okay. I'll upload this. We'll review and get back to you."

"Thank you," she replied.

Does that sound like a scripted call? Later, the government coerced this rep into saying I had given him a script to obstruct justice. Nonsense. It was a verification call, nothing more.

And then I discovered something far more explosive in EC's file: an attachment labeled "Discovery File." Inside was an email several months old. It was from the very developer EC hired us to help her escape. The developer wrote: "We've decided to cancel your $71,569 debt. But do us a favor—don't tell VO." (VO was my company.) A smoking gun of collusion between the developer and the FBI. EC had been lying—pretending she was victimized while secretly freed from her debt and still trying to milk my company for a refund.

If I had truly been trying to obstruct justice, wouldn't I have paid her off immediately, silenced her, and sent her away? Instead, I denied her refund, unaware she was being groomed as a government witness. Common sense alone makes it clear that there was no obstruction.

But the government buried the truth. At trial, they barred the recording and email from evidence, later charging the rep to ensure he flipped against me. On the stand, EC claimed that we had lied to her, that she had been foreclosed on, and that her credit had been ruined. None of it was true.

And when I refused, at this evidentiary hearing, to validate their lies, the prosecutor pounced. The judge wrote: "When confronted with this history of obstruction, the petitioner was evasive and belligerent... I find his testimony wholly unworthy of belief."

But my skepticism wasn't obstruction—it was survival. It was known that the evidence had been poisoned, the testimony coerced. The Supreme Court has long warned against stripping defendants' rights based on uncharged conduct (Townsend v. Burke, 334 U.S. 736 (1948)). Yet this judge claimed my insistence on innocence meant I never would have taken a plea. That conclusion ignores reality. Defendants across this country maintain innocence every day and still accept pleas to lesser charges. The Supreme Court in North Carolina v. Alford upheld exactly that—pleas are constitutionally valid even when defendants protest factual guilt.

Collateral allegations are not proven and not tested before a jury, yet they are used to deny relief. That is not justice. That is judicial activism dressed in robes.

If you think this corruption stops with me, look no further than the president himself. Donald Trump was convicted in New York under the gavel of a radical judge for one reason alone—his name. Like him or not, the man broke no law. But in this era, innocence is irrelevant. Outcomes are political. Truth is expendable. When a black-robed radical judge strides into the courtroom as they do every day in this country, those present can feel the atmosphere shift. Many Americans, including our president, have felt their aura, thick and suffocating, disguised as something almost priestly, an almost God-like demeanor. Sadly, this is what I, along with many in the public, have come to expect. As I look at this ruling, which makes no sense, I find myself wondering where this mystique originates and why it's spreading instead of being reined in, especially as I wait for the appeal.

The answer can be found in a single, brilliantly calculated decision two centuries ago, which is the fuse that shaped every lawyer and judge who has come since: Marbury v. Madison. What followed this decision is the story of how the Judicial Branch appropriated power from 'We the people, ' which was not granted to them by the Constitution, and how that precedent still warps today's balance among the branches.

The framers drafted Article III to create an independent judiciary, not an omnipotent one. Nowhere in the Constitution, the Federalist Papers, the ratification debates, or the state conventions does a clause proclaim, "The Supreme Court shall have the final say." Indeed, Alexander Hamilton, James Madison, and John Jay engaged in extensive debate, and those discussions were recorded for all of us to review. They spoke about how they wanted the courts to interpret statutes, yes, but always in concert with checking the power of Congress and the Executive. The founders envisioned that there needed to be three coequal branches of government and not one branch silently elevated above the rest.

Fast-forward to the chaotic transfer of power from John Adams to Thomas Jefferson. In the whirlwind final hours of the federalist administration, Adams signed "midnight" commissions, including William Marbury's appointment as a justice of the peace in the District of Columbia. When Jefferson's new secretary of state, James Madison, refused to deliver Marbury's commission, Marbury sued, invoking a writ of mandamus authorized under section 13 of the Judiciary Act of 1789.

Chief Justice John Marshall saw an opportunity and seized the moment. He declared that while Marbury had the right to his commission, Section 13 itself, in his view, was unconstitutional, thus ruling that Congress lacked the authority to expand the court's original jurisdiction. In the same breath, he expanded the court's jurisdiction, taking more authority for the court than he was relinquishing in an elegant opinion in which he both chastised Jefferson and proclaimed that henceforth, the Supreme Court possessed the power of "judicial review," the last decisive voice. In this moment, the Judicial Branch effectively crowned itself the final arbiter without a single elector or state legislature ever consenting to grant it this authority.

This newly forged power was not merely theoretical, and it paved the way for some of the darkest chapters in American jurisprudence, where the court has ruled on the constitutionality of issues in America, the present, and beyond. Dred Scott v. Sanford told an entire class of human beings that they could never be citizens. Plessy v. Ferguson legitimized Jim Crow and segregation. Each opinion was ruled constitutional. Both were littered with the same self-bestowed authority that Marshall claimed in 1803. The same self-bestowed authority Judge Marchuin showed Trump. The same my judges have shown me. History shows that when unchecked, any human institution tends to drift towards hubris, precisely the corruption the framers feared.

Today, the pattern persists and is out of control. Radical judges and judicial overreach are becoming an epidemic. In 1787, the framers pledged that the Constitution would secure "the blessing of liberty" through a delicate dance of ambition counteracting ambition. When one of those dancers seizes the spotlight and refuses to share the stage, the choreography collapses. Today, that dancer is the judiciary. As a nation, our task should never be to push the courts off stage but remind them and ourselves that the robe they wear was meant to serve the republic, never rule it.

So now I wait on appeal.

And even after all of this, I am not jaded. I love my country and believe in it. I believe in the rule of law. I believe in 'we the people,' but as the years have passed, the sludge that was covering my eyes has faded away, and never have I seen the world more clearly. Because of this, I can no longer live my life, regardless of where I am, without trying to do something to change it for the better, even if it is while I reside within the Penumbra of existence.

# Acknowledgments

I would like to thank my editor, Elisheva Balkany, for her brilliance and sharp eye and for always being there to help me find my voice when I needed it most. I would like to thank Steve Bannon and the team at WarRoom for their unconditional support on this project and for our brainstorming sessions over tasters and rice cakes. A special thanks to Tony Lyons, Daniela Rapp, and the team at Skyhorse for taking a chance on a new author when others might have shied away. Last but certainly not least, I would like to thank my family for never losing faith in me and always remaining by my side. All of you have made this possible and I am eternally grateful.